Hanoi & Northern Vietnam

Claire Boobbyer

Credits

Footprint credits

Editor: Alan Murphy
Production and layout: Angus Dawson, Emma Bryers
Maps: Kevin Feeney

Managing Director: Andy Riddle
Commercial Director: Patrick Dawson
Publisher: Alan Murphy
Publishing Managers: Felicity Laughton, Nicola Gibbs.
Digital Editors: Jo Williams, Tom Mellors
Marketing and PR: Liz Harper
Sales: Diane McEntee
Advertising: Renu Sibal
Finance and Administration: Elizabeth Taylor

Photography credits

Front cover: Denis R/Shutterstock
Back cover: Michaelstockfoto/Shutterstock

Printed in Great Britain by CPI Antony Rowe, Chippenham, Wiltshire

Every effort has been made to ensure that the facts in this guidebook are accurate. However, travellers should still obtain advice from consulates, airlines, etc about travel and visa requirements before travelling. The authors and publishers cannot accept responsibility for any loss, injury or inconvenience however caused.

Publishing information

Footprint *Focus Hanoi & Northern Vietnam*
1st edition

ISBN: 978 1 908206 07 7
CIP DATA: A catalogue record for this book is available from the British Library

Published by Footprint
6 Riverside Court
Lower Bristol Road
Bath BA2 3DZ, UK
T +44 (0)1225 469141
F +44 (0)1225 469461
footprinttravelguides.com

Distributed in the USA by Globe Pequot Press, Guilford, Connecticut

The content of Footprint *Focus Hanoi & Northern Vietnam* has been taken directly from Footprint's *Vietnam Handbook* which was researched and written by Claire Boobbyer.

Contents

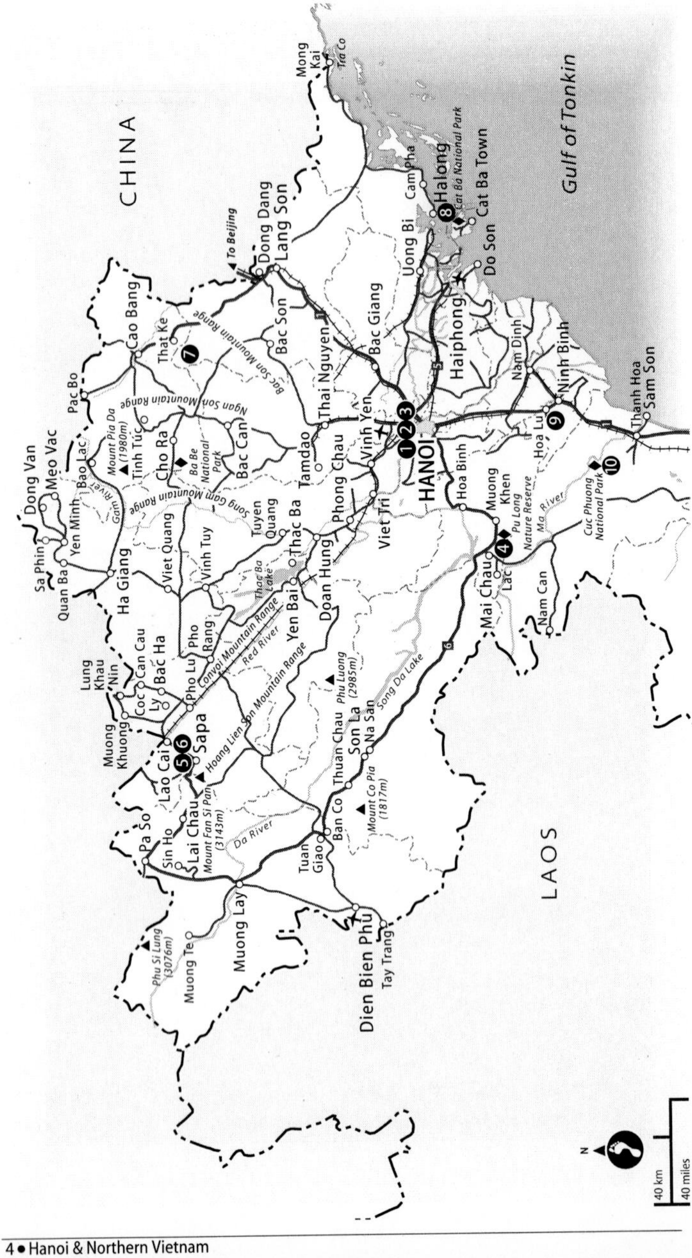
CHINA
LAOS
Gulf of Tonkin
HANOI
Mong Kai
Tra Co
Cam Pha
Halong
Cat Ba National Park
Cat Ba Town
Do Son
Uong Bi
Haiphong
Dong Dang
Lang Son
To Beijing
Bac Son
Bac Son Mountain Range
Bac Giang
Thai Nguyen
Cao Bang
That Ke
Pac Bo
Ngan Son Mountain Range
Mount Pia Da (1980m)
Tinh Túc
Cho Ra
Ba Be National Park
Bac Can
Tamdao
Vinh Yen
Phong Chau
Viet Tri
Nam Dinh
Ninh Binh
Thanh Hoa
Sam Son
Hoa Lu
Hoa Binh
Muong Khen
Pu Long Nature Reserve
Ma River
Cuc Phuong National Park
Dong Van
Meo Vac
Bao Lac
Gam River
Song Gam Mountain Range
Sa Phin
Yen Minh
Quan Ba
Ha Giang
Viet Quang
Vinh Tuy
Tuyen Quang
Thac Ba
Thac Ba Lake
Doan Hung
Yen Bai
Mai Chau
Lac
Nam Can
Lung Khau Nin
Can Cau
Bac Ha
Coc Ly
Pho Lu
Pho Rang
Convoi Mountain Range
Red River
Hoang Lien Son Mountain Range
Phu Luong (2985m)
Song Da Lake
Muong Khuong
Lao Cai
Sapa
Mount Fan Si Pan (3143m)
Thuan Chau
Son La
Na San
Mount Co Pia (1817m)
Ban Co
Tuan Giao
Pa So
Sin Ho
Lai Chau
Da River
Muong Lay
Phu Si Lung (3076m)
Muong Te
Dien Bien Phu
Tay Trang
N
40 km
40 miles

In an age of urban sprawl, Hanoi remains small, compact and charming: a city of broad, tree-lined boulevards, lakes, parks, weathered colonial buildings and elegant squares. The city has a wealth of historical sights, lying as it does at the heart of a region rich in history and landscapes. It also has stylish shops and plentiful market stalls and increasingly diverse restaurants from French haute cuisine to Vietnamese street food. And though Hanoians may be dour and xenophobic and their leaders austere, the large diplomatic community brings a cosmopolitan feel, and a younger generation has proved willing to engage with the outside world. Consequently the feel of Hanoi is very different – and pleasantly so – from what it was just 15 years ago.

To many the Northwest represents the finest Vietnam has to offer. In terms of scenery, colour, human interest and for the thrill of discovering the unknown, it is unrivalled. The region has wider significance too: the course of world history was altered at Dien Bien Phu in 1954. It is, in short, that myth of travellers' folklore: unspoilt Vietnam. There are good reasons for this. The distance, rugged environment and primitive infrastructure have all contributed to placing the Northwest at the edge of Vietnamese space. Pockets of the north have already been discovered – Sapa, for example, is no longer a secret. But for those who wish to avoid the backpacker trail and are prepared to put up with a little discomfort, the rewards are great.

Rugged, but lacking the lofty grandeur of Northwest Vietnam, the scenery of the Northeast consists of limestone hills dissected by fast-flowing streams – tributaries of the Gam and Red rivers – hurrying south with their burden of silt. Localized landscapes draw admiration but extensive tracts are unremarkable. Hilltribe minorities, particularly the Dao, Nung and Tay, are much in evidence.

Planning your trip

When to go

Climatically the best time to see Vietnam is around December to March when it should be dry and not too hot. In the south it is warm but not too hot with lovely cool evenings. Admittedly the north and the highlands will be a bit chilly but they should be dry with clear blue skies. The tourist industry high season is normally November to May when hotel prices tend to rise and booking flights can be hard. Travel in the south and Mekong Delta can be difficult at the height of the monsoon (particularly September, October and November). The central regions and north sometimes suffer typhoons and tropical storms from May to November. Hué is at its wettest from September to January.

Despite its historic and cultural resonance Tet, or Vietnamese New Year, is not a good time to visit. This movable feast usually falls between late January and March and, with aftershocks, lasts for about a fortnight. It is the only holiday most people get in the year. Popular destinations are packed, roads are jammed and for a couple of days almost all restaurants are shut. All hotel prices increase, and car hire prices are increased by 50% or more. The best prices are from May to October.

During the school summer holidays some resorts get busy. At Cat Ba, Sapa, Phan Thiet, Long Hai and Phu Quoc, for example, prices rise, there is a severe squeeze on rooms and weekends are worse. The Central Highlands tend to fare much better with cool temperatures and a good availability of rooms.

Getting there

Air

Vietnam is relatively isolated in comparison with Bangkok, Hong Kong and Singapore. Most major airlines have direct flights from Europe, North America and Australasia to these hubs. Ho Chi Minh City, and to a lesser extent Hanoi, is pretty well connected with other Southeast Asian countries which remain the source of most foreign visitors. Connections have also increased in the last few years with the rise of budget airlines. Prices vary according to high (November to April, July and August) and low season.

Flights from Europe In Western Europe, there are direct flights to Vietnam from Paris and Frankfurt with **Vietnam Airlines/Air France**. These code-shared flights last 12 hours. **Vietnam Airlines** has an office in the UK or book flights online. There are also direct **Vietnam Airlines** flights from Moscow.

Flights from London and other European hubs go via Bangkok, Singapore, Kuala Lumpur, Hong Kong or UAE states. From London to Vietnam, flights take 16 to 18 hours, depending on the length of stopover. Airlines include **Air France**, **Cathay Pacific**, **Emirates**, **Gulf Air**, **Thai International**, **Singapore Airlines**, **Malaysia Airlines**, **Lufthansa**, and **Qatar**. It is possible to fly into Hanoi and depart from Ho Chi Minh City although this does seem to rack up the return fare. Check details with flight agents and tour operators (see pages 5 and 5).

Flights from the USA and Canada By far the best option is to fly via **Bangkok**, **Taipei**, **Tokyo** or **Hong Kong** and from there to Vietnam. The approximate flight time from Los

Don't miss...

1 **Huan Kiem Lake**, page 27
2 **Old Quarter**, page 29
3 **Water Puppet Theatre**, page 57
4 **Mai Chau**, page 72
5 **Dragon's Jaw Hill**, page 89
6 **Around Sapa**, page 90
7 **Far North and Northeast**, page 99
8 **Halong Bay**, page 123
9 **Tam Coc**, page 136
10 **Cuc Phuong National Park**, page 138

Numbers relate to numbers on map on page 4.

Angeles to **Bangkok** is 21 hours. **United** flies from LA and Chicago via Tokyo and from San Francisco via Seoul to Vietnam. **Thai, Delta, United** and **Air Canada** fly to Bangkok from a number of US and Canadian cities.

Flights from Australia and New Zealand There are direct flights from Adelaide, Melbourne, Sydney, Perth, Auckland and Wellington with **Cathay Pacific, Malaysia Airlines, Singapore Airlines** and **Thai. Qantas** flies from Sydney, Adelaide and Melbourne to Ho Chi Minh City.

Budget airlines from Australia include **Jetstar** and **Tiger Airways**. From Sydney the flights to Vietnam are eight hours 45 minutes direct.

Flights from Asia **Thai** flies from Bangkok to Ho Chi Minh City and Hanoi. **AirAsia** flies from Bangkok and Kuala Lumpur to Ho Chi Minh City and from Kuala Lumpur and Bangkok to Hanoi. **Vietnam Airlines** flies from Bangkok, Phnom Penh, Siem Reap, Vientiane, Luang Prabang, Beijing, Guangzhou, Kunming, Hong Kong, Kuala Lumpur, Singapore, Manila, Busan, Seoul, Japan and Taipei. **Laos Airlines** flies from Luang Prabang and Vientiane. **Malaysia Airlines** flies from Kuala Lumpur to Hanoi and Ho Chi Minh City. **Tiger Airways** flies from Singapore to Ho Chi Minh City and Hanoi. **Cathay Pacific** flies from Hong Kong. **China Airlines** flies from Taipei to Ho Chi Minh City. **Japan Airlines** flies from Tokyo to Ho Chi Minh City and Hanoi. **Korean Air** flies from Seoul to Ho Chi Minh City and Hanoi. **Philippine Airlines** flies from Manila to Ho Chi Minh City. **Singapore Airlines** flies to Hanoi and Ho Chi Minh City. **Thai International** flies from Bangkok to Ho Chi Minh City and from Sydney and Melbourne to Ho Chi Minh City and Hanoi.

Airport information There are two main international airports in Vietnam: **Tan Son Nhat Airport** (SGN) in Ho Chi Minh City, see page 306, and **Noi Bai Airport** (HAN) in Hanoi, see page 22.

Getting around

Air

Vietnam Airlines is the national carrier and flies to multiple domestic destinations. **Vietnam Airlines** changes its schedule every six months so check before making any plans.

Refunds, rebookings and rerouting may not be allowed on certain ticket fares. Remember that during holiday periods flights get extremely busy. ▸▸ *See also map, page 6.*

Rail

Train travel is exciting and overnight journeys are a good way of covering long distances. The Vietnamese rail network extends from Hanoi to Ho Chi Minh City. **Vietnam Railways** (www.vr.com.vn) runs the 2600-km rail network down the coast. With overnight stays at hotels along the way to see the sights, a rail sightseeing tour from Hanoi to Ho Chi Minh City should take a minimum of 10 days but you would need to buy tickets for each separate section of the journey.

The difference in price between first and second class is small and it is worth paying the extra. There are three seating classes and four sleeping classes including hard and soft seats and hard and soft sleepers; some are air-conditioned, others are not. The prices vary according to the class of cabin and the berth chosen; the bottom berth is more expensive than the top berth. All sleepers should be booked three days in advance. The kitchen on the Hanoi to Ho Chi Minh City service serves soups and simple, but adequate, rice dishes (it is a good idea to take additional food and drink on long journeys). First-class long-distance tickets include the price of meals. The express trains (**Reunification Express**) take between an advertised 29½ to 34 hours; odd-numbered trains travel from Hanoi to Ho Chi Minh City, even-numbered trains vice versa.

Most ticket offices have some staff who speak English. Queues can be long and some offices keep unusual hours. If you are short of time and short on patience it may well pay to get a tour operator to book your ticket for a small commission or visit the Ho Chi Minh City railway office in Pham Ngu Lao or the Hanoi agency in the Old Quarter.

There are also rail routes from Hanoi to Haiphong, to Lang Son and to Lao Cai. The **Victoria** hotel chain (www.victoriahotels-asia.com) runs a luxury carriage on the latter route.

River

In the south, there are services from Chau Doc to Phnom Penh, see page 383. The **Victoria** hotel chain (www.victoriahotels-asia.com) runs a Mekong Delta service for its guests. Ferries operate between Ho Chi Minh City and Vung Tau; Rach Gia and Phu Quoc; Ha Tien and Phu Quoc; Haiphong and Cat Ba Island; and Halong City and Cat Ba and Mong Cai.

Road

Open Tour Buses, see below, are very useful and cheap for bridging important towns. Many travellers opt to take a tour to reach remote areas because of the lack of self-drive car hire and the dangers and slow speed of public transport.

Bus Roads in Vietnam are notoriously dangerous. As American humourist PJ O'Rourke wrote: "In Japan people drive on the left. In China people drive on the right. In Vietnam it doesn't matter." Since Highway 1 is so dangerous and public transport buses are poor and slow, most travellers opt for the cheap and regular **Open Tour Bus** (private minibus or coach) that covers the length of the country. Almost every Vietnamese tour operator/travellers' café listed in this guide will run a minibus service or act as an agent. The ticket is a flexible, one-way ticket from Ho Chi Minh City to Hanoi and vice versa, see box page 23. The buses run daily from their own offices and include the following stops: Ho Chi Minh City, Mui Ne, Nha Trang, Dalat, Hoi An, Hué, Ninh Binh and Hanoi. They will also stop off at tourist destinations along the way such as Lang Co, Hai Van Pass, Marble Mountains and Po Klong Garai for quick visits. You may join at any leg of the journey, paying for one trip or several as you go. The Hanoi to Hué and vice versa is an overnight trip but although you might save on a night's accommodation you are unlikely to get much sleep.

If you do opt for **public buses** note that most bus stations are on the outskirts of town; in bigger centres there may be several stations. Long-distance buses invariably leave very early in the morning (0400-0500). Buses are the cheapest form of transport, although sometimes foreigners find they are being asked for two to three times the correct price. Prices are normally prominently displayed at bus stations. It helps if you can find out what the correct fare should be in advance. Less comfortable but quicker are the minibus services, which ply the more popular routes.

Car hire Self-drive car hire is not available in Vietnam. It is, however, possible to hire cars with drivers and this is a good way of getting to more remote areas with a group of people. Cars with drivers can be hired for around US$60-110 per day. Longer trips would see a reduced cost. All cars are air-conditioned. Car hire prices increase by 50% or more during Tet.

Motorbike and bicycle hire Most towns are small enough to get around by bicycle, and this can also be a pleasant way to explore the surrounding countryside. However, if covering large areas (touring around the Central Highlands, for example) then a motorbike will mean you can see more and get further off the beaten track.

Motorbikes and bicycles can be hired by the day in the cities, often from hotels and travellers' cafés. You do not need a driver's licence or proof of motorbike training to hire a motorbike in Vietnam, however, it became compulsory in 2007 to wear a helmet. Take time to familiarize yourself with road conditions and ride slowly. Motorbikes cost around US$6 per day including helmet; bicycles can be hired for US$1-2 including a lock. Always park your bicycle or motorbike in a gui xe (guarded parking place) and ask for a ticket. The small cost is worth every dong, even if you are just popping into the post office to post a letter.

Motorbike taxi and cyclo Motorcycle taxis, known as *honda ôm* or *xe ôm* (*ôm* means to cuddle) are ubiquitous and cheap. You will find them on most street corners, outside hotels or in the street. With their baseball caps and dangling cigarette, *xe ôm* drivers are readily recognizable. If they see you before you see them, they will shout 'moto' to get your attention. In the north and upland areas the Honda is replaced with the Minsk. The shortest hop would be at least 10,000d. Always bargain though.

Cyclos are bicycle trishaws. Cyclo drivers charge double or more that of a *xe ôm*. A number of streets in the centres of Ho Chi Minh City and Hanoi are one-way or out of bounds to cyclos, necessitating lengthy detours which add to the time and cost. Do not take a cyclo after dark unless the driver is well known to you or you know the route. It is a wonderful way to get around the Old Quarter of Hanoi, though, and for those with plenty of time on their hands it is not as hazardous in smaller towns.

Taxi Taxis ply the streets of Hanoi and Ho Chi Minh City and other large towns and cities. They are cheap, around 12,000d per kilometre, and the drivers are better English speakers than cyclo drivers. Always keep a small selection of small denomination notes with you so that when the taxi stops you can round up the fare to the nearest small denomination. At night use the better known taxi companies rather than the unlicensed cars that often gather around popular nightspots.

Sleeping

Accommodation ranges from luxury suites in international five-star hotels and spa resorts to small, family hotels (mini hotels) and homestays with local people in the Mekong Delta and with the ethnic minorities in the Central Highlands and northern Vietnam. During peak seasons – especially December to March and particularly during busy holidays such as Tet, Christmas, New Year's Eve and around Easter – booking is essential. Expect staff to speak English in all top hotels. Do not expect it in cheaper hotels or in more remote places, although most places employ someone with a smattering of a foreign language.

Private, mini hotels are worth seeking out as, being family-run, guests can expect good service. Mid-range and tourist hotels may provide a decent breakfast which is often included in the price. Many luxury and first-class hotels and some three-star hotels charge extra for breakfast and, on top of this, also charge 10% VAT and 5% service charge. When quoted a hotel price you should ask whether that includes these two taxes; it is marked as ++ (plus plus) on the bill.

There are some world-class beach resorts in Phu Quoc, Nha Trang, Mui Ne, Hoi An and Danang. In the northern uplands, in places like Sapa, Ha Giang province and Mai Chau, it is possible to stay in an ethnic minority house. Bathrooms are basic and will consist of a cold shower or warm shower and a natural or western toilet. To stay in a homestay, you must book through a tour operator or through the local tourist office; you cannot just turn up. Homestays are also possible on farms and in orchards in the Mekong Delta. Guests sleep on camp beds and share a Western bathroom. National parks offer everything from air-conditioned bungalows to shared dormitory rooms to campsites where, sometimes, it is possible to hire tents. Visitors may spend a romantic night on a boat in Halong Bay or on the Mekong Delta. Boats range from the fairly luxurious to the basic. Most people book through tour operators. In remote places where there is no competition, dour and surly service remain the order of the day. **The Vietnam Hostelling International Association** (www.hihostels.com) has been established, operating hostels in Hanoi, Hoi An and Sapa.

You will have to leave your passport at hotel reception desks for the duration of your hotel stay. It will be released to you temporarily for bank purposes or buying an air ticket. Credit cards are widely accepted but there is often a 2-4% fee for paying in this manner. Tipping is not expected in hotels in Vietnam.

Camping in Vietnam is limited mainly because the authorities insist on foreign visitors sleeping in registered accommodation. There are no campsites but visitors bringing tents may be able to use them around Sapa or on Cat Ba and surrounding islands. Some guesthouses in Mui Ne and other seaside places have tents.

If you wish to stay at the **house of a friend** this is normally permitted but your hosts will need to take your passport and arrival form to their local police station. Police and People's Committee regulations in some towns mean that a foreigner travelling with his Vietnamese wife must bring a marriage certificate in order to share a hotel room with her.

The age of consent in Vietnam is 18. There are rules relating to a Vietnamese person of the opposite sex being in your hotel room. It depends on the attitude of the hotel. If the Vietnamese person is your partner, as opposed to a one-night stand, hotels are more relaxed. However, Hoi An is the exception and you will have to rent a second room. This is also the policy in international hotels in big cities, not because international chains have moral qualms but because they get penalized by the police. Local hotels from which the police can collect bribes tend to be more 'accommodating'.

Sleeping and eating price codes

Sleeping

$$$$ over US$100 | $$$ US$46-100 | $$ US$20-45
$ under US$20

Prices include taxes and service charge, but not meals. They are based on a double room, except in the $ range, where prices are almost always per person.

Eating

TTT over US$12 | TT US$6-12 | T under US$6

Prices refer to the cost of a two-course meal for one person, excluding drinks or service charge.

Travellers normally get their laundry done in hotels. In cheap hotels it's inexpensive. Cheaper hotels and laundries in the hotel districts charge by weight. The smarter places charge by the item and the bill can be a shock! Always check bills; overcharging is common.

Eating and drinking

Food

Food is a major attraction of Vietnam and it is one of the paradoxes of this enigmatic country that so much food should be so readily and deliciously available. Eating out is so cheap that practically every meal eaten by the visitor will be taken in a restaurant or café. Ho Chi Minh City and Hanoi offer a wide range of cuisines besides Vietnamese, so that only Congolese, Icelandic and English tourists will be deprived of home cooking.

Vietnam offers outstanding Vietnamese, French and international cuisine in restaurants that range from first class to humble foodstalls. The quality will be, in the main, exceptional. The accent is on local, seasonal and fresh produce and the rich pickings from the sea, along Vietnam's 2000-km coastline will always make it far inland too. You will find more hearty stews in the more remote north and more salad dishes along the coast. All restaurants offer a variety of cuisine from the regions and some specialize in certain types of food – Hué cuisine, Cha Ca Hanoi, etc. *Pho* (pronounced *fer*), a bowl of flat, white, noodle soup served with chicken or beef, is utterly delicious. The soup is made from stock flavoured with star anise, ginger and other spices and herbs but individual recipes often remain a closely guarded secret. Vietnamese usually eat *pho* in the morning, often in the evening but rarely at lunchtime, when they require a more filling meal accompanied by rice. On each table of a *pho* restaurant sits a plate of fresh green leaves: mint, cinnamon, basil and the spiky looking *ngo gai*, together with bean sprouts, chopped red chillies, barbecue sauce and sliced lemons, enabling patrons to produce their own variations on a theme.

Another local speciality which visitors often overlook is *com tam* or broken rice. *Com tam* stalls abound on the streets and do brisk trade at breakfast and lunch. They tend to be low-cost canteens, but in many cities they have appeal to the wealthier office market and have started to abandon tiny plastic stools in favour of proper tables and chairs and concentrate more on cleanliness and presentation. The steamed broken rice is eaten with fried chicken, fish, pork and vegetables and soup is normally included in the price.

There are many types of Vietnamese roll: the most common are deep-fried spring rolls (confusingly, *cha gio* in the south and *nem ranh* in the north) but if these appear on your table too frequently, look for the fresh or do-it-yourself types, such as *bi cuon* or *bo bia*. Essentially, these are salads with prawns or grilled meats wrapped in rice paper. Customers who roll their own cigarettes are at a distinct advantage while innocents abroad are liable to produce sagging Camberwell Carrots that collapse in the lap.

Vietnamese salads (*goi* in the south and *nom* in the north) are to die for. The best known is the green papaya salad with dried beef (*nom du du bo kho*); others include *goi xoai* (mango salad) and *goi buoi* (pomelo salad). They all involve a wonderful fusion of herbs and vegetables with sweet and spicy tastes rolled in.

Delicious seafood is a staple across the land. It would be invidious to isolate a particular seafood dish when there are so many to chose from. Prawns are prawns – the bigger and the less adulterated the better. But a marvellous dish that does deserve commendation is crab in tamarind sauce. This glorious fusion of flavours, bitter tamarind, garlic, piquant spring onion and fresh crab is quite delicious. To the Vietnamese, part of the fun of eating crab is the fiddly process of extracting meat from the furthest recesses of its claws and legs. A willingness to crack, crunch, poke and suck is required to do it justice, not a task for the squeamish but great for those who aren't.

All Vietnamese food is dipped, whether in fish sauce, soy sauce, chilli sauce, peanut sauce or pungent prawn sauce (*mam tom* – avoid if possible) before eating. As each course is served so a new set of dips will accompany. Follow the guidance of your waiter or Vietnamese friends to get the right dip with the right dish.

When it comes to food, Vietnamese do not stand on ceremony and (perhaps rather like the French) regard peripherals such as furniture, service and ambience as mere distractions to the task of ploughing through plates, crocks, casseroles and tureens charged with piping hot meats, vegetables and soups. Do not expect good service, courses to arrive in the right order, or to eat at the same time as your companions, but do expect the freshest and tastiest food you will find anywhere.

While it is possible to eat very cheaply in Vietnam (especially outside Hanoi and Ho Chi Minh City) the higher class of restaurant, particularly those serving foreign cuisine, can prove quite expensive, especially with wine. But with judicious shopping around it is not hard to find excellent value for money, particularly in the small, **family restaurants**. In the listing sections we describe a range of diners which should satisfy every palate and every pocket and in the Hanoi chapter we provide information on street stalls. Some restaurants (mostly expensive ones) add 5% service charge and the government tax of 10% to the bill. See box, page 11 on restaurant classification.

For day trips, an early morning visit to the **markets** will produce a picnic fit for a king. Hard-boiled quails' eggs, thinly sliced garlic sausage and salami, pickled vegetables, beef tomatoes, cucumber, pâté, cheese, warm baguettes and fresh fruit. And, far from costing a king's ransom, it will feed four for around US$1 a head.

The thing that separates India from China is that in the former there are prohibitions governing the consumption of just about everything. In the latter anything and everything can be – and is – eaten. Vietnam of course falls under Chinese sway. Therefore anyone who self imposes restrictions on his eating habits is regarded as a bit of a crank. There are **vegetarian restaurants** in Vietnam but these usually sell different types of tofu dressed to look like meat. The vegetable section of most 'normal' restaurants has vegetables – but cooked with pork, with beef or with prawns, rarely pure vegetables. Nevertheless there are a few Vietnamese vegetarians and twice a month a great many people eat vegetarian so restaurants are aware of the concept. We have listed for most bigger towns some highly acclaimed vegetarian restaurants and places on the backpacker trail that are on the ball.

Given the large proportion of the population aged 16 and under no Vietnamese restaurant is put out by **children**. Indeed any restaurant frequented by Vietnamese families will have kids running around everywhere. So parents need have no fears about their children's behaviour upsetting anyone. Obviously in smarter places unruly children may not be so popular so beware invitations to 'take a tour of the kitchen'.

Note that Vietnamese get up early and so lunch time starts at 1100 although restaurants catering for foreigners stay open until 1400, but don't leave lunch later than that as many places close the kitchen until the dinner trade at around 1700.

Drink

Locally produced fresh beer is called *bia hoi*. It is cold and refreshing, and weak and cheap enough to drink in quite large volumes. It is usually consumed in small pavement cafés where patrons sit on small plastic stools. Most *bia hoi* cafés serve simple and inexpensive food. Almost all customers are men and they can get a bit jolly. As the beer is fresh it has to be consumed within a short period of brewing hence most towns, even quite small ones, have their own brewery and impart to their beer a local flavour in a way that used to happen in England before the big brewers took over. Unfortunately bars and restaurants do not sell *bia hoi* as it's too cheap, at just 4000d per litre. Hence bar customers have a choice of Tiger, Heineken, Carlsberg, San Miguel, 333, Saigon Beer or Huda. All are brewed in Vietnam but many visitors try to stick to the local beers (333, Saigon and Huda) as they are cheaper and, to many, more distinctively flavoursome than the mass produced international brands. Unfortunately this is not always possible as many bars and restaurants stock only the more expensive beers of the big international brewers because they have higher mark-ups.

Rice and **fruit wines** are produced and consumed in large quantities in upland areas, particularly in the north of Vietnam. Rice wines are fairly easily found, however. There are two types of rice wine, *ruou nep* and *ruou de*. *Ruou nep* is a viscous wine made from sticky rice. It is purple and white due to the different types of rice used to make it. Among the ethnic minorities, who are recognized as masters of rice wine, *ruou nep* is drunk from a ceramic jar through a straw. This communal drinking is an integral part of their way of life and no doubt contributes substantially to strengthening the ties of the clan. It is possible to become very drunk drinking *ruou nep* without realizing it. *Ruou de* is a rice spirit and very strong.

The Chinese believe that **snake wines** increase their virility and are normally found in areas with a large Chinese population. It is called a wine despite being a spirit. Other wines include the body and parts of seahorses, gecko, silkworms and bees.

There is a fantastic range of different **fruit wines** but unless you make a real effort it can be quite hard to find them. Wines are made from just about all upland fruits: plum, strawberry, apple and, of course, grapes, although grape wine in Vietnam is generally disappointing. The others are fiery and warm, strong and, bought by the bottle, cheap.

Local customs and laws

Vietnam is remarkably relaxed and easy going with regard to conventions. The people, especially in small towns and rural areas, can be pretty old-fashioned, but it is difficult to cause offence unwittingly. The main complaint Vietnamese have of foreigners is their fondness for dirty and torn clothing. Backpackers come in for particularly severe criticism and the term *tay ba lo* (literally 'Western backpacker') is a contemptuous one reflecting the low priority many budget travellers seem to allocate to personal hygiene and the antiquity and inadequacy of their shorts and vests.

Shoes should be removed before entering temples and before going into people's houses. Modesty should be preserved and excessive displays of bare flesh are not considered good form, particularly in temples and private houses. (Not that the Vietnamese are unduly prudish, they just like things to be kept in their proper place.) Shorts are fine for the beach and travellers' cafés but not for smart restaurants.

Kissing and canoodling in public are likely to draw attention, not much of it favourable. But walking hand in hand is now accepted as a Western habit. Hand shaking among men is a standard greeting and although Vietnamese women will consent to the process, it is often clear that they would prefer not to. The head is held by some to be sacred and people would rather you didn't pat them on it. The Vietnamese do not share the concern about having someone's feet higher than their head.

Terms of address

Vietnamese names are written with the surname first, followed by the first name. Thus Nguyen Minh is not called Nguyen as we would presume in the West but Minh. In addressing people who are the same age as you but who you don't know, you would call them *anh* (for a man) and *chi* (for a woman). When you know their first name you would say 'anh Minh', for example.

Religion

The Vietnamese are open to religious experiences of all kinds. Vietnam is predominantly a Buddhist country. Following Chinese tradition, ancestor worship is widely practiced and animism (the belief in and worship of spirits of inanimate objects such as venerable trees, the land, mountains and so on) is widespread. The government is hostile to proselytizing, particularly by Christians. But the Catholic Church is more vital than in many European countries and foreigners are perfectly free to attend services. In Ho Chi Minh City one or two services in the Notre Dame Cathedral are in French and in English. Protestant churches are found throughout the country to a lesser degree then the Roman Catholic Church but all services are in Vietnamese.

Essentials A-Z

Accident and emergency

Contact the relevant emergency service and your embassy. Make sure you obtain police/medical records in order to file insurance claims. If you need to report a crime, visit your local police station and take a local with you who speaks English.

Ambulance T115, **Fire** T114, **Police** T113.

Disabled travellers

Considering the proportion of the country's population that is seriously disabled, foreigners might expect better facilities and allowances for the immobile. But there are very few. However, some of the more upmarket hotels do have a few designated rooms for the disabled. For those with walking difficulties many of the better hotels do have lifts. Wheelchair access is improving with more shopping centres, hotels and restaurants providing ramps for easy access. People sensitive to noise will find Vietnam, at times, almost intolerable.

RADAR, 12 City Forum, 250 City Rd, London, EC1V 8AF, T020-7250 3222, www.radar.org.uk.

SATH, 347 Fifth Av, Suite 605, New York City, NY 10016, T212-447 7284, www.sath.org.

Electricity

Voltage 110-240. Sockets are round 2-pin. Sometimes they are 2 flat pin. A number of top hotels now use UK 3 square-pin sockets.

Embassies and consulates

Australia, 6 Timbarra Cres, O'Malley Canberra, ACT 2606, T+61-2 6286 6059, www.vietnamembassy.org.au.

Cambodia, 436 Monivong, Phnom Penh, T+855 23-726274, www.vietnamembassy-cambodia.org.

Canada, 470 Wilbrod St, Ottawa, Ontario, K1N 6M8, T+1 613-236 0772, www.vietnamembassy-canada.ca.

China, 32 Guanghua R, Jiangou menwai, PO Box 00600, Beijing, T+86-10 6532 1155; 5/F, Great Smart Tower, 230 Van Chai Rd, Wan Chai, Hong Kong, T852-2591 4517, http://www.vnemba.org.cn/en.

France, 62 R Boileau-75016, Paris, T+33 144-146400, www.vietnamembassy-france.org/en.

Laos, 85 23 Singha Rd, Vientiane, T+856 21-413409, www.mofa.gov.vn/vnemb.la.

South Africa, 87 Brooks St, Brooklyn, Pretoria, T+27 12-362 8119, www.vietnamembassy-southafrica.org/en/.

Thailand, 83/1 Wireless Rd, Lumpini, Pathumwan, Bangkok 10330, T+66 2-251 5837, www.vietnamembassy-thailand.org/en.

UK, 12-14 Victoria Rd, London W8 5RD, T+44 (0)20-7937 1912, www.vietnamembassy.org.uk/consular.html.

USA, 1233, 20th St, NW Suite 400 Washington DC, 20036, T+1 202 861 0737, www.vietnamembassy-usa.org.

Health

See your doctor or travel clinic at least 6 weeks before your departure for general advice on travel risks, malaria and vaccinations (see also below). Make sure you have travel insurance, get a dental check-up (especially if you are going to be away for more than a month), know your own blood group and if you suffer a long-term condition such as diabetes or epilepsy make sure someone knows or that you have a **Medic Alert** bracelet/necklace with this information on it (www.medicalert.co.uk).

Health risks

Malaria exists in rural areas in Vietnam. However, there is no risk in the Red River Delta and the coastal plains north of Nha Trang. Neither is there a risk in Hanoi, HCMC, Danang and Nha Trang. The choice of malaria prophylaxis will need to be something other than chloroquine for most people, since there is such a high level of resistance to it. Always check with your doctor or travel clinic for the most up-to-date advice.

Malaria can cause death within 24 hrs. It can start as something just resembling an attack of flu. You may feel tired, lethargic, headachy, feverish; or more seriously, develop fits, followed by coma and then death. Have a low index of suspicion because it is very easy to write off vague symptoms, which may actually be malaria. If you have a temperature, go to a doctor as soon as you can and ask for a malaria test. On your return home if you suffer any of these symptoms, get tested as soon as possible, even if any previous test proved negative; the test could save your life.

The most serious viral disease is **dengue fever**, which is hard to protect against as the mosquitos bite throughout the day as well as at night. Bacterial diseases include **tuberculosis** (TB) and some causes of the more common traveller's **diarrhoea**. Lung fluke (**para-gonimiasis**) occurs in Vietnam. A fluke is a sort of flattened worm. In the Sin Ho district the locals like to eat undercooked or raw crabs, but our advice is to leave them to it. The crabs contain a fluke which, when eaten, travels to the lungs. The lung fluke may cause a cough, coughing 'blood', fever, chest pain and changes on your X-ray which will puzzle a British radiologist. The cure is the same drug that cures schistosomiasis (another fluke which can be acquired in some parts of the Mekong delta).

Each year there is the possibility that **avian flu** or **SARS** may again rear their ugly heads. Check the news reports. If there is a problem in an area you are due to visit you may be advised to have an ordinary flu shot or to seek expert advice. Vietnam has had a number of fatalities from Avian influenza. Consult the WHO website, www.who.int, for further information and heed local advice on the ground. There are high rates of **HIV** in the region, especially among sex workers. See also box, page 11.

Medical services

Western hospitals staffed by foreign and Vietnamese medics exist in Hanoi and HCMC. See under medical services in each area for listings.

Useful websites

www.btha.org British Travel Health Association (UK). This is the official website of an organization of travel health professionals.
www.cdc.gov US government site that gives excellent advice on travel health and details of disease outbreaks.
www.fitfortravel.scot.nhs.uk A-Z of vaccine/health advice for each country.
www.who.int The WHO *Blue Book* lists the diseases of the world.

Vaccinations

The following vaccinations are advised: BCG, Hepatitis A, Japanese Encephalitis, Polio, Rabies, Tetanus, Typhoid and Yellow Fever.

Insurance

Always take out travel insurance before you set off and read the small print carefully. Check that the policy covers the activities you intend or may end up doing. Also check exactly what your medical cover includes, such as ambulance, helicopter rescue or emergency flights back home. Also check the payment protocol. You may have to pay up first before the insurance company reimburses you. Keep receipts for expensive personal effects, such as jewellery or cameras. Take photos of these items and note down all serial numbers. You are advised to shop around. **STA Travel** and other reputable student travel organizations offer good value policies. Companies like **BUPA** offer good and comprehensive cover. Young travellers from North America can try the **International Student Insurance Service** (ISIS), which is available through **STA Travel**, T1-800-781-4040, www.sta-travel.com. Other recommended companies in North America include: **Access America**, www.accessamerica.com; **Travel Insurance**

Services, www.travelinsure.com; and **Travel Assistance International**, www.travelassistance.com. Older travellers should note that some companies will not cover people over 65 years old, or may charge higher premiums. The best policies for older travellers in the UK are offered by **Age UK**, www.ageuk.org.uk.

Language

You are likely to find some English spoken wherever there are tourist services but outside tourist centres communication can be a problem for those who have no knowledge of Vietnamese. Furthermore, the Vietnamese language is not easy to learn. For example, pronunciation presents enormous difficulties as it is tonal: it has 6 tones, 12 vowels and 27 consonants. On the plus side, Vietnamese is written in a Roman alphabet making life much easier; place and street names are instantly recognizable. French is still spoken and often very well by the more elderly and educated Vietnamese.

In HCMC, language courses of several months' duration are offered by various organizations. In Hanoi, contact www.hiddenhanoi.com.vn.

Money

➔ *US$1 = 20,584d, £1 = 33,875, €1 = 29,457 (May 2011)*

The unit of currency is the dong. Under law, shops should only accept dong but in practice this is not enforced and dollars are accepted almost everywhere. If possible, however, try to pay for everything in dong as prices are usually lower and in more remote areas people may be unaware of the exchange rate. Also, to ordinary Vietnamese, 18,000d is a lot of money, while US$1 means nothing.

ATMs are plentiful in HCMC and Hanoi and are now pretty ubiquitous in other major tourist centres, but it is a good idea to travel with US dollars cash as a back up. Try to avoid tatty notes. ATM withdrawals are limited to 2 million dong per transaction. Banks in the main centres will change other major currencies including UK sterling, Hong Kong dollars, Thai baht, Swiss francs, Euros, Australian dollars, Singapore dollars and Canadian dollars. **Credit cards** are increasingly accepted, particularly Visa, MasterCard, Amex and JCB. Large hotels, expensive restaurants and medical centres invariably take them but beware a surcharge of between 2.5% and 4.5%. Most hotels will not add a surcharge onto your bill if paying by credit card. Traveller's cheques are best denominated in US dollars and can only be cashed in banks in the major towns. Commission of 2-4% is payable if cashing into dollars but not if you are converting them direct to dong.

Cost of travelling

On a budget expect to pay around US$6-15 per night for accommodation and about US$6-12 for food. A good mid-range hotel will cost US$12-30. There are comfort and cost levels anywhere from here up to more than US$200 per night. For travelling, many use the Open Tour Buses as they are inexpensive and, by Vietnamese standards, 'safe'. Slightly more expensive are trains followed by planes.

Opening hours

Banks Mon-Fri 0800-1600. Many close 1100-1300 or 1130-1330.
Offices Mon-Fri 0730-1130, 1330-1630.
Restaurants, cafés, bars Daily from 0700 or 0800 although some open earlier. Bars are supposed to close at 2400 by law.
Shops Daily 0800-2000. Some stay open for another hour, especially in tourist centres.

Police and the law

If you are robbed in Vietnam, report the incident to the police (for your insurance claim). Otherwise, the police are of no use whatsoever. They will do little or nothing (apart from log the crime on an incident sheet that you will need for your claim). Vietnam is not the best place to come into conflict with the law. Avoid getting arrested. If you are arrested, however, ask for consular assistance and English-speaking staff.

Involvement in politics, possession of political material, business activities that have not been licensed by appropriate authorities, or non-sanctioned religious activities (including proselytizing) can result in detention. Sponsors of small, informal religious gatherings such as bible-study groups in hotel rooms, as well as distributors of religious materials, have been detained, fined and expelled (source: US State Department). The army are extremely sensitive about all their military buildings and become exceptionally irate if you take a photo. Indeed there are signs to this effect outside all military installations.

Post

Postal services are pretty good. Post offices open daily 0700-2100; smaller ones close for lunch. Outgoing packages are opened and checked by the censor.

Safety

Travel advisories

The US State Department's travel advisory: **Travel Warnings & Consular Information Sheets**, www.travel.state.gov, and the **UK Foreign and Commonwealth Office**'s travel warning section, www.fco.gov.uk, are useful. Do not take any valuables on to the streets of HCMC as bag and jewellery snatching is a common problem. Thieves work in teams, often with beggar women carrying babies as a decoy. Beware of people who obstruct your path (pushing a bicycle across the pavement is a common ruse); your pockets are being emptied from behind. Young men on fast motorbikes also cruise the central streets of HCMC waiting to pounce on victims. The situation in other cities is not so bad but take care in Nha Trang and Hanoi. Never go by cyclo in a strange part of town after dark.

Lone women travellers have fewer problems than in many other Asian countries. The most common form of harassment usually consists of comic and harmless displays of macho behaviour.

Unexploded ordnance is still a threat in some areas. It is best not to stray too far from the beaten track and don't unearth bits of suspicious metal.

Single Western men will be targeted by prostitutes on street corners, in tourist bars and those cruising on motorbikes.

Beware of the following scams: being overcharged on credit cards; the pretend tearing up of a credit card transaction and the issuing of a new one; massage parlours where your money is stolen when you're having a massage; newspapers being sold for 5 times their value; and motorbikes that go 'wrong' and need repairs costing the earth.

Telephone

Telephone numbers beginning with 091 or 090 are mobile phone numbers. Vietnam's IDD is 0084; directory enquiries: 1080; operator-assisted domestic long-distance calls 103; international directory enquiries 143; yellow pages 1081.

To make a domestic call dial 0 + area code + phone number. Note that all numbers in this guide include the area code. Most shops or cafés will let you call a local number for 2000d; look for the blue sign *'dien thoai cong cong'* (public telephone). All post offices provide international telephone services. The cost of calls has been greatly reduced but some post offices and hotels still insist on charging for a minimum of 3 mins. You start paying for an overseas call from the moment you ring even if the call is not answered. By dialling 171 or 178 followed by 0 or 00 to make an international call, it is around 30% cheaper.

Pay-as-you-go sim cards are available from a number of operators including **Mobiphone** and **Vinaphone**. A sim card costs around £10 and top-up cards are available. Calls are very cheap and it's the most convenient and cheapest way to keep in touch in country.

Time

Vietnam is 7 hrs ahead of GMT.

Tipping

Vietnamese do not normally tip if eating in small restaurants but may tip in expensive bars. Foreigners leave small change, which is appreciated. Big hotels and restaurants add 5-10% service charge and the government tax of 10% to the bill. Taxis are rounded up to the nearest 5000d, hotel porters 20,000d.

Tourist information

Contact details for tourist offices and other resources are given in the relevant Ins and outs sections throughout the text.

The national tourist office is **Vietnam National Administration of Tourism** (www.vietnamtourism.com), whose role is to promote Vietnam as a tourist destination rather than to provide tourist information. Visitors to its offices can get some information and maps but they are more likely to be offered tours. Good tourist information is available from tour operators in the main tourist centres.

Visas and immigration

Tourist visa extensions need careful planning as, although hotels will accept photocopies of passports and visas, you cannot buy a ticket or fly with Vietnam Airlines without the original.

Valid passports with visas issued by a Vietnamese embassy are required by all visitors, irrespective of citizenship. Visas are normally valid only for arrival by air at Hanoi and HCMC. Those wishing to enter or leave Vietnam by land must specify the border crossing when applying. It is possible to alter the point of departure at immigration offices in Hanoi and HCMC. Contact the Vietnamese embassy in your country for specific application details. Visas on arrival at land crossings are not available and visas on arrival at airports are not exactly as they appear; they must be arranged in advance with licensed companies, paperwork signed before arriving and handed at desks at airports to get the visa. This may or may not work out cheaper than the embassy approach.

The standard tourist visa is valid for 1 month for 1 entry (*mot lan*) only. Tourist visas cost £44 and generally take 5 days to process. Express visas cost more and take 2 days. 2-month tourist visas are now available for £85. If you are planning on staying for a while or making a side trip to Laos or Cambodia with the intention of coming back to Vietnam then a 1-month multiple entry visa will make life much simpler. Business visas cost the same as multiple entry visas. Visa regulations are ever changing; usually it is possible to extend visas within Vietnam. Travel agencies and hotels will probably add their own mark-up but for many people it is worth paying to avoid the difficulty of making 1 or 2 journeys to an embassy. Visas can be extended for 1 month. Depending on where you are it will take between 1 day and a week. A visa valid for 1 month can only be extended for 1 month; a further 1 month extension is then possible. Citizens of Sweden, Norway, Denmark, and Finland may visit, visa free, for not more than 15 days.

Vietnam now operate a quasi 'visa on arrival' programme. An online application must be made through a company such as www.visa-vietnam.org. A pre-approved letter is granted and a service fee paid but payment for the actual visa is made on collection at the airport.

Hanoi

Contents

Footprint features

Ins and outs

Getting there

Noi Bai Airport is 35 km from the city, about a one-hour drive. There are official taxis and a minibus service that drops passengers at their hotels and thus receives commission. Hotels also have their own buses. There are regular flights to a number of international destinations as well as many domestic connections. The train station is central, about a five- to 10-minute taxi ride from the Old Quarter of the city north of Hoan Kiem Lake. There are regular trains from Ho Chi Minh City, and all points on the route south, as well as from Haiphong and Lao Cai (for Sapa) in the north. There is not just one bus terminal but several receiving buses from destinations in the north and major towns all the way south from Ho Chi Minh City. ▸▸ *See also Transport, page 64*.

Getting around

Hanoi is getting more frenetic by the minute. With its elegant, tree-lined boulevards walking and bicycling can be delightful. If you like the idea of being pedalled, then a cyclo is the answer – but be prepared for some concentrated haggling. There are also motorbike taxis (*xe ôm*) and self-drive motorbikes for hire as well as a fleet of metered taxis. Local buses are a last resort.

Orientation

Hanoi can be parcelled up into a number of districts each with its own feel and function. At the heart of the city is Hoan Kiem Lake. The majority of visitors make straight for the Old City (36 Streets and Guilds) area north of the lake, which is densely packed and bustling with commerce. The French Quarter, which still largely consists of French buildings, is south of the lake. Here you'll find the Opera House and the grandest hotels, shops and offices. A large block of the city west of Hoan Kiem Lake (Ba Dinh District) represents the heart of government and the civil and military administration of Vietnam. Imposing colonial architecture, the mark of authority of the French administration, now houses Vietnamese government ministries. All around this district colonial villas are occupied by foreign embassies. To the north of the city is the West Lake, Tay Ho District, fringed with the suburban homes of the new middle class and a new emerging expat quarter with bars and restaurants. Away to the southern and eastern edges of the city are the industrial and residential zones.

Best time to visit

For much of the year Hanoi's weather is decidedly non-tropical. It benefits from glorious European-like springs and autumns when temperatures are warm but not too hot and not too cold. From May until early November Hanoi is fearfully hot and steamy. You cannot take a step without breaking into a sweat. The winter months from November to February can be decidedly chilly and Hanoians wrap themselves up well in warm coats, woolly hats, gloves and scarves. Most museums are closed on Mondays.

Tourist information

The **Tourist Information Center** ⓘ *7 Dinh Tien Hoang St, T4-3926 3366, www.ticvietnam.com, daily 0800-2200*, at the northern end of the lake, is proving useful. It provides information and maps and will book hotels and transport tickets at no extra cost; also currency exchange and ATM. The website www.hanoitourism.gov.vn is also useful. Good tourist information is available from the multitude of tour operators in the city. ▸▸ *See also Tour operators, page 61*.

History

Precolonial era

The original village on the site of the present city was located in a district with the local name of Long Do. The community seems to have existed as a small settlement as early as the third century AD, although the early history of the Red River Delta largely passed it by. At the beginning of the eighth century a general named Lu Yu became so enchanted with the scenery around the village of An Vien (close to Long Do), that he decided to move his headquarters there. Here he built a shrine to the Emperor Hsuan Tsung, erected an inscribed tablet, and dedicated a statue of the local earth spirit on which was inscribed a poem extolling the beauty of the spot.

The origins of Hanoi as a great city lie with a temple orphan, Ly Cong Uan. Ly rose through the ranks of the palace guards to become their commander and in 1010, four years after the death of the previous King Le Hoan, was enthroned, marking the beginning of the 200-year-long Ly Dynasty. On becoming king, Ly Cong Uan moved his capital from Hoa Lu to Dai La, which he renamed **Thang Long** (Soaring Dragon). Thang Long is present-day **Hanoi**. During the Ly Dynasty the heart of Thang Long was the king's sanctuary in the Forbidden City (Cam Thanh). Drawing both spiritual and physical protection, as well as economic well-being from their proximity to the king and his court, a city of commoners grew up around the walls of Cam Thanh. The Ly kings established a Buddhist monarchical tradition, which mirrored other courts in Southeast Asia. A number of pagodas were built at this time – most have since disappeared, although the One Pillar Pagoda and the Tran Vu Temple both date from this period (see below).

Thang Long, renamed **Tay Do** (Western Capital), was to remain the capital of Vietnam until 1400 when the Ho Dynasty (1400-1407) established a new capital at Thanh Hoa. But soon afterwards, the focus of power shifted back to Thang Long which, in turn, was renamed **Dong Kinh** (Eastern Capital). It is from Dong Kinh that the French name for North Vietnam – Tonkin – is derived. From 1786 to 1802 when Quang Trung established his capital in Hué the city was known as **Bac Thanh** (Northern Citadel). The present name of the city dates from 1831 when the Nguyen Emperor Tu Duc (1847-1883) made it the capital of the province of Hanoi. Hanoi celebrated its 1000th anniversary with a series of special events in October 2010.

Colonial era

During the period of French expansion into Indochina, the Red River was proposed as an alternative trade route to the Mekong. Indeed, the oldest name for Hanoi seems to have been Ke Cho, which means, 'a place where markets are'. Francis Garnier, a French naval officer, was dispatched to the area in 1873 to ascertain the possibilities of establishing such a route. Despite having only a modest force of men under arms, when negotiations with Emperor Tu Duc failed in 1882, Garnier attacked and captured the citadel of Hanoi under the dubious pretext that the Vietnamese were about to attack him. Recognizing that if a small expeditionary force could be so successful, then there would be little chance against a full-strength army, Tu Duc acceded to French demands. At the time that the French took control of Annam, Hanoi could still be characterized more as a collection of villages than a city. As late as the 1870s, the French scholar André Masson, for example, argued that Hanoi "was not a city but a composite agglomeration where an administrative capital, a commercial town and numerous villages were juxtaposed".

1 Hanoi

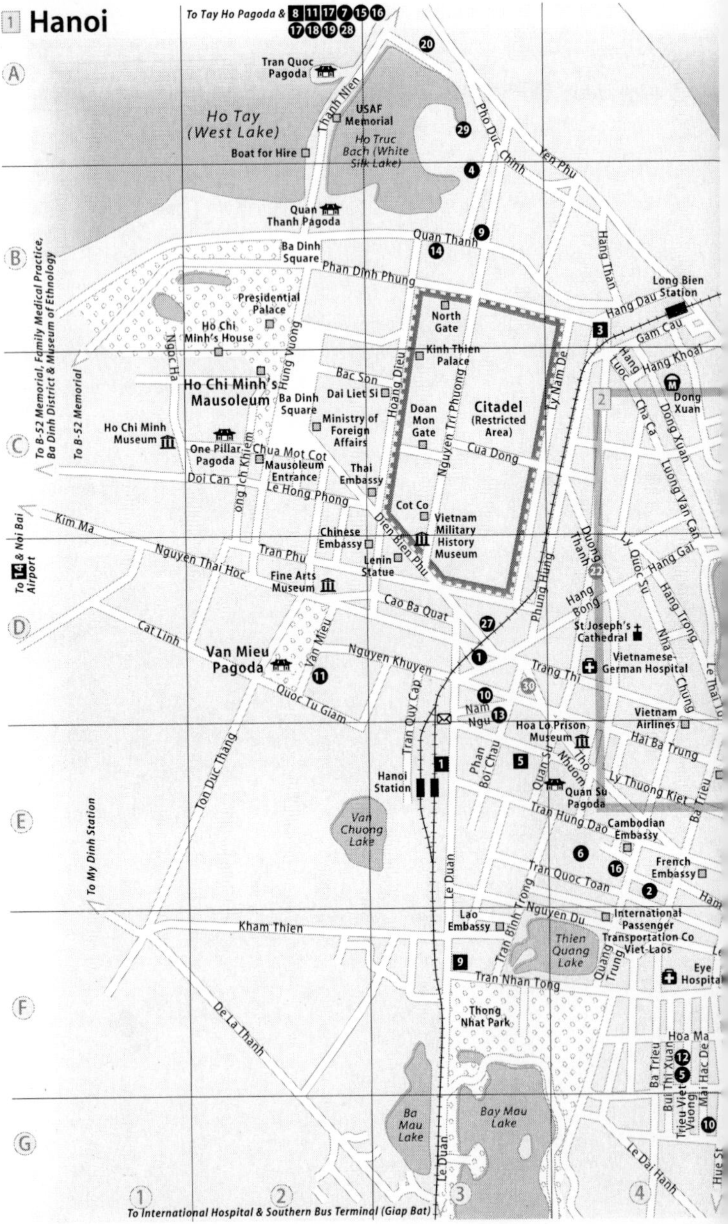

To Tay Ho Pagoda & 8 11 17 7 15 16 17 18 19 28
Tran Quoc Pagoda
Ho Tay (West Lake)
Thanh Nien
USAF Memorial
Ho Truc Bach (White Silk Lake)
Boat for Hire
Pho Duc Chinh
Yen Phu
Quan Thanh Pagoda
Quan Thanh
Ba Dinh Square
Phan Dinh Phung
Hang Than
Long Bien Station
Hang Dau
Gam Cau
Hang Khoai
Hang Luoc
Dong Xuan
Cha Ca
Luong Van Can
Presidential Palace
Ho Chi Minh's House
North Gate
Kinh Thien Palace
Ngoc Ha
Hung Vuong
Hoang Dieu
Nguyen Tri Phuong
Ly Nam De
Bac Son
Ho Chi Minh's Mausoleum
Ba Dinh Square
Dai Liet Si
Ministry of Foreign Affairs
Doan Mon Gate
Citadel (Restricted Area)
Ho Chi Minh Museum
One Pillar Pagoda
Chua Mot Cot
Mausoleum Entrance
Thai Embassy
Cua Dong
Ong Ich Khiem
Doi Can
Le Hong Phong
Cot Co
Vietnam Military History Museum
To B-52 Memorial, Family Medical Practice, Ba Dinh District & Museum of Ethnology
To B-52 Memorial
To 14 & Noi Bai Airport
Kim Ma
Nguyen Thai Hoc
Tran Phu
Chinese Embassy
Lenin Statue
Dien Bien Phu
Duong Thanh
Ly Quoc Su
Hang Gai
Hang Trong
Fine Arts Museum
Cao Ba Quat
Phung Hung
Hang Bong
St Joseph's Cathedral
Cat Linh
Van Mieu Pagoda
Van Mieu
Nguyen Khuyen
Trang Thi
Vietnamese-German Hospital
Nha Chung
Le Thai To
Quoc Tu Giam
Tran Quy Cap
Nam Ngu
Hoa Lo Prison Museum
Vietnam Airlines
Hai Ba Trung
Ton Duc Thang
Phan Boi Chau
Quan Su
Tho Nhuom
Hanoi Station
Quan Su Pagoda
Ly Thuong Kiet
Ba Trieu
Van Chuong Lake
Tran Hung Dao
Cambodian Embassy
Le Duan
Tran Quoc Toan
French Embassy
To My Dinh Station
Lao Embassy
Nguyen Du
International Passenger Transportation Co Viet-Laos
Kham Thien
Tran Binh Trong
Thien Quang Lake
Quang Trung
Eye Hospital
Tran Nhan Tong
Thong Nhat Park
De La Thanh
Hoa Ma
Ba Trieu
Bui Thi Xuan
Mai Hac De
Trieu Viet Vuong
Ba Mau Lake
Bay Mau Lake
Le Dai Hanh
Hue St
To International Hospital & Southern Bus Terminal (Giap Bat)

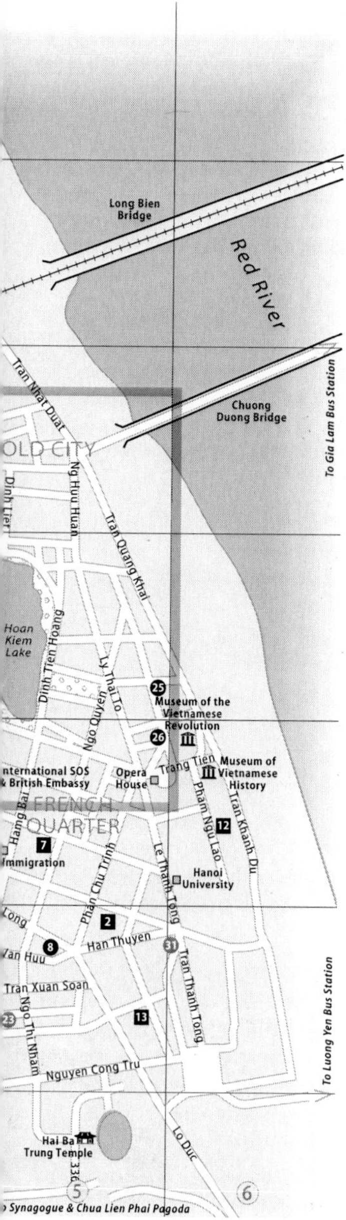

➡ **Hanoi maps**
1 **Hanoi, page 24**
2 Hoan Kiem, page 28

N

400 metres
400 yards

Sleeping
Army **12** *E6*
Cay Xoai **1** *E3*
De Syloia & Cay Cau Restaurant **2** *F5*
Intercontinental Hanoi Westlake **8** *A2*
Galaxy **3** *B4*
Movenpick **5** *E3*
Hanoi Daewoo **14** *D1*
Hoa Binh **7** *E5*
Nikko Hanoi **9** *F3*
Sheraton **17** *A2*
Sofitel Plaza Hanoi **11** *A2*
Sunway **13** *F5*

Eating
252 Hang Bong **1** *D3*
Bobby Chinn **7** *A2*
Café 129 **10** *F4*
Café Puku **27** *D3*
Chien Beo **28** *A3*
Club de l'Oriental **26** *E5*
Com Chay Nang Tam **6** *E4*
Cong Café **5** *F4*
Daluva **17** *A3*
Don's Bistro **16** *A3*
Foodshop 45 **29** *A3*
Hanoi Cooking Centre **4** *B3*
Hanoi Gourmet **8** *F5*
La Badiane **10** *D3*
Le Co-operative **18** *A3*
Khazana **25** *D5*
Kitchen **19** *A3*
KOTO **11** *D2*
Mau House & Ceramic **20** *A3*
Pho Yen **9** *B3*
Quan An Ngon **13** *D3*
Seasons of Hanoi **14** *B3*
Shim Sáo **12** *F4*
Song Thu **16** *E4*
Verticale **2** *E4*
Vine Wine Boutique Bar & Café **15** *A3*

Bars & clubs
Finnegan's Irish Pub **22** *D4*
Hoa Vien **31** *F6*
House of Son Tinh **24** *A3*
R&R Tavern **30** *D3*
Tadiato **23** *F5*

From 1882 onwards, Hanoi, along with the port city of Haiphong, became the focus of French activity in the north. Hanoi was made the capital of the new colony of Annam, and the French laid out a 2-sq-km residential and business district, constructing mansions, villas and public buildings incorporating both French and Asian architectural styles. Many of these buildings still stand to the south and east of the Old City and Hoan Kiem Lake – almost as if they were grafted onto the older Annamese city. In the 1920s and 1930s, with conditions in the countryside deteriorating, there was an influx of landless and dispossessed labourers into the city. In their struggle to feed their families, many were willing to take jobs at subsistence wages in the textile, cigarette and other industries that grew up under French patronage. Before long, a poor underclass, living in squalid, pathetic conditions, had formed. At the end of the Second World War, with the French battling to keep Ho Chi Minh and his forces at bay, Hanoi became little more than a service centre. By 1954 there were about 40,000 stallholders, shopkeepers, peddlars and hawkers operating in the city – which at that time had a population of perhaps 400,000. It has been calculated that half of all families relied on the informal sector for their livelihoods.

War damage

After the French withdrew in 1954, Ho Chi Minh concentrated on building up Vietnam and in particular Hanoi's industrial base. At that time the capital had only eight, small, privately owned factories. By 1965, more than 1000 enterprises had been added to this figure. However, as the US bombing of the north intensified with Operation Rolling Thunder in 1965, so the authorities began to evacuate non-essential civilians from Hanoi and to disperse industry into smaller, less vulnerable, units of operation. Between 500,000 and 750,000 people were evacuated between 1965 and 1973, representing 75% of the inner-city population. Nevertheless, the cessation of hostilities led to a spontaneous migration back into the capital. By 1984 the population of the city had reached 2.7 million, and today it is in excess of three million.

Urban renewal

Although Ho Chi Minh City has attracted the lion's share of Vietnam's foreign inward investment, Hanoi, as the capital, also receives a large amount. But whereas Ho Chi Minh City's investment tends to be in industry, Hanoi has received a great deal of attention from property developers, notably in the hotel and office sectors. Much of the development has been in prestigious and historical central Hanoi and has included the construction of a huge office complex on the site of the notorious 'Hanoi Hilton' prison, much to the mortification of Vietnamese war veterans, see page 34. Some commentators applauded the authorities for this attempt at putting the past behind them.

Although some architecturallly insensitive schemes have dominated the cityscape, in the past 15 years numerous old colonial villas have been tastefully restored as bars, restaurants and homes cater to the growing numbers of Western visitors, dipomats and businessmen with a very positive effect on Hanoi's architectural heritage.

Pollution levels in Hanoi have soared as a result of the construction boom: dust from demolition, piling, bricks and tiles and sand blown from the back of trucks add an estimated 150 cubic metres of pollutants to the urban atmosphere every day. But while asthmatics may wheeze, Hanoi's army of builders grows daily ever stronger. Hundreds of farmers join the urban job market each week and one can see bands of men standing around at strategic points waiting to be recruited; on Duong Thanh Street, for example, carpenters with their tool boxes wait patiently for the call to a day's work. But can Hanoi's economy keep pace with the rate of migration in from the countryside? Against the background of the Asian financial crisis of the late 1990s the situation looked ominous but the stage now seems set for a period of sustained growth. In addition, by means of a strict system of residential permits the Party is able to control the rate at which people settle in the capital. Without the proper papers stamped with a round red seal children cannot go to school. As education is one of the highest priorities for many Vietnamese parents it curbs their enthusiasm for moving to the city.

Hanoi is, in a great many ways, very different from Ho Chi Minh City. The Hanoians have an agreeable sense of history and appreciation for old buildings: indeed a great many of Hanoi's citizens also appear elderly. Whether practicing t'ai chi around one of the city's many lakes or squatting at a tiny pavement café the elderly are part of Hanoi's historical structure and charm. The old buildings, small scale and compact nature of Hanoi will make many Europeans feel very much at home and quickly develop a strong sense of attachment.

Sights

Much of the charm of Hanoi lies not so much in the official 'sights' but in the unofficial and informal: the traffic, small shops, stalls, the bustle of pedestrians, clothing, parents treating their children to an ice cream, an evening visit to Hoan Kiem Lake. Like China when it was 'opening up' to Western tourists in the late 1970s, the primary interest lies in the novelty of exploring a city which, until recently, has opted for a firmly socialist road to development and has been insulated from the West. Today, you'll find it enlivened by an entrepeneurial spirit manifest in new shops, bars, companies and building developments.

Hoan Kiem Lake and Central Hanoi

Hoan Kiem Lake

Hoan Kiem Lake or Ho Guom (the Lake of the Restored Sword) as it is more commonly referred to in Hanoi, is named after an incident that occurred during the 15th century. Emperor Le Thai To (1428-1433), following a momentous victory against an army of invading Ming Chinese, was sailing on the lake when a golden turtle appeared from the depths to take back the charmed sword which had secured the victory and restore it to the lake whence it came. Like the sword in the stone of British Arthurian legend, Le Thai To's sword assures Vietnamese of divine intervention in time of national crisis and the story is graphically portrayed in water puppet theatres across the country. There is a modest and rather dilapidated tower (the **Tortoise Tower**) commemorating the event on an islet in the southern part of the lake. In fact, the lake does contain large turtles; one captured in 1968 was reputed to have weighed 250 kg. The creatures that inhabit the lake are believed to be a variety of Asian softshell tortoise. It is thought that they were the species *Rafetus swinhoei* but a scientist reported that these species were in fact different from Ho Guom tortoises; the Ho Guom tortoise has now been named *Rafetus leloii*. In 2004 the water level fell quite dramatically and turtles were seen more often. The park that surrounds the lake is used by the residents of the city every morning for jogging and t'ai chi (Chinese shadow boxing) and is regarded by locals as one of the city's beauty spots. The light around the lake has a filmic quality, especially in the early morning. When the French arrived in Hanoi at the end of the 19th century, the lake was an unhealthy lagoon surrounded by so many huts that it was impossible to see the shore.

Ngoc Son Temple and Sunbeam Bridge

ⓘ *3000d.*

The northeast corner of Hoan Kiem Lake is the place to have your photo taken, preferably with the **Ngoc Son Temple** in the background. The temple was built in the early 19th century on a small island on the foundations of the old Khanh Thuy Palace. The island is linked to the shore by the The Huc (Sunbeam) Bridge, constructed in 1875. The temple is dedicated to Van Xuong, the God of Literature, although the 13th-century hero Tran Hung Dao, the martial arts genius Quan Vu and the physician La To are also worshipped here. Shrouded by trees and surrounded by water, the pagoda's position is its strongest attribute. To the side of the temple is a room containing a preserved turtle and photographs of the creatures in the lake.

Hoan Kiem

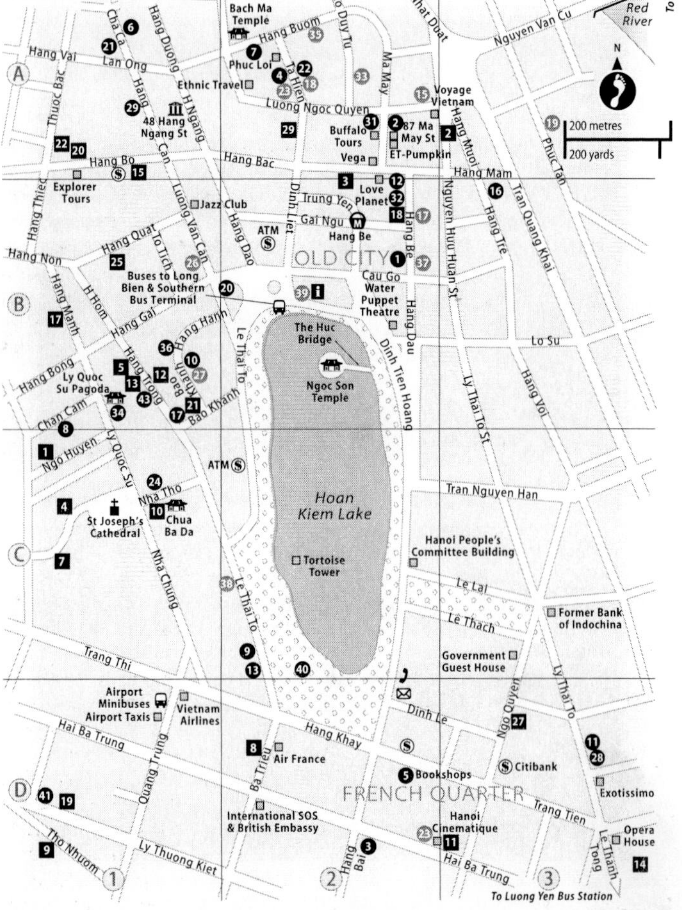

Old City and 36 Streets

Stretching north from the lake is the Old City (36 Streets and Guilds or 36 Pho Phuong). Previously, it lay to the east of the citadel, where the emperor had his residence, and was squalid, dark, cramped and disease-ridden. This part of Hanoi has survived surprisingly intact, and today is the most beautiful area of the city. Narrow streets, each named after the produce that it sells or used to sell (**Basket Street**, **Paper Street**, **Silk Street**, etc), create an intricate web of activity and colour, see box, page 30.

By the 15th century there were 36 short lanes here, each specializing in a particular trade and representing one of the 36 guilds. Among them, for example, were the **Phuong Hang Dao** (**Dyers' Guild Street**), and the **Phuong Hang Bac** (**Silversmiths' Street**). In fact, Hang Bac (*hang* means merchandise) is the oldest street in Hanoi, dating from the 13th century. The 36 streets have interested European visitors since they first started coming to Hanoi. For example, in 1685 Samuel Bacon, noted how "all the diverse objects sold in this town have a specially assigned street", remarking how different this was from "companies and corporations in European cities". The streets in question not only sold different products, but were usually also populated by people from different areas of the country – even from single villages. They would live, work and worship together because each of the occupational guilds had its own temple and its own community support networks.

Some of this past is still in evidence: at the south end of Hang Dau Street, for example, is a mass of stalls selling nothing but shoes, while Tin Street is still home to a community of pot and pan menders (and sellers). Generally, however, the crafts and trades of the past have given way to new activities – karaoke bars and tourist shops – but it is remarkable the extent to which the streets still specialize in the production and sale of just one type of merchandise.

The dwellings in this area are known as *nha ong* (**tube houses**). The majority were built at the end of the 19th century and the beginning of the 20th; they are narrow, with shop fronts sometimes only 3 m wide, but can be up to 50 m long (such as the one at 51 Hang Dao). In the countryside the dimensions of houses were calculated on the basis of the owner's own physical dimensions; in urban areas the tube houses

➡ **Hanoi maps**
1 Hanoi, page 24
2 Hoan Kiem, page 52

Sleeping
Artist **11** *D3*
Church **10** *C1*
Cinnamon **4** *C1*
Eden Hanoi & Luna d'Autunno Restaurant **9** *D1*
Freedom **12** *B1*
Gold Spring **2** *A3*
Golden Lotus **5** *B1*
Hang Trong **13** *B1*
Hanoi Backpackers' Hostel **1** *C1*
Hilton Hanoi Opera **14** *D3*
Hoa Linh **15** *A1*
Hong Ngoc **17** *B1*
Hong Ngoc 3 **3** *B2*
Joseph's **7** *C1*
Mai Phuong **18** *B2*
Melia Hanoi **19** *D1*
My Lan **20** *A1*
Nam Phuong **21** *B1*
Ngoc Diep **22** *A1*
Real Darling Café **25** *B1*
Sofitel Legend Metropole Hanoi & Le Beaulieu Restaurant **27** *D3*
Thuy Nga **29** *A2*
Zephyr **8** *D2*

Eating
69 **2** *A2*
Al Fresco's **3** *D2*
Baan Thai **6** *A1*
Bit Tet **7** *A2*
Bon Mua **9** *C2*
Café des Arts & Stop Café **10** *B1*
Café Moca **24** *C1*
Café Puku **43** *B1*
Cha Ca La Vong **21** *A1*
Chica **4** *A2*
Club Opera **11** *D3*
Fanny Ice Cream **13** *C2*
Green Tangerine **1** *B2*
Hanoi Press Club **28** *D3*
Highlands Coffee **40** C2
Highway 4 **16** *B3*
Kangaroo Café **17** *B1*
Kem Trang Tien **5** *D2*
Lá **34** *B1*
Little Hanoi (Ta Hien St) **22** *A2*
Little Hanoi (Hang Gai St) **20** *B2*
Madame Hiem **8** *B1*
My Burger My **12** *B2*
Pepperonis **36** *B1*
Restaurant 22 **29** *A1*
San Ho **41** *D1*
Tamarind & Handspan Adventure Travel **31** *A2*
Tandoor **32** *B2*

Bars & clubs
Cheeky Quarter, Tet **33** *A2*
Dragonfly **35** *A2*
Funky Buddha **37** *B2*
Ho Guom Xanh **38** *C2*
Jo Jo's **30** *D2*
Half Man/Half Noodle **15** *A2*
Le Pub **17** *B2*
Mao's Red Lounge **18** *A2*
Legends **39** *B2*
Phuc Tan **19** *A3*
Polite Pub **27** *B1*
Roots **23** *A2*
Solace **25** *A3*
Rock Billy **26** *B2*

Guild street name meanings and their current trades

Bat Dan St – clay bowls
Bat Su – ceramic bowls
Hang Bac – silver, jewellery
Hang Bo – baskets, motorbike stickers, barbecue squid (late night)
Hang Bong – cotton
Hang Buom – sails, coffee, chocolate, booze
Hang But – calligraphy brushes
Hang Can – weighing scales
Hang Dao – silk (Pho Hang Dao means 'street where red-dyed fabrics are sold'), sewing things, feathers
Hang Dieu – smoking pipes, fake brand name handbags
Hang Duong – sugar
Hang Gai – hemp, silk, souvenirs, galleries, tailor shops
Hang Ma – votive paper, headstones
Hang Manh – bamboo screens/mats
Hang Non – conical hats
Hang Phen St – alum sulphate
Hang Quat – paper fans, religious artefacts
Hang Thiec – tinsmiths, tin ovens
Hang Tre – bamboo
Hang Trong – drums, boutiques, galleries
Lan Ong – traditional medicine
Hang Vai – cloth street
Ngo Gach – bricks
Thuoc Bac – medicine street
To Tich – undecorated mats, fruit cups
Yen Thai Alley – embroidery

evolved so that each house owner could have an, albeit very small, area of shop frontage facing onto the main street; the width was determined by the social class of the owner. The houses tend to be interspersed with courtyards or 'wells' to permit light into the house and allow some space for outside activities like washing and gardening. As geographers Brian Shaw and R Jones note in a paper on heritage conservation in Hanoi, the houses also had a natural air-conditioning system: the difference in ambient temperature between the inner courtyards and the outside street created air flow, and the longer the house the greater the velocity of the flow.

A common wall can sometimes still be seen between tube houses. Built in a step-like pattern, it not only marked land boundaries but also acted as a fire break. The position of the house frontages were not fixed until the early 20th century and consequently some streets have a delightfully irregular appearance. The structures were built of bricks 'cemented' together with sugar-cane juice.

The older houses tend to be lower; commoners were not permitted to build higher than the Emperor's own residence. Other regulations prohibited attic windows looking down on the street; this was to prevent assassination and to stop people from looking down on a passing king. As far as colour and decoration were concerned, purple and gold were strictly for royal use only, as was the decorative use of the dragon. By the early 20th century inhabitants were replacing their traditional tube houses with buildings inspired by French architecture. Many fine buildings from this era remain, however, and are best appreciated by standing back and looking upwards. Shutters, cornices, columns and wrought-iron balconies and balustrades are common decorative features. An ornate façade sometimes conceals the pitched roof behind. There are some good examples on **Nguyen Sieu Street**.

A fear among conservationists is that this unique area will be destroyed as residents who have made small fortunes with the freeing-up of the economy, redevelop their houses insensitively. The desire is understandable: the tube houses are cramped and squalid, and often without any facilities.

48 Hang Ngang Street ⓘ *at the north end of Hang Dao St, before it becomes Hang Duong*

Syndicated loans keep the sharks away

Throughout Vietnam, and indeed across the world wherever there are large numbers of Vietnamese, one will find *hui* in operation. *Hui* (or *ho* as it is called in the north) is a credit circle of 10 to 20 people who meet every month; the scheme lasts as many months as there are participants. In a blind auction the highest bidder takes home that month's capital. Credit is expensive in Vietnam, partly because there are few banks to make personal loans, so in time of crisis the needy have to borrow from money-lenders at crippling rates of interest. Alternatively they can join a *hui* and borrow at more modest rates.

It works like this: the *hui* is established with members agreeing to put in a fixed amount, say 100,000d, each month. Each month the members bid according to their financial needs, entering a zero bid if they need no cash. If, in month one, Mr Nam's daughter gets married he will require money for the wedding festivities and, moreover, he has to have the money so he must bid high, maybe 25,000d. Assuming this is the highest bid he will receive 75,000d from each member (ie 100,000d less 25,000d). In future months Mr Nam cannot bid again but must pay 100,000d to whoever collects that month's pot. Towards the end of the cycle several participants (those whose buffalo have not died and those whose daughters remain unmarried) will have taken nothing out but will have paid in 100,000d (minus x) dong each month; they can enter a zero bid and get the full 100,000d from all participants and with it a tidy profit. There is, needless to say, strategy involved and this is where the Vietnamese love of gambling ("the besetting sin of the Vietnamese" according to Norman Lewis) colours the picture. One day, Mr Muoi wins one million dong on the Vinh Long lottery. He lets it be known that he intends to buy a Honda Dream, but to raise the necessary purchase price he must 'win' that month's *hui* and will be bidding aggressively. In the same month Thuy, Mrs Phuoc's baby daughter, celebrates her first birthday so Mrs Phuoc needs money to throw a lavish *thoi noi* party. She has heard of old Muoi's intentions but doesn't know if he is serious. In case he is, she will have to bid high. On the day, nice Mrs Phuoc enters a knock-out bid of 30,000d but wily old Muoi was bluffing all along and he and the others make a lot of interest that month.

St, 0800-1130, 1330-1630, 10,000d, is the spot where Ho Chi Minh drew up the **Vietnamese Declaration of Independence** in 1945, ironically modelled on the US Declaration of Independence. It now houses a **museum** with black and white photographs of Uncle Ho.

The house at **87 Ma May Street** ⓘ *daily 0800-1200, 1300-1700, 5000d, guide included*, is a wonderfully preserved example of an original shop house now open to the public. The house was built in the late 1800s as a home for a single family. The importance of the miniature interior courtyards providing light, fresh air and gardens can be appreciated. The wooden upstairs and pitched fish-scale-tiled roofs are typical of how most houses would have looked. From 1954 to 1999 five families shared the building as the urban population rose and living conditions declined. The **Bach Ma (White Horse) Temple** ⓘ *76 Hang Buom St*, dating from the ninth century, honours Long Do and is the oldest religious building in the Old Quarter. In 1010, King Ly Thai To honoured Long Do with the title of the capital. It is said that a horse revealed to King Ly Thai To where to build the walls of the citadel.

A walk through **Hang Be Market** (actually on Gai Ngu Street) reveals just how far Hanoi has developed over the past decade. There is a wonderful variety of food on sale – live, dead, cooked and raw. Quacking ducks, newly plucked chickens, saucers of warm blood, pigs' trotters, freshly picked vegetables as well as pickled ones; the quality of produce is remarkable and testimony to the rapid strides Vietnamese agriculture has made. In this market and surrounding streets beautiful cut flowers are on sale.

Venturing further north, is **Cua Quan Chuong**, the last remaining of Hanoi's 16 gates. In the 18th century a system of ramparts and walls was built around Hanoi. Quan Chuong Gate was built in 1749 and rebuilt in 1817.

Further north still, on Dong Xuan Street, is the large and varied **Dong Xuan Market**. This large covered market was destroyed in a disastrous fire in 1994. Stall holders lost an estimated US$4.5 million worth of stock and complained bitterly at the inadequacy of the fire services; one fire engine arrived with no water. The market has been rebuilt. It specializes mainly in clothes and household goods.

To the west, along Phung Hung Street is another live market of fish, dog, birds, vegetables and betel nut. It makes for a wonderful wander.

West of Hoan Kiem Lake

To the west of Hoan Kiem Lake in a little square stands the rather sombre, twin-towered neo-Gothic **Saint Joseph's Cathedral** ⓘ *open 0500-1130, 1400-1930 through a door at the back; Mass Mon-Fri 0530, 0815, Sat 0530, 1800, Sun 0500, 0700, 0900, 1100, 1600, 1800*. Built in 1886, the cathedral is important as one of the very first colonial-era buildings in Hanoi finished, as it was, soon after the Treaty of Tientsin which gave France control over the whole of Vietnam (see page 412). It was at located at the centre of the Catholic Mission. Some fine stained-glass windows remain.

About 100 m in front of the cathedral on Nha Tho Street is a much older religious foundation, the **Stone Lady Pagoda** (**Chua Ba Da**), down a narrow alley. It consists of an old pagoda and a Buddhist school. On either side of the pagoda are low buildings where the monks live. Although few of the standing buildings are of any antiquity it is an ancient site and a tranquil and timeless atmosphere prevails. Originally built in 1056 as Sung Khanh Pagoda, by the late 15th century it needed rebuilding. A stone statue of a woman was found in the foundations and was worshipped in the pagoda. By 1767 the walls needed rebuilding. Each time they were built they collapsed. The foundations were dug deeper and the stone statue was found again. Since then the walls have held fast. Although now a pagoda for the worship of Buddha it is clear that the site has had a mixed spiritual history.

North of the cathedral on Ly Quoc Su Street is the **Ly Quoc Su Pagoda**, once home to Minh Khong, a physician and the chief adviser to Ly Than Tong, the Ly dynasty emperor. He became famous in the 12th century after curing the emperor of a disease that other doctors had failed to treat. It was restored in 2010.

South of Hoan Kiem Lake

Opera House

ⓘ *Not open to the public except during public performances. See the billboards outside or visit the box office for details.*

To the south and east of Hoan Kiem Lake is the proud-looking French-era Opera House. It was built between 1901-1911 by François Lagisquet and is one of the finest French colonial buildings in Hanoi. Some 35,000 bamboo piles were sunk into the mud of the Red River to provide foundations for the lofty edifice. The exterior is a delightful mass of shutters, wrought-iron work, little balconies and a tiled frieze. The top balustrade is nicely capped with griffins. Inside, there are dozens of little boxes and fine decoration evocative of the French era. Having suffered years of neglect the Opera House was eventually lavishly restored, opening in time for the Francophone Summit held in 1997. Original drawings in Hanoi and Paris were consulted and teams of foreign experts were brought in to supervise local craftsmen. Slate was carried from Sin Ho to re-tile the roof, Italians oversaw the relaying of the mosaic floor in the lobby and French artists repainted the fine ornamental details of the auditorium. The restoration cost US$14 million, a colossal sum to spend on the reappointment of a colonial edifice. A Hanoi planning department architect explained that although the Opera House was French in style it was built by Vietnamese hands and represented an indelible part of Vietnamese history.

Sofitel Metropole

ⓘ *15 Ngo Quyen St.*

The Metropole, built in French-colonial style in 1901 is an icon of elegance in the French quarter of the city. It quickly became the focal point of colonial life for 50 years. In 1916, it screened the first movie shown in Indochina. In 1944, Japanese POWS were temporarily housed here. In the 1950s the Vietnamese government appropriated it, named it the **Thong Nhat Hotel**, and used it as a hotel for VIPs; during the Vietnam War years the press and diplomats used it as their headquarters. Many famous celebrities and diplomats have stayed here including Graham Greene (writing *The Quiet American*), Somerset Maugham, Noel Coward, Stephen Hawking, Oliver Stone, Charlie Chaplin, Sir Roger Moore, Jane Fonda, Mick Jagger, Catherine Deneuve, George Bush Senior, Fidel Castro, Robert McNamara, Jacques Chirac and Boutros Boutros Ghali. ▸▸ *See also Sleeping, page 45.*

Museum of the Vietnamese Revolution

ⓘ *216 Tran Quang Khai St, T4-3825 4151, Tue-Sun 0800-1145, 1330-1615, 20,000d.*

The Museum of the Vietnamese Revolution (Bao Tang Cach Mang Vietnam), housed in an old French villa, traces the struggle of the Vietnamese people to establish their independence. Following the displays, it becomes clear that the American involvement in Vietnam has been just one episode in a centuries-long struggle against foreign aggressors. The 3000 exhibits are dryly presented across 29 rooms and in chronological order. They start with the cover the struggle for independence (1858-1945); the final rooms show the peace and prosperity of reunification: bountiful harvests, the opening of large civil engineering projects, and smiling peasants.

Museum of Vietnamese History

ⓘ *1 Trang Tien St, T4-325 3518, Tue-Sun 0800-1130, 1330-1630, 15,000d.*

A short distance south of the Museum of the Vietnamese Revolution is the History Museum (**Bao Tang Lich Su**). It is housed in a splendid building, completed in 1931. It was built as the home of the École Française d'Extrême-Orient, a distinguished archaeological, historical and ethnological research institute, by Ernest Hébrard. Hébrard, who was responsible for so many fine colonial-era buildings in Vietnam, here employed a distinctly Indochinese style appropriate to its original and, indeed, its current function. The museum remains a centre of cultural and historical research. The École Française d'Extrême-Orient played an important role in the preservation and restoration of ancient Vietnamese structures and temples, many of which were destroyed or came under threat of demolition by the French to enable the growth of their colonial city.

The museum remains a centre of cultural and historical research. The collection spans Vietnamese history from the neolithic to the 20th century of Ho Chi Minh and is arranged in chronological order. Galleries lead from the Neolithic (Bac Son) represented by stone tools and jewellery; the Bronze Age (Dong Son) with some fine bronze drums; Funan and the port of Oc-Eo; Champa is represented by some fine stone carvings of *apsaras*, mythical dancing girls. There are relics such as bronze temple bells and urns of successive royal dynasties from Le to Nguyen. An impressive giant turtle, symbol of longevity, supports a huge stela praising the achievements of Le Loi, founder of the Le Dynasty, who harnessed nationalist sentiment and forced the Chinese out of Vietnam. Unfortunately some of the pieces (including a number of the stelae) are reproductions.

Other French Quarter buildings

Other buildings of the 'French Concession' include the impressive **Government Guest House** ⓘ *12 Ngo Quyen St*, diagonally opposite the Metropole. The bright ochre building was the former residence of the French Resident Superior of Tonkin.

The enormous **Post Office** ⓘ *6 Dinh Le St*, facing Hoan Kiem lake, was designed by Henri Cerruti in 1942. Next door is the **Post and Telegraphic Office** ⓘ *75 Dinh Tien Hoang St*, designed by Auguste-Henri Vildieu and completed in 1896. Further up Dinh Tieng Hoang is the **Hanoi People's Committee** building, formerly the town hall and built by Vildieu between 1897 and 1906. The main section at the front dates from the late 1980s and early 1990s demonstrating brutalist communist architecture. Vildieu also designed the **Supreme Court** ⓘ *48 Ly Thuong Kiet*, between 1900 and 1906. It's a fine symmetrical building with a grey-tiled roof, two staircases and balustrades.

Ernest Hébrard, who worked at the Central Services of Urban Planning and Architecture, designed the **Indochina University**, now **Hanoi University** ⓘ *19 Le Thanh Tong St*, which was completed in 1926. It bears a remarkable resemblance to the history museum, which he also designed. Furthermore, Hébrard designed the **Ministry of Foreign Affairs** (then the **Bureau des Finances**) ⓘ *Dien Bien Phu St*, in 1931.

The architecturally remarkable former **Bank of Indochina** ⓘ *49 Ly Thai To St*, was built in 1930 by architect Georges-André Trouvé. Its grey, heavy art deco appearance and isolated position evokes a bit of fear. One wonders what the bank vaults look like inside.

Around 1000 colonial villas are still scattered around Hanoi, especially west of the Old Quarter. Many of them have been superbly restored and are used by embassies.

Hoa Lo Prison

ⓘ*1 Hoa Lo, T4-3824 6358, Tue-Sun 0800-1130, 1330-1630, 10,000d.*

Hoa Lo Prison (Maison Centrale), better known as the **Hanoi Hilton**, is the prison where US POWs were incarcerated, some for six years, during the Vietnamese War. Up until 1969, prisoners were also tortured here. Two US Airforce officers, Charles Tanner and Ross Terry, rather than face torture, concocted a story about two other members of their squadron who had been court-martialled for refusing to fly missions against the north. Thrilled with this piece of propaganda, visiting Japanese communists were told the story and it filtered back to the US. Unfortunately for Tanner and Terry they had called their imaginary pilots Clark Kent and Ben Casey (both TV heroes). When the Vietnamese realized they had been made fools of, the two prisoners were again tortured. The final prisoners were not released until 1973, some having been held in the north since 1964.

At the end of 1992 a US mission was shown around the prison where 2000 inmates were housed in cramped and squalid conditions. Despite pleas from war veterans and party members, the site was sold to a Singapore-Vietnamese joint venture and is now a hotel and shopping complex, **Hanoi Towers**. As part of the deal the developers had to leave a portion of the prison for use as a museum, a lasting memorial to the horrors of war.

'Maison Centrale', reads the legend over the prison's main gate, which leads in to the museum. There are recreations of conditions under colonial rule when the barbarous French incarcerated patriotic Vietnamese from 1896: by 1953 they were holding 2000 prisoners in a space designed for 500. Many well-known Vietnamse were incarcerated here: Phan Boi Chau (founder of the Reformation Party; 1867-1940), Luong Van Can (Reformation Party leader and school founder; 1854-1927), Nguyen Quyen (founder along with Luong Van Can of the School for the Just Cause; 1870-1942) and five men who were later to become general secretaries of the Communist Party: Le Duan (served as general secretary 1976-1986), Nguyen Van Cu (served 1938-1940), Truong Chinh (served 1941-1956 and July-December 1986), Nguyen Van Linh (served 1986-1991) and Do Muoi (served 1991-1997). Less prominence is given to the role of the prison for holding American pilots, but Douglas 'Pete' Peterson, the first post-war American Ambassador to Vietnam (1997-2001), who was one such occupant (imprisoned 1966-1973) has his mug-shot on the wall, as does John McCain (imprisoned 1967-1973), now a US senator.

Ambassadors' Pagoda (Quan Su) and around

ⓘ*73 Quan Su St.*

In the 15th century there was a guesthouse on the site of the Ambassadors' Pagoda (Quan Su Pagoda) for visiting Buddhist ambassadors. The current structure was built between 1936 and 1942. Chinese in appearance from the exterior, the temple contains some fine stone sculptures of the past, present and future Buddhas. It is very popular and crowded with scholars, pilgrims, beggars and incense sellers. The pagoda is one of the centres of Buddhist learning in Vietnam (it is the headquarters of the Vietnam Central Buddhist Congregation): at the back is a school room which is in regular use, students often spill-over into the surrounding corridors to listen.

Nearby, on Le Duan Street just south of the railway station, stalls sell a remarkable array of US, Soviet and Vietnamese army-surplus kit.

Ho Chi Minh's Mausoleum complex and around

Ho Chi Minh's Mausoleum

ⓘ*Summer Tue-Thu, Sat and Sun 0730-1100. Winter Tue-Thu, Sat and Sun 0800-1100, closed 6 weeks from Sep for conservation. Before entering the mausoleum, visitors must leave cameras and possessions at the office (Ban To Chuc) on Huong Vuong, just south of and a few mins' walk from the Mausoleum. Visitors must be respectful: dress neatly, walk solemnly, do not talk and do not take anything in that could be construed as a weapon, for example a penknife.*

The Vietnamese have made Ho Chi Minh's body a holy place of pilgrimage and visitors march in file to see Ho's embalmed corpse inside the mausoleum (Lang Chu Tich Ho Chi Minh).

The mausoleum, built between 1973 and 1975, is a massive, square, forbidding structure and must be among the best constructed, maintained and air-conditioned buildings in Vietnam. Opened in 1975, it is a fine example of the mausoleum genre and is modelled closely on Lenin's Mausoleum in Moscow. Ho lies, with a guard at each corner of his bier. The embalming of his body was undertaken by the chief Soviet embalmer Dr Sergei Debrov who also pickled such communist luminaries as Klement Gottwald (President of Czechoslovakia), Georgi Dimitrov (Prime Minister of Bulgaria) and Forbes Burnham

(President of Guyana). Debrov was flown to Hanoi from Moscow as Ho lay dying, bringing with him two transport planes packed with air conditioners (to keep the corpse cool) and other equipment. To escape US bombing, the team moved Ho to a cave, taking a full year to complete the embalming process. Russian scientists still check-up on their handiwork, servicing Ho's body regularly. Their embalming methods and the fluids they use are still a closely guarded secret, and in a recent interview, Debrov noted with pleasure the poor state of China's Chairman Mao's body, which was embalmed without Soviet help.

The embalming and eternal display of Ho Chi Minh's body was however contrary to Ho's own wishes: he wanted to be cremated and his ashes placed in three urns to be positioned atop three unmarked hills in the north, centre and south of the country. He once wrote that "cremation is not only good from the point of view of hygiene, but it also saves farmland".

Ba Dinh Square

In front of Ho Chi Minh's Mausoleum is Ba Dinh Square where Ho read out the Vietnamese Declaration of Independence on 2 September 1945. Following Ho's declaration, 2 September became Vietnam's National Day. Coincidentally 2 September was also the date on which Ho died in 1969, although his death was not officially announced until 3 September.

In front of the mausoleum on Bac Son Street is the **Dai Liet Si**, a memorial to the heroes and martyrs who died fighting for their country's independence. It appears to be modelled as a secular form of stupa and inside is a large bronze urn.

Ho Chi Minh's house and the Presidential Palace

ⓘ *Ho Chi Minh's house, 1 Bach Thao St, T4-3804 4529; Summer Tue-Thu, Sat and Sun, 0730-1100, 1400-1600, Fri 0730-1100; winter Tue-Thu, Sat and Sun 0800-1100, 1330-1600, Fri 0800-1100; 15,000d; the Presidential Palace is not open to the public.*

From the mausoleum, visitors are directed to Ho Chi Minh's house built in the compound of the former Presidential Palace. The palace, now a Party guesthouse, was the residence of the Governors-General of French Indochina and was built between 1900 and 1908 by Auguste-Henri Vildieu. In 1954, when North Vietnam's struggle for independence was finally achieved, Ho Chi Minh declined to live in the palace, saying that it belonged to the people. Instead, he stayed in what is said to have been an electrician's house in the same compound. Here he lived from 1954 to 1958, before moving to a new stilt house built on the other side of the small lake (Ho Chi Minh's 'Fish Farm', swarming with massive and well-fed carp). The house was designed by Ho and an architect, Nguyen Van Ninh. This modest house made of rare hardwoods is airy and personal and immaculately kept. Ho conducted meetings under the house, which is raised up on wooden pillars, and slept and worked above (his books, slippers and telephones are still here) from May 1958 to August 1969. Built by the army, the house mirrors the one he lived in while fighting the French from his haven near the Chinese border. Behind the house is Ho's bomb shelter, and behind that, the hut where he actually died in 1969.

One Pillar Pagoda

Close by is the One Pillar Pagoda (Chua Mot Cot), one of the few structures remaining from the original foundation of the city. It was built in 1049 by Emperor Ly Thai Tong, although the shrine has since been rebuilt on several occasions, most recently in 1955 after the French destroyed it before withdrawing from the country. The emperor built the pagoda in a fit of religious passion after he dreamt that he saw the goddess Quan Am (Vietnam's equivalent of the Chinese goddess Kuan-yin) sitting on a lotus and holding a young boy, whom she handed to the emperor. On the advice of counsellors who interpreted the

The story of Quan Am

Quan Am was turned onto the streets by her husband for some unspecified wrong-doing and, dressed as a monk, took refuge in a monastery. There, a woman accused her of fathering, and then abandoning, her child. Accepting the blame (why, no one knows), she was again turned out onto the streets, only to return to the monastery much later when she was on the point of death – to confess her true identity. When the Emperor of China heard the tale, he made Quan Am the Guardian Spirit of Mother and Child, and couples without a son now pray to her.

Quan Am's husband is sometimes depicted as a parakeet, with the Goddess usually holding her adopted son in one arm and standing on a lotus leaf (the symbol of purity).

dream, the Emperor built this little lotus-shaped temple in the centre of a water-lily pond and shortly afterwards his queen gave birth to a son. As the name suggests, it is supported on a single (concrete) pillar with a brick and stone staircase running up one side. The pagoda symbolizes the 'pure' lotus sprouting from the sea of sorrow. Original in design, with dragons running along the apex of the elegantly curved tiled roof, the temple is one of the most revered monuments in Vietnam. But the ungainly concrete pillar and the pond of green slime in which it is embedded detract considerably from the enchantment of the little pagoda. Adjacent is the inhabited Dien Huu Pagoda; a sign says they don't like people in shorts, but they are quite friendly and it has a nice courtyard.

Ho Chi Minh Museum

ⓘ*19 Ngoc Ha St, T4-3846 3752, Tue-Thu and Sat 0800-1130, 1400-1600, Fri 0800-1130, 10,000d, 40,000d for a guide.*

Overshadowing the One Pillar Pagoda is the Ho Chi Minh Museum – opened in 1990 in celebration of the centenary of Ho's birth. Contained in a large and impressive modern building, likened to a white lotus, it is the best-arranged and most innovative museum in Vietnam. The displays trace Ho's life and work from his early wanderings around the world to his death and final victory over the south.

Temple of Literature (Van Mieu Pagoda)

ⓘ*The entrance is on Quoc Tu Giam St, T4-3845 2917, open daily summer 0730-1730, winter 0730-1700, 5000d, 45-min tour in French or English 50,000d, 3000d for brochure. ATM inside.*

The Temple of Literature (Van Mieu Pagoda) is the largest, and probably the most important, temple complex in Hanoi. It was founded in 1070 by Emperor Ly Thanh Tong, dedicated to Confucius who had a substantial following in Vietnam, and modelled, so it is said, on a temple in Shantung, China, the birthplace of the sage. Some researchers, while acknowledging the date of foundation, challenge the view that it was built as a Confucian institution pointing to the ascendancy of Buddhism during the Ly Dynasty. Confucian principles and teaching rapidly replaced Buddhism, however, and Van Mieu subsequently became the intellectual and spiritual centre of the kingdom as a cult of literature and education spread among the court, the mandarins and then among the common people. At one time there were said to be 20,000 schools teaching the Confucian classics in northern Vietnam alone.

The temple and its compound are arranged north-south, and visitors enter at the southern end from Quoc Tu Giam Street. On the pavement two pavilions house stelae

The examination of 1875

The examinations held at the Temple of Literature and which enabled, in theory, even the most lowly peasant to rise to the exalted position of a Mandarin, were long and difficult and conducted with great formality.

André Masson quotes Monsieur de Kergaradec, the French Consul's, account of the examination of 1875.

"On the morning of the big day, from the third watch on, that is around one o'clock in the morning, the big drum which invites each one to present himself began to be beaten and soon students, intermingled with ordinary spectators, approached the Compound in front of the cordon formed around the outer wall by soldiers holding lances. In the middle of the fifth watch, towards four or five o'clock in the morning, the examiners in full dress came and installed themselves with their escorts at the different gates. Then began the roll call of the candidates, who were thoroughly searched at the entrance, and who carried with them a small tent of canvas, and mats, cakes, rice, prepared tea, black ink, one or two brushes and a lamp. Everyone once inside, the gates were closed, and the examiners met in the central pavilion of the candidates' enclosure in order to post the subject of the composition. During the afternoon, the candidates who had finished withdrew a few at a time through the central gate, the last ones did not leave the Compound until midnight."

bearing the inscription *ha ma* (climb down from your horse), a nice reminder that even the most elevated dignitaries had to proceed on foot. The main **Van Mieu Gate** (Cong Van Mieu Mon) is adorned with 15th-century dragons. Traditionally, the large central gate was opened only on ceremonial occasions. The path leads through the Cong Dai Trung to a second courtyard and the **Van Khue Gac Pavilion** which was built in 1805 and dedicated to the Constellation of Literature. The roof is tiled according to the yin-yang principle.

Beyond lies the **Courtyard of the Stelae** at the centre of which is the rectangular pond or Cieng Thien Quang (Well of Heavenly Clarity). More important are the stelae themselves, 82 in all, on which are recorded the names of 1306 successful examination scholars (*tien si*). Of the 82 that survive (30 are missing) the oldest dates back to 1442 and the most recent to 1779. Each stela is carried on the back of a tortoise, symbol of strength and longevity but they are arranged in no order; three chronological categories, however, can be identified. Fourteen date from the 15th and 16th centuries; they are the smallest and are embellished with floral motifs and yin-yang symbols but not dragons (a royal emblem). Twenty-five stelae are from the 17th century and are ornamented with dragons (by then permitted), pairs of phoenix and other creatures mythical or real. The remaining 43 stelae are of 18th-century origin; they are the largest and are decorated with two stylized dragons, some merging with flame clouds.

Passing the examination was not easy: in 1733, out of some 3000 entrants only eight passed the doctoral examination (*Thai Hoc Sinh*) and became Mandarins – a task that took 35 days. This tradition was begun in 1484 on the instruction of Emperor Le Thanh Tong, and continued through to 1878, during which time 116 examinations were held. The Temple of Literature was not used only for examinations, however: food was also distributed to the poor and infirm, 500 g of rice at a time. In 1880, the French Consul Monsieur de Kergaradec recorded that 22,000 impoverished people came to receive this meagre handout.

Continuing north, the **Dai Thanh Mon** (Great Success Gate) leads on to a courtyard flanked by two buildings which date from 1954, the originals having been destroyed in

1947. These buildings were reserved for 72 disciples of Confucius. Facing is the **Dai Bai Duong** (Great House of Ceremonies), which was built in the 19th century but in the earlier style of the Le Dynasty. The carved wooden friezes with their dragons, phoenix, lotus flowers, fruits, clouds and yin-yang discs are all symbolically charged, depicting the order of the universe and by implication reflecting the god-given hierarchical nature of human society, each in his place. It is not surprising that the communist government has hitherto had reservations about preserving a temple extolling such heretical doctrine. Inside is an altar on which sit statues of Confucius and his closest disciples. Adjoining is the **Dai Thanh Sanctuary** (Great Success Sanctuary), which also contains a statue of Confucius.

To the north once stood the first university in Vietnam, Quoc Tu Giam, which from the 11th to 18th centuries educated first the heir to the throne and later sons of mandarins. It was replaced with a temple dedicated to Confucius' parents and followers, which was itself destroyed in 1947.

Fine Arts Museum

ⓘ66 Nguyen Thai Hoc St, T4-3733 2131, www.vnfineartsmuseum.org.vn, Tue-Sun 0830-1700, Wed and Sat 0800-2100, 7000d. Free tours in English or French, register in advance, no photography. Restaurant in museum grounds.

Not far from the northern walls of the Van Mieu Pagoda is the Fine Arts Museum (Bao Tang My Thuat), contained in a large colonial building. The oriental roof was added later when the building was converted to a museum. The ground-floor galleries display pre-20th-century art – from Dongsonian bronze drums to Nguyen Dynasty paintings and sculpture, although many works of this later period are on display in the Museum of Royal Fine Arts in Hué. There are some particularly fine stone Buddhas. The first floor is given over to folk art. There are some lovely works from the Central Highlands and engaging Dong Ho woodblock prints – one block for each colour – and Hang Trong woodblock prints, a single black ink print which is coloured in by hand. There are also some fine lacquer paintings. The top floor contains 20th-century work including some excellent water colours and oil paintings. Contemporary Vietnamese artists are building a significant reputation for their work (see box, Modern Vietnamese Art, page 465). There is a large collection of overtly political work, posters and propaganda (of great interest to historians and specialist collectors), and a collection of ethnic minority clothes is exhibited in the annex.

Vietnam Military History Museum and Citadel

ⓘ28 Dien Bien Phu St, T4-3733 6453, www.btlsqsvn.org.vn, Tue-Thu, Sat and Sun 0800-1130, 1300-1630, 20,000d, camera use, 5000d, ATM and Highlands Coffee Café on site.

A five-minute walk east from the Fine Arts Museum, is the Military History Museum (Bao Tang Quan Doi). Tanks, planes and artillery fill the courtyard. Symbolically, an untouched Mig-21 stands at the museum entrance while wreckage of B-52s, F1-11s and Q2Cs is piled up at the back. The museum illustrates battles and episodes in Vietnam's fight for independence from the struggles with China (there is a good display of the Battle of Bach Dang River of AD 938) through to the resistance to the French and the Battle of Dien Bien Phu (illustrated by a good model). Inevitably, of course, there are lots of photographs and exhibits of the American War and although much is self-evident, unfortunately a lot of the explanations are in Vietnamese only.

In the precincts of the museum is the Cot Co, a flag tower, raised up on three platforms. Built in 1812, it is the only substantial part of the original citadel still standing. There are good views over Hanoi from the top. The walls of the **citadel** were destroyed by the French in 1894 to 1897, presumably as they symbolized the power of the Vietnamese emperors. The French were highly conscious of the projection of might, power and authority through large structures, which helps explain their own remarkable architectural legacy. Other remaining parts of the citadel are in the hands of the Vietnamese army and out of bounds to visitors. Across the road from the museum's front entrance is a **statue of Lenin**.

The North Gate of the Citadel is on Phan Dinh Phung St and can be visited, 10,000d. The new Kinh Thien Palace is due to open on Hoang Dieu St. Further south on Hoang Dieu is the Doan Mon Gate (free, 0800-1130, 1400-1630) where you can nose at the previously off-limits citadel exploration and get a new view of Cot Co and the citadel complex from the roof. The citadel was named a UNESCO World Heritage Site in August 2010.

Outer Hanoi

North of the Old City

North of the Old City is **Ho Truc Bach** (**White Silk Lake**). Truc Bach Lake was created in the 17th century by building a causeway across the southeast corner of Ho Tay. This was the site of the 11th-century **Royal Palace** which had, so it is said, 'a hundred roofs'. All that is left is the terrace of Kinh Thien with its dragon staircase, and a number of stupas, bridges, gates and small pagodas.

At the southwest corner of the lake, on the intersection of Hung Vuong, Quan Thanh and Thanh Nien streets is the **Quan Thanh Pagoda** ⓘ*2000d*, originally built in the early 11th century in honour of Huyen Thien Tran Vo (a genie) but since much remodelled. Despite renovation, it is still very beautiful. The large bronze bell was cast in 1677.

To the east of here the Long Bien and Chuong Duong bridges cross the Red River. The former of these two bridges was built as a road and rail bridge by Daydé & Pillé of Paris and named **Paul Doumer Bridge** after the Governor General of the time. Construction was begun in 1899 and it was opened by Emperor Thanh Thai on 28 February 1902. Today it is used by trains, bicycles, motorbikes and pedestrians. Over 1.5 km in length, it was the only river crossing in existence during the Vietnam War and suffered repeated attacks from US planes, only to be quickly repaired. The Chuong Duong Bridge was completed at the beginning of the 1980s.

The much larger **Ho Tay** (**West Lake**) was originally a meander in the Red River. The **Tran Quoc Pagoda**, an attractive brick-red building, can be found on an islet on the east shores of the lake, linked to the causeway by a walkway. It was originally built on the banks of the Red River before being transferred to its present site by way of an intermediate location. The pagoda contains a stela dated 1639 recounting its unsettled history. Just south, on a white boat is a **Highlands Coffee** café. Pedaloes are available for hire (US$2.50 per hour; motorboat US$16 per 20 minutes). Opposite, facing Truc Bach Lake, is a monument recording the shooting down of USAF's John (now US Senator) McCain on 26 October 1967. It reveals the pilot falling out of the sky, knees bent.

A few kilometres north, on the tip of a promontory, stands **Tay Ho Pagoda**, notable chiefly for its setting. It is reached along a narrow lane lined with stalls selling fruit, roses and paper votives and a dozen restaurants serving giant snails with *bun oc* (noodles) and fried shrimp cakes. Dominating it is an enormous bronze bell held by a giant dragon hook supported by concrete dragons and two elephants; notice the realistic glass eyes of the elephants.

However, West Lake is fast losing its unique charm as development spreads northwards. The nouveau riche of Hanoi are rapidly turning the area into a middle-class suburb and

The Trung sisters

Vietnamese history honours a number of heroines, of whom the Trung sisters are among the most revered. At the beginning of the Christian era, the Lac Lords of Vietnam began to agitate against Chinese control over their lands. Trung Trac, married to the Lac Lord Thi Sach, was apparently of a 'brave and fearless disposition' and encouraged her husband and the other lords to rise up against the Chinese in AD 40. The two sisters often fought while pregnant, apparently putting on gold-plated armour over their enlarged bellies. Although an independent kingdom was created for a short time, ultimately the uprising proved fruitless; a large Chinese army defeated the rebels in AD 43, and eventually captured Trung Trac and her sister Trung Nhi, executing them and sending their heads to the Han court at Lo-yang. An alternative story of their death has it that the sisters threw themselves into the Hat Giang River to avoid being captured, and turned into stone statues. These were washed ashore and placed in Hanoi's Hai Ba Trung Temple for worship.

new restaurants and bars have clustered around Xuan Dieu Street. New houses go up in an unplanned and uncoordinated sprawl. Nguyen Ngoc Khoi, director of the Urban Planning Institute in Hanoi, estimates that the area of the lake has shrunk by 20%, from 500 ha to 400 ha, as residents and hotel and office developers have reclaimed land. The lake is also suffering encroachment by water hyacinths, which are fed by organic pollutants from factories (especially a tannery) and untreated sewage. The view from Nghi Tam Road, which runs along the Red River dyke, presents a contrasting spectacle of sprawling houses interspersed with the remaining plots of land which are intensively and attractively cultivated market gardens supplying the city with flowers and vegetables.

Museum of Ethnology and B-52 memorials

ⓘ*Some distance west of the city centre in Cau Giay District (Nguyen Van Huyen Rd), T4-3756 2193, www.vme.org.vn, Tue-Sun 0830-1730, 25,000d, photography 50,000d, tour guide, 50,000d. Catch the No 14 minibus from Dinh Tien Hoang St, north of Hoan Kiem Lake, to the Nghia Tan stop; turn right and walk down Hoang Quoc Viet St for 1 block, before turning right at the Petrolimex station down Nguyen Van Huyen; the museum is down this street, on the left. Alternatively take a taxi. Branch of Baguette & Chocolat bakery on site.*

The museum opened in November 1997 in a modern, purpose-built structure. The collection here of some 25,000 artefacts, 15,000 photographs and documentaries of practices and rituals is excellent and, more to the point, is attractively and informatively presented with labels in Vietnamese, English and French. It displays the material culture (textiles, musical instruments, jewellery, tools, baskets and the like) of the majority Kinh people as well as Vietnam's 53 other designated minority peoples. While much is historical, the museum is also attempting to build up its contemporary collection. There is a shop attached to the museum and in the grounds of the museum, ethnic minorities' homes have been recreated.

On the routes out to the Ethnology Museum are two B-52 memorials. The remains of downed B-52s have been hawked around Hanoi over many years but seem to have found a final resting place at the **Bao Tang Chien Tang B-52 (B-52 Museum)** ⓘ *157 Doi Can St, free*. This curious place is not really a museum but a military hardware graveyard, but this doesn't matter because what everyone wants to do is walk over the wings and tail of a shattered B-52, and the B-52 in question lies scattered around the yard. As visitors to

Vietnamese museums have by now come to expect, any enemy objects are literally heaped up as junk while the 'heroic' Vietnamese pieces are painted, tended for and carefully signed with the names of whichever heroic unit fought in them. Here we have anti-aircraft guns, the devastating SAMs that wreaked so much havoc on the USAF and a MIG21. Curiously the signs omit to mention the fact that all this hardware was made in Russia. The size and strength of the B-52 is simply incredible and needs to be seen to be believed.

On Hoang Hoa Tham Street, between Nos 55 and 57, a sign points 100 m down an alley to the wreckage of a B-52 bomber sticking up out of the pond-like Huu Tiep Lake. There's a plaque on the wall stating that at 2305 on 27 December 1972, Battalion 72 of Regiment 285 shot down the plane. At the time Huu Tiep was a flower village and the lake a lot bigger.

South of Hanoi

Down Hué Street is the hub of motorcycle sales, parts and repairs. Off this street, for example along Hoa Ma, Tran Nhan Tong and Thinh Yen, are numerous stalls and shops, each specializing in a single type of product – TVs, electric fans, bicycle parts and so on. It is a fascinating area to explore. At the intersection of Thinh Yen and Pho 332, people congregate to sell new and second-hand bicycles, as well as bicycle parts.

Not far away is the venerable **Den Hai Ba Trung** (**Hai Ba Trung Temple**) ⓘ *open 1st and 15th of each lunar month, 0600-1800, free*, the temple of the two Trung Sisters – overlooking a lake. The temple was built in 1142, but like others, has been restored on a number of occasions. It contains crude statues of the Trung sisters, Trung Trac and Trung Nhi (see box, page 41), which are carried in procession once a year during February.

Further south still from the Hai Ba Trung, is another pagoda – **Chua Lien Phai**. This quiet pagoda, which can be found just off Bach Mai Street, was built in 1732, although it has since been restored.

Around Hanoi

Compared with Ho Chi Minh City and the south, Hanoi and its surrounds are rich in places of interest. Not only is the landscape more varied and attractive, but the 1000-year-old history of Hanoi has generated dozens of sights of architectural appeal, many of which can be visited on a day trip.

Co Loa Citadel

ⓘ *16 km north of Hanoi. Drive north up Highway 3, Co Loa is signposted to the east.*

In the third-century BC Co Loa Citadel was the region's capital, built by King An Duong with walls in three concentric rings; the outer ring is 8 km in circumference. It is an important Bronze Age site and thousands of arrow heads and three bronze ploughshares have been excavated here. Today there is little to see as electricity sub-stations and farms have obliterated much of archaeological interest.

Hung Kings' Temples

ⓘ *South of Yen Bai and approximately 100 km northwest of Hanoi near the industrial town of Viet Tri in Vinh Phu Province; turn off Highway 2 about 12 km north of Viet Tri; it's a morning or afternoon excursion by car from Hanoi.*

The Hung Kings' Temples (Phong Chau) are popular with Vietnamese visitors especially during the **Hung Kings' Festival**. In purely topographical terms the site is striking, an almost perfectly circular hill rising unexpectedly out of the monotonous Red River floodplain with two lakes at the bottom. Given its peculiar physical setting it is easy to understand how the site acquired its mythical reputation as the birthplace of the Viet people and why the Hung Vuong kings chose it as the capital of their kingdom.

In this place, myth and historical fact have become intertwined. Legend has it that the Viet people are the product of the union of King Lac Long Quan, a dragon, and his fairy wife Au Co. Au Co gave birth to a pouch containing 100 eggs that hatched 50 boys and 50 girls. Husband and wife decided to separate in order to populate the land and propagate the race, so half the children followed their mother to the highlands and half remained with their father on the plains, giving rise to the Montagnards and lowland peoples of Vietnam. Historically easier to verify is the story of the Hung kings (Hung Vuong) who built a temple in order to commemorate the legendary progenitors of the Vietnamese people.

A new **Hung Kings' Museum** ⓘ *0800-1130, 1300-1600*, was opened in mid-2010 and displays interesting items excavated from the province. Exhibits include pottery, jewellery, fish hooks, arrow heads and axe heads (dated 1000-1300 BC), but of particular interest are the bronze drums dating from the Dongsonian period. The Dongsonian was a transitional period between the neolithic and bronze ages and the drums are thought to originate from around the fifth to the third centuries BC. Photographs show excavation in the 1960s when these items were uncovered.

Ascending the hill, a track leads to a **memorial to Ho Chi Minh**. Ho said he hoped that people would come from all over Vietnam to see this historic site. Nearby is the **Low Temple** dedicated to Au Co, mother of the country and supposedly the site where the 100 eggs were produced. At the back of the temple is a statue of the Buddha of a thousand arms and a thousand eyes. Continuing up the hill is the **Middle Temple** where Prince Lang Lieu was

Hung King's Temples

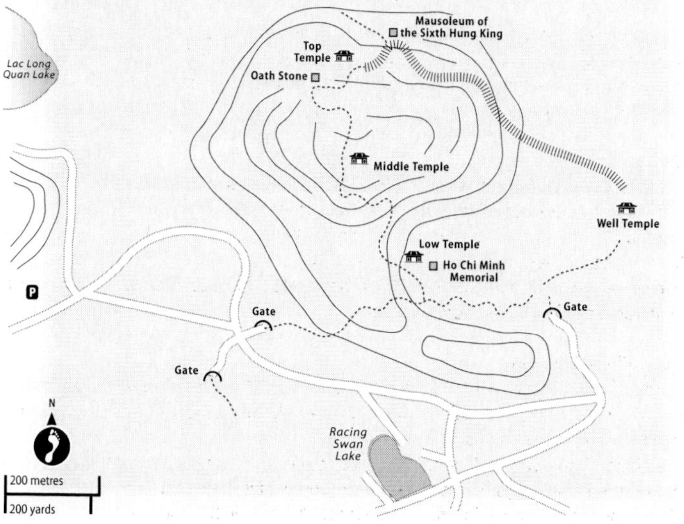

crowned seventh Hung king and where the kings would play chess and discuss pressing affairs of state. Prince Lang Lieu was (like the English King Alfred) something of a dab hand in the kitchen and his most enduring creation is a pair of cakes, *banh trung* and *banh day*, which to this day remain popular, eaten at Tet. This temple has three altars and attractive murals.

Further on, towards the top of the hill is the **oath stone** on which the 18th Hung king, Thuc Phan, swore to defend the country from its enemies. Adjacent is the **Top Temple** dating from the 15th century. The roof is adorned with dragons and gaudily painted mural warriors stand guard outside. A not particularly ancient drum hangs from the ceiling but smoke rising from burning incense on the three altars helps add to the antiquity of the setting. Here it was that the kings would supplicate God for peace and prosperity.

Steps lead from the back right-hand side of this temple down the hill to the mausoleum of the sixth Hung king. These steps then continue down the far side of the hill to the **Well Temple** built in memory of the last princess of the Hung Dynasty. Inside is a well in the reflection of which this girl used to comb her hair. Today worshippers throw money in and, it is said, they even drink the water. Turn right to get back to the car park.

Perfume Pagoda

ⓘ *30,000d entrance plus 210,000d for the boat (maximum 4 people). Taking a tour is the best way to get here.*

The Perfume Pagoda (Chua Huong or Chua Huong Tich) is 60 km southwest of Hanoi. A sampan takes visitors along the Yen River, a diverting 4-km ride through a flooded landscape to the Mountain of the Perfume Traces. From here it is a 3-km hike up the mountain to the cool, dark cave wherein lies the Perfume Pagoda. Dedicated to Quan Am (see page 37), it is one of a number of shrines and towers built among limestone caves and is regarded as one of the most beautiful spots in Vietnam. The stone statue of Quan Am in the principal pagoda was carved in 1793 after Tay Son rebels had stolen and melted down its bronze predecessor to make cannon balls. Emperor Le Thanh Tong (1460-1497) described it as "Nam Thien de nhat dong" ("foremost cave under the Vietnamese sky"). It is a popular pilgrimage spot, particularly during the festival months of March and April.

Pagodas around Hanoi

Tay Phuong Pagoda is about 6 km from the Thay Pagoda in the village of Thac Xa. It may date back to the eighth century, although the present structure was rebuilt in 1794. Constructed of ironwood, it is sited at the summit of a hill and is approached by means of a long stairway. The pagoda is best known for its collection – all 74 of them – of 18th-century *arhat* statues (statues of former monks). They are thought to be among the best examples of the woodcarver's art from the period.

Thay Pagoda (Master's Pagoda), also known as Thien Phuc Tu Pagoda, lies 40 km southwest of Hanoi in the village of Sai Son, in Ha Son Binh Province. Built in the 11th century, the pagoda honours a herbalist, Dao Hanh, who lived in Sai Son village. It is said that he was reborn as the son of Emperor Le Thanh Tong after he and his wife had come to pray here. The pagoda complex is divided into three sections. The outer section is used for ceremonies, the middle is a Buddhist temple, while the inner part is dedicated to the herbalist. The temple has some fine statues of Buddhas, as well as an array of demons. Water puppet shows are performed during holidays and festivals on a stage built in the middle of the pond at the front of the pagoda (see page 57). Dao Hanh, who was a water puppet enthusiast, is said to have created the pond. It is spanned by two bridges built at the beginning of the 17th century. There are good views from the nearby Sai Son Hill – a path leads up from the pagoda.

Handicraft villages

Many tour operators arrange excursions to villages just outside of Hanoi including Van Phuc, where silk is produced, Bat Trang, where ceramics and bricks are made, and Le Mat, a snake village; here visitors can try eating snake meat.

Further afield

Cuc Phuong National Park (see page 138 for details) is about 160 km south of Hanoi and can be visited as a day trip or over-nighter from Hanoi or as an excursion from Ninh Binh. Other possible day trips are excursions to **Hoa Binh** (see page 71) and **Mai Chau** (see page 72) **Haiphong** (see page 117) **Ninh Binh** (see page 135), **Hoa Lu** (see page 135), **Tam Coc** (see page 136) and **Phat Diem Cathedral** (see page 164).

Hanoi and around listings

For sleeping and eating price codes and other relevant information, see page 10-13.

Sleeping

There has been a spate of hotel building and renovation in recent years. There's still a lack of good, attractive 3- to 4-star hotels in Hanoi. The more expensive hotels offer a full range of services. Cheaper hotels tend to be found in the Old Quarter. Old Quarter buildings are tightly packed and rooms small, sometimes without windows. Hotels in this area offer the best value for money, most budget travellers head straight for this area. Many hotels now offer Wi-Fi, if not in the room, in the lobby. Watch out for scams. Tourists are often told by taxi drivers that their hotel is full or has closed and are taken to another hotel where they will receive commission. Have a booking in advance and be insistent. Readers may read reviews of the Green Mango. We cannot recommend it. We were shown one room with a dirty bathroom and duvet; the second room's bathroom featured a sink overflowing with green candle wax. Breakfast service was slow and other customers complained at the service continuously. We have received other reports of unsatisfactory service too.

Hoan Kiem Lake and Central Hanoi *p27, maps p24 and p28*

$$$$ Sofitel Legend Metropole Hanoi, 15 Ngo Quyen St, T4-3826 6919, www.accorhotelsasia.com. The only hotel in its class in central Hanoi. The French-colonial-style cream building with green shutters is beautifully and lusciously furnished and exudes style. The historic **Metropole** wing contains the original more classically stylish rooms while the new wing is named the **Opera** with rooms exhibiting a modern flair. It boasts a diversity of bars and restaurants including the new Italian Angelina restaurant. **Le Beaulieu** is one of the finest restaurants in Hanoi; a pianist plays nightly at **Le Club** bar. The new **Le Spa du Metropole** is seriously chic. There's also a business centre, cluster of luxury shops and smart deli, and a small pool with attractive poolside **Bamboo Bar**. The hotel has retained most of its business despite competition from newer business hotels away from the city centre and remains a hub of activity and the classiest hotel address in the country. The Graham Greene suite is sumptuous Indochine chic.

$$$ Church Hotel, 9 Nha Tho St, T4-3928 8118, www.churchhotel.com.vn. Markets itself as a boutique hotel, which it isn't. It has 16 small rooms with wooden floors and attractive bed linen with nice en suite bathrooms. Ask for a room away from the street to avoid the noise.

$$$ Cinnamon Hotel, 26 Au Trieu St, T4-3993 8430, http://cinnamonhotel.net. This is a cute, stylish hotel with lovely, comfortable rooms. However, the regular bong of the cathedral bell is disturbing so you may wish to avoid the cute balconied rooms overlooking the cathedral square and opt for a back room with a lesser view. Breakfast service is slow and watch for overcharging on laundry. Little English is spoken.

$$$ Galaxy, 1 Phan Dinh Phung St, T4-3828 2888, www.tctgroup.com.vn. Well-run 3-star business hotel (built in 1918) with 50 carpeted rooms and full accessories including the all-important bedside reading lights, which too many expensive hotels forget.

$$$ Golden Lotus Hotel, 32 Hang Trong St, T4-3928 8583, www.goldenlotushotel.com.vn. On Hang Trong street, home to many galleries, the **Golden Lotus** has a series of smart, attractive rooms from standard single to deluxe. Balcony rooms afford a better view but anything facing the street is bound to be noisier.

$$$ Hong Ngoc, 30-34 Hang Manh St, T4-3828 5053, www.hongngochotel.com. This is a real find. A small, family-run hotel with comfortable rooms and huge bathrooms with bathtubs. It's spotlessly clean throughout and run by cheerful and helpful staff. Breakfast is included. This **Hong Ngoc** has put its prices up but there are 2 other cheaper **Hong Ngocs** in the Old Quarter.

$$$ Joseph's Hotel, 5 Au Trieu St, T4-3938 1048, www.josephshotel.com. Right near St Joseph's Cathedral, on Au Trieu St – a cosy street filled with good cafés, salons and souvenir shops – **Joseph's Hotel** is small, with just 10 rooms. However small can equal cosy, and it does here. This mid-range hotel has Wi-Fi in all rooms, as well as standards such as a/c, cable and mini-bar. Breakfast is included in the price.

$$ Freedom, 57 Hang Trong St, T4-3826 7119. freedomhotel@hn.vnn.vn. Not far from Hoan Kiem lake and the cathedral. 11 spacious rooms with desks. Some have bathtubs; those without have small bathrooms. Friendly family. Breakfast not included on the cheaper rate.

$$ Gold Spring Hotel, 22 Nguyen Huu Huan St, T4-3926 3057, www.goldspringhotel.com.vn. On the edge of the Old Quarter. 22 fine rooms that are attractively decorated. Breakfast and free internet included.

$$ Hang Trong, 56 Hang Trong St, T4-3825 +1346, thiencotravelvn@yahoo.com. A/c and hot water (showers only), a few unusual and quite decent rooms set back from the road, either on a corridor or in a courtyard. The ones that don't overlook the courtyard are dark and airless. Very convenient position for every part of town. Internet and booking office for **Sinh Tourist** tours. Staff are very helpful.

$$ Hong Ngoc 3, 39 Hang Bac St, T4-3926 0322, www.hongngochotel.com. Some staff here are exceptionally helpful, others are not. A real mixed bag. Rooms are clean and comfortable with TVs, a/c and bathtubs in the bathrooms and it's in a great central location and surprisingly quiet. You may want to pass on the breakfast.

$$-$ Hanoi Backpackers' Hostel, 48 Ngo Huyen St, T4-3828 5372 (last-minute reservations T1800 1552 toll free), www.hanoibackpackershostel.com. Dorm rooms (with bedside lights, lockers and a/c) and double suites in a house that belonged to a Brazilian ambassador. This is a friendly and busy place to stay with plenty of opportunities to meet other travellers and gather advice. Breakfast, internet, tea and coffee and luggage store is included. Don't miss the BBQs on the roof terrace and the Sunday sessions. There is also a busy bar. Many kinds of tours, including more off-the-beaten-track options such as island stays near Ha Long Bay, can be arranged.

$$-$ Hoa Linh, 35 Hang Bo St, T4-3824 3887, hoalinhhotel@hn.vnn.vn. Right in the centre of the 36 Streets area, attractive lobby and willing staff. 17 rooms, price includes breakfast.

$ Mai Phuong, 32 Hang Be St, T4-3092 63269, www.maiphuonghotel.com. Fan and a/c rooms that are slightly cramped, but the place is friendly and clean.

$ My Lan, 70 Hang Bo St, T4-3824 5510, hotelmylan@yahoo.com. Go through the dentist's surgery where an elderly French-speaking dentist has 10 rooms to rent, a/c or fans. Rather tightly packed but light and breezy; nice apartment with kitchen and terrace, US$400 a month. Super-friendly family. Recommended.

$ Nam Phuong, 16 Bao Khanh St, T4-3825 8030, www.ktscom@vnn.vn. Pleasant position near Hoan Kiem Lake, 9 a/c rooms with soundproofing. Rooms at the back are cheaper. Breakfast and free internet included.

$ Ngoc Diep, 83 Thuoc Bac St, through the Chinese pharmacy, T4-3825 0020, thugiangguesthouse@yahoo.com. Cheaper rooms have fan; more expensive rooms a/c. All rooms have hot water and TV, and free internet; breakfast can be included. Bus station and railway station pick-up, popular and friendly. Long-stay discounts available.

$ Real Darling Café, 33 Hang Quat St, T4-3826 9386, darling_cafe@hotmail.com. Travellers' café which has 16 rooms, though only 10 have a/c. Food is available, excellent English is spoken and visas for both overseas and extensions for within Vietnam can be organized. Wi-Fi.

$ Thuy Nga, 24C Ta Hien St, T4-3826 6053, thuyngahotel@hotmail.com. Just 6 rooms. A/c, hot water, cramped, but friendly with good English and good value. Wi-Fi included.

South of Hoan Kiem Lake *p32, maps p24 and p28*

$$$$ Hilton Hanoi Opera, 1 Le Thanh Tong St, T4-3933 0500, www1.hilton.com. Opened in 1999 and built adjacent to, and architec-turally sympathetically with, the Opera House. It is a splendid building and provides the highest levels of service and hospitality. But whereas the **Metropole** is normally busy the **Hanoi Opera** is often quieter.

$$$$ Melia Hanoi, 44B Ly Thuong Kiet St, T4-3934 3343, www.meliahanoi.com. A huge tower block in Central Hanoi. Well-appointed rooms but not a welcoming feel and a small swimming pool. There's an ATM and **Thai Airways** office on site. Popular venue for international conferences and national days held by many embassies, usually with excellent food.

$$$$ Movenpick, 83A Ly Thuong Kiet St, T4-3822 2800, www.moevenpick-hotels.com. Formerly the **Guoman** this Swiss-run hotel chain is housed in an attractive building on Ly Thuong Kiet street, in the middle of Hanoi's business district. Rooms are smart and stylish.

$$$$ Sunway Hotel, 19 Pham Dinh Ho St, T4-3971 3888, www.sunway-hotel.com. This extremely comfortable, quiet and friendly hotel is located just south of the lake and close to **Hanoi Gourmet**, which is an attraction in itself, see Eating, below. The breakfast is good and varied and the fact that you can control all the room's lighting from a panel by your bed is a huge plus. There are 145 rooms in this business hotel.

$$$$ Zephyr, 4 Ba Trieu St, T4-3934 1256, www.zephyrhotel.com.vn. Popular among business travellers, **Zephyr** is under a minute's walk to the lake and sits at the end of Ba Trieu street, which heads south to the city's interesting Hai Ba Trung district, home to Hanoi's only international-standard cinema. There is a café and restaurant downstairs. Special deals are offered in the low season.

$$$$-$$$ De Syloia, 17A Tran Hung Dao St, T4-3824 5346, www.desyloia.com. Very attractive and friendly small boutique, business hotel with 33 rooms and suites, a business centre and gym in a good central location. The popular **Cay Cau** restaurant specializes in Vietnamese dishes and the daily set-lunch is excellent value.

$$$$-$$$ Hoa Binh, 27 Ly Thuong Kiet St, T4-3825 3315, www.hoabinhhotel.com. Old but renovated hotel with quite large rooms. **Le Splendide** French restaurant attached.

$$$ Army Hotel, 33C Pham Ngu Lao St, T4-3825 2896, armyhotel@fpt.vn. Owned and run by the Army this is a surprisingly pleasant and attractive hotel. Set around a decent-sized swimming pool, which some people worry about swimming in, it is quiet and comfortable. The hotel has a total of 78 a/c rooms and a restaurant. Reception could be more welcoming though.

$$$-$$ Eden Hanoi, 78 Tho Nhuom St, T4-3942 3273, www.edenhanoihotel.com. Good location but small rooms; worth paying more for the suites. Nevertheless popular and handy for **Luna d'Autunno** restaurant.

$ Artist Hotel, 22A Hai Ba Trung St, T4-3824 4433, artist_hotel@yahoo.com.This small hotel is set above the pleasant and quiet courtyard of the **Hanoi Cinematique**. Some of the rooms, all with a/c, are a little dark but the price is great for such a central and unusual location. Although there is no breakfast you can always snack at the **Cinemateque** instead.

$ Cay Xoai (**Mango**), formerly the **Railway Hotel**, 118 Le Duan St, T4-3942 3704. Adjacent to the station, *bia hoi* and *pho* stalls in the compound. Expensive for what it is. Busy, noisy area but quite friendly with 35 rooms. Reception can be indifferent.

Outer Hanoi *p40, map p24*

Hanoi's relatively small central district means that some new office complexes and hotels have tended to open a short distance out of the centre.

$$$$ Hanoi Daewoo, 360 Kim Ma St, Ba Dinh District, T4-3831 5000, www.hanoi-daewoo.com. Giant hotel with 411 rooms and suites opened in 1996. Adjoining apartment complex and office tower. The hotel is one of Vietnam's most luxurious with a large pool, shops and 4 restaurants; Chinese, Japanese, Italian and international. The hotel has also accumulated a large collection of Vietnamese modern art. Popular with large busloads of well-heeled Koreans and surrounded by Korean restaurants, many not very good.

$$$$ InterContinental Hanoi Westlake, 1A Nghi Tam, Tay Ho District, T4-3829 3939, www.intercontinental.com. One of the newer 5-stars in the city, the **InterContinental** sits on West Lake, almost beside the **Sheraton**. Rooms are large and decorated using traditional Vietnamese elements. The bar and pool areas facing the lake are lovely, especially in early evening when *den choi* (fire-powered paper balloons) drift across the sky above the water. Cocktails are good but prices are international standard.

$$$$ Nikko Hanoi, 84 Tran Nhan Tong St, T4-3822 3535, www.hotelnikkohanoi.com. Rather a forbidding appearance from the outside but a tranquil marble lobby. Somewhat impersonal but a nice pool and good Japanese restaurant. Particularly popular with Japanese businessmen.

$$$$ Sheraton Hotel, K5 Nghi Tam, 11 Xuan Dieu, Tay Ho District, T4-3719 9000, wwwsheraton.com/hanoi. Opened in early 2004, the **Sheraton** is many miles out of town on a scenic spot overlooking the West Lake. Its position will attract some but probably prove awkward for many visitors. It is opulent and luxurious and rooms are fully equipped. The swimming pool backs onto a lawn that leads down to the lakeshore.

$$$$ Sofitel Plaza Hanoi, 1 Thanh Nien St, T4-3823 8888, www.Sofitel.com. The 2nd Sofitel in town, it lacks the cache of the **Metropole** but is in an equally good location, by Truc Bach Lake. Restaurants, galleries, wine cellars and rice wine restaurants are all within walking distance. The rooftop has one of the best views in town, but the prices, music and garish carpet do leave something to be desired. The 322-room hotel offers Italian and Chinese restaurants, excellent business facilities and a large all-weather swimming pool with retractable roof.

Eating

Hanoi has Western-style coffee bars, restaurants and watering holes. It also has a good number of excellent Vietnamese restaurants catering both to local people and visitors from overseas. Korean and Japanese food is found everywhere thanks to huge expat populations, see box page 51.

In short, there is a super-abundance of food in Hanoi: shortage of time means most people will only sample a few of the places recommended below.

A few words of caution: dog (*thit chó* or *thit cay*) is a delicacy in the north – "who can resist a steaming bowl of broth with a pair of dogs paws?" demands one restaurateur – but dog is usually served only in specialist outlets – usually shacks on the edge of town – so is unlikely to be ordered inadvertently.

Eating on the street is one of the joys of a trip to Hanoi.

Hoan Kiem Lake and Central Hanoi *p27, maps p24 and p28*

TTT Club de l'Oriental, 22 Tong Dan St, T4-3826 8801. From the same people who run **Emperor**, this newer iteration serves traditional Vietnamese in a very high-end manner: don't expect to escape without a lighter wallet. Though the setting is gorgeous, and the downstairs wine cellar and dining area cosy, you may ask, at some stage, why you are paying several times as much for competently rendered, high-end versions of quite usual Vietnamese cuisine.

TTT Hanoi Press Club, 59A Ly Thai To St, T4-3934 0888, www.hanoi-pressclub.com. This is an odd building with some style inside directly behind the **Sofitel Metropole Hotel**: **The Restaurant** has remained one of the most popular dining experiences in Hanoi. The dining room is luxuriously furnished with polished, dark wood floors and print-lined walls. The food is superb and there's a fine wine list. Service has slipped though. **The Terrace**, a large outdoor space, hosts live music events and at the time of writing is still holding big parties popular with every hard-networking local and expat in town the 1st Fri of each month. The **Library Bar** stocks a good range of cigars and whiskies.

TTT Lá, 25 Ly Quoc Su St, T4-3928 8933. This attractive green and cream building houses a restaurant serving up marvellous Vietnamese and international food. Behind the modest exterior is one of the best-loved restaurants in the city. Chef Wayne Sjothun's menu offers traditional Vietnamese as well as a range of unpretentious fusion meals and daily specials. The bistro atmosphere is comfortable and the wine list excellent. The small bar is, on close inspection, surprisingly well stocked.

TTT Le Beaulieu, 15 Ngo Quyen St (in the **Metropole Hotel**), T4-3826 6919. A good French and international restaurant open for breakfast, lunch and dinner; last orders 2200. Its Sun brunch buffet is regarded as one of the best in Asia. A great selection of French seafood, oysters, prawns, cold and roast meats and cheese. The buffet is good enough that even *Forbes* magazine waxed ecstatic over it. Famous chef Didier Corlou has left to open his own restaurants (see **Verticale**, page 53) and **Madame Hien**, below, but remains a culinary consultant.

TTT-TT Club Opera, 59 Ly Thai To St, T4-3824 6950, clubopera@fpt.vn. 1100-1400, 1730-2230. Good restaurant with extensive Vietnamese menu in the attractive setting of a restored French villa. The menu is varied, the tables are beautifully laid and the food is appealingly presented.

TTT-T Green Tangerine, 48 Hang Be St, T4-3825 1286, greentangerine@vnn.vn. This is a gorgeous French restaurant with a lovely spiral staircase, wafting fans, tasselled curtain cords and abundant glassware. It's a Hanoi stalwart in a lovely 1928 house in the centre of the Old Quarter serving fusion and Vietnamese food. Recommended dining areas are the courtyard and downstairs; upstairs can lack atmosphere. Many have decried the drop in quality but it remains popular with the tourist crowd. However, the set lunch is still excellent and good value. The cheese platter is intriguing and delicious.

ΨΨΨ-Ψ Madame Hien, 15 Chan Cam St, T4-3938 1588, madame.hien@didiercorlou.com. 1100-2200. Closed during Tet. An addition to the Didier Corlou empire, this charming restaurant is in the former Spanish embassy building and named after Corlou's wife's grandmother. Its small proportions encourage intimate dining. Tasty and intricate Vietnamese fare. You won't go hungry. Exceptional service.

ΨΨ Baan Thai, 3B Cha Ca St, T4-3828 8588. 1030-1400, 1630-2200. Longstanding Thai restaurant. Food is good, service decent to indifferent, and the atmosphere sometimes like a shut-down shopping mall before the zombies attack.

ΨΨ Khazana, 1C Tong Dan St, T4-3934 5657. A longstanding Indian restaurant once famous for its amiable and helpful owner. It has since changed hands but the large menu of south and north Indian dishes remains top notch. All curries come served in traditional copper bowls, and breads arrive at the table soft and piping hot. Hugely popular with the often unseen Indian expatriate crowd.

ΨΨ Pepperonis, 31 Bao Khanh St, T4-3928 7030. Mon-Sat 1130-1330. A popular pizza and pasta chain, marketed to Vietnamese more than foreigners, right in the heart of a busy bar/restaurant area. Cheap and cheerful. Known for its buffet lunch.

ΨΨ-Ψ 69 Restaurant Bar, 69 Ma May St, T4-3926 1720. 0700-2300. Set in a nicely restored 19th-century house in the Old Quarter, this is an atmospheric experience. Try and get 1 of the 2 tables squeezed onto the tiny balcony. The restaurant is up a steep flight of wooden stairs. There's a good menu with plenty of Vietnamese and seafood dishes and some with a Chinese influence – the Hong Kong duck is good, as is the sunburnt beef (beef strips deep-fried in 5-spice butter). There's a bar downstairs serving mulled wine on chilly nights and other traditional rice wines.

ΨΨ-Ψ Highway 4, 3 Hang Tre St, T4-3926 4200. 0900-0200. Therea are other branches too. The original restaurant has moved next door. It specializes in ethnic minority dishes from North Vietnam (Highway 4 is the most northerly road in Vietnam running along the Chinese border and favoured by owners of Minsk motorbikes) but now includes a full menu of dishes from other provinces. The fruit and rice wines – available in many flavours – are the highlight of this place. For those unable to make up their minds sampler shots are available, but after a couple of these they all taste good. Upstairs, guests sit cross-legged on cushions; downstairs there's conventional dining. There's plenty to eat and it's a great fun and memorable experience.

ΨΨ-Ψ Restaurant Number Five, 5 Hang Be St, T4-3926 3761. The smart, classy interior and large windows are inviting. The menu is eclectic but offering something a little different in the old quarter such as Lebanese lamb pizza and spinach, ricotta and walnut ravioli. The profiteroles stuffed with peanut butter ice cream and served with chocolate sauce are a treat!

ΨΨ-Ψ Tandoor, 24 Hang Be St, T4-3824 5359. 1100-1430, 1800-2230. A smallish but long-standing restaurant serving excellent Indian food freshly prepared. Authentic curries, tandooris and breads. Don't miss the branch in HCMC.

Ψ Bit Tet (Beefsteak), 51 Hang Buom St, T4-3825 1211. 1700-2100. If asked to name the most authentic Vietnamese diner in town it would be hard not to include this on the list. The soups and steak frites are simply superb: it's rough and ready and you'll share your table as, at around US$2-3 per head, it is understandably crowded. (Walk to the end of the alley and turn right for the dining room.)

Ψ Café des Arts and **Stop Café**, 11b Ngo Bao Khanh St, T4-3828 7207, www.cafedesarts.com. Housed in 1 building and owned by the same people: upstairs is home to a fine dining French restaurant, **Café des Arts**, and downstairs, **Stop Café**, a more pared-back

Bites but no bark in a Vietnamese restaurant

Quang Vinh's restaurant was the ideal place for the ordeal to come. The palm-thatched house near the West Lake, on the outskirts of the Vietnamese capital Hanoi, was far from the accusing eyes of fellow Englishmen.

It was dark outside. At one table, a Vietnamese couple were contentedly finishing their meal. At another, a man smoked a bamboo pipe. A television at the end of the room showed mildly pornographic Chinese videos.

But then came the moment of truth: could an Englishman eat a dog? Could he do so without his stomach rebelling, without his thoughts turning to labradors snoozing by Kentish fireplaces, Staffordshire bull terriers collecting sticks for children, and Pekinese perched on the laps of grandmothers?

One Englishman could: I ate roast dog, dog liver, barbecued dog with herbs and a deliciously spicy dog sausage, for it is the custom to dine on a selection of dog dishes when visiting a dog restaurant. The meat tastes faintly gamey. It is eaten with noodles, crispy rice-flour pancakes, fresh ginger, spring onions, apricot leaves and, for cowardly Englishmen, plenty of beer.

I had been inspired to undergo this traumatic experience – most un-British unless one is stranded with huskies on a polar ice cap – by a conversation earlier in the week with Do Duc Dinh, a Vietnamese economist, and Nguyen Thanh Tam, my official interpreter and guide.

They were much more anxious to tell me about the seven different ways of cooking a dog, and how unlucky it was to eat dog on the first five days of the month, than they were to explain Vietnam's economic reforms. "My favourite," began Tam, "is minced intestines roasted in the fire with green beans and onions." He remembered proudly how anti-Vietnamese protesters in Thailand in the 1980s had carried placards saying "Dog-eaters go home!"

During the Vietnam War, he said, a famous Vietnamese professor had discovered that wounded soldiers recovered much more quickly when their doctors prescribed half a kilogram of dog meat a day. Dinh insisted I should eat dog in Hanoi rather than Saigon. "I went to the south and ate dog, but they don't know how to cook it like we do in the north," he said. I asked where the dogs came from. "People breed it, then it becomes the family pet." And then they eat it? "Yes," he said with a laugh. I told myself that the urban British, notorious animal lovers that they are, recoil particularly at the idea of eating dogs only because most of them never see the living versions of the pigs, cows, sheep and chickens that they eat in meat-form every day. And the French, after all, eat horses. Resolutely unsentimental, we put aside our dog dinner and went to Vinh's kitchen. Two wire cages were on the floor; there was one large dog in the first and four small dogs in the second. Two feet away, a cauldron of dog stew steamed and bubbled. Vinh told us about his flourishing business. The dogs are transported from villages in a nearby province. A 10 kg dog costs him about 120,000d, or just over US$10. At the end of the month – peak dog-eating time – his restaurant gets through about 30 dogs a day. The restaurant, he said, was popular with Vietnamese, Koreans and Japanese. Squeamish Westerners were sometimes tricked into eating dog by the Vietnamese friends, who would entertain them at the restaurant and tell them afterwards what it was they had so heartily consumed.

Source: Extracted from an article by Victor Mallet, *The Financial Times*.

bistro with cheap steaks and excellent pizza. Stop Café also delivers. Popular among the French community.

Café Moca, 14-16 Nha Tho, T4-3825 6334. 0700-2400. From cinnamon-flavoured cappuccino to smoked salmon, and from dry martinis to Bengali specials, this is a good place to come and snack. It's a longstanding tourist favourite though these days less beloved than the days when foreign dining options were scant. The high ceilings and marble floors still make it a comfortable spot for a coffee and it's a favourite for people-watching.

Cha Ca La Vong, 14 Cha Ca St, T4-3825 3929. 1100-2100. Serves 1 dish only, the eponymous *cha ca Hanoi*, fried fish fillets in mild spice and herbs served with noodles. It's utterly delicious and popular with visitors and locals, although expensive at 1,300,000d for the meal and the service is now complacent, slap dash and verging on the rude. They've definitely had too much of a good thing and treat the customers now with disdain rather than a warm welcome.

Little Hanoi, 9 and 14 Ta Hien St, T4-3926 0168. Reputedly the original Little Hanoi, these small restaurants offer inexpensively priced traditional Vietnamese food and are incredibly popular. Try the steamed tuna in beer with rice. Watch out for the staircase if you're heading upstairs.

Little Hanoi, 21 Hang Gai St, T4-3828 8333. 0730-2300. An excellent little place. An all-day restaurant/café serving outstanding sandwiches. The cappuccinos, home-made yoghurt with honey and the apple pie are also top class.

My Burger My, 5 Hang Bac St, T4-7309 0777. Though portions are small, American Burger My serves US-style burgers with many toppings, on grilled buns in a small but comfortable shop in the Old Quarter. Those preferring gut-busters are advised to look elsewhere but for a snack it's worth the stop. Also has a Mexican menu. Delivery available.

Restaurant 22, 22 Hang Can St, T4-3826 7160. 1200-2100. Good menu, popular and tasty Vietnamese food, succulent duck. At just a couple of dollars per main course it represents excellent value for money.

Tamarind, 80 Ma May St, T4-3926 0580, tamarind_café@yahoo.com. A vegetarian restaurant that goes beyond traditional 'veggie' fare. There is a comfortable café at the front and a smart restaurant behind in the Handspan Adventure Travel office. There's a lengthy vegetarian selection, delicious juices and the recommended Thai glass noodle salad.

Cafés

Bon Mua, 38-40 Le Thai To St, T4-3825 6923. 0700-2300. Popular ice cream shop on the west bank of Hoan Kiem Lake.

Cafe Puku, 16/18 Tong Duy Tan St, T4-3928 5244. An old favourite recently relocated to a new location in a large colonial villa. Puku has kept everything that made it good and still managed improvements, such as cheaper beer and an astonishing 24-hr licence. Set on famous Food Street now, it still even smells the same: like your university café, all friendly garlic and fresh brewed coffee.

Fanny Ice Cream, 48 Le Thai To St, T4-3828 5656, www.fanny.com.vn. Refreshing ice cream and sorbet with an ice cream buffet at 95,000d.

Highlands Coffee, southwest corner of Hoan Kiem Lake. Lovely spot under the trees overlooking the lake. Great place for a coffee or cold drink. This home-grown chain is often referred to by people as equally lacking in taste and imagination as 'Vietnam's Starbucks'. It is more than that, and better. While an iced coffee is twice or more what you'd pay in a smaller café, quality is assured and ambience relaxing. Food is reasonable and desserts are more of a draw for most than mains.

Kem Trang Tien, 35 Trang Tien St. This is probably the most popular ice cream parlour in the city and it's a drive-in and park your moto affair. It's also a flirt joint for Hanoian young things. Flavours are cheap and change as to what's available.

South of Hoan Kiem Lake *p32, maps p24 and p28*

₸₸₸-₸₸ Chica, 27 Hang Be St. Inside the **Hoa Binh Hotel**, floor 9, T4-2243 4370. One of the city's more hidden gems, Chica is an 8-floor ride at the top of the **Hoa Binh Hotel**. Known best for its steaks, Chica has a small but loyal following. Desserts come recommended too.

₸₸₸-₸₸ La Badiane, 10 Nam Ngu St, T4-3942 4509. A relative newcomer to Hanoi, from a couple of Hanoi old hands, **La Badiane's** French aesthetic stops at the food. Fusion, and of more than Vietnamese and French, is what this restaurant is about and while its intricately decorated plates of seasonal meals won't appeal to everyone there are many who swear this is the best restaurant in town. Service is good, if over-attentive at times. Portions have increased but order a starter too if you're hungry. The converted colonial villa is delightful. The set lunch menu, a bargain US$10.

₸₸₸-₸₸ San Ho, 58 Ly Thuong Kiet St, T4-3934 9184, ando@hn.vnn.vn. 1100-1400, 1700-2200. This is Hanoi's most popular seafood restaurant. Located in a colonial villa in Hoan Kiem district, it's a better bet than some of the seafood barns closer to the river. Set menus, fish tanks, and local seafood.

₸₸₸-₸₸ Verticale, 19 Ngo Van So St, T4-3944 6317, verticale@didiercorlou.com. 0900-1400, 1700-2400. Didier Corlou, former chef at the **Sofitel Metropole**, opened this new restaurant in a small street in the French quarter. The tall, multi-storey building includes a spice shop, restaurant, private rooms and a terrace bar. The food and presentation are an adventurous culinary journey of gustatory delight; this is certainly one of the best dining experiences in the city. Highly recommended.

₸₸ Al Fresco's, 23L Hai Ba Trung St, T4-3826 7782. Part of a chain, **Al Fresco's** is a popular Australian-run grill bar serving ribs, steak, pasta, pizza and fantastic salads. Portions are large, hugely so, and it's a very child-friendly place, with paper table cloths and crayons on every table. Recommended.

₸₸ Luna d'Autonno, 78 Tho Nhuom St, T4-3823 7338. Regarded as one of the city's best Italian restaurants, **Luna** has a large menu of pizza, pasta and mains. Though it has recently moved to a far less prepossessing setting, the food, if not ambience, remains good.

₸₸ Song Thu, 28A Ha Hoi St (off Tran Hung Dao St), T4-3942 4448, www.hoasuaschool.com. 0700-2200. French training restaurant for disadvantaged youngsters where visitors can eat excellently prepared French and Vietnamese cuisine in an attractive and secluded courtyard setting. Reasonably cheap and popular. Cooking classes now available, see Activities and tours, page 61.

₸₸-₸ Cay Cau, 17A Tran Hung Dao St, T4-3933 1010. In the **De Syloia Hotel**. Good Vietnamese fare at reasonable prices in this popular place. Daily set lunch at 130,000d is good value.

₸₸-₸ Chim Sáo, 65 Ngo Hue St, T4-3976 0633, www.chimsao.com. Set in an atmospheric old colonial villa, **Chim Sao** is famous for its Northern Vietnamese food, cooked by a French chef. Seating is on the floor upstairs.

₸ Café 129, 129 Mai Hac De St. Does excellent breakfast fry-ups and cheap but filling Mexican meals in what is still one of Hanoi's most basic settings. Despite serving a mostly Western menu, **Café 129** has never moved past its pho shop vibe of low tables and plastic stools. And its long-standing fan club wouldn't have it any other way.

₸ Com Chay Nang Tam, 79A Tran Hung Dao St, T4-3942 4140. 1100-1400, 1700-2200. This popular little a/c vegetarian restaurant is down an alley off Tran Hung Dao St and serves excellent and inexpensive 'Buddhist' dishes in a small, family-style dining room. There are numerous options and jugs full of freshly squeezed juices.

₸ Hanoi Gourmet, 1B Ham Long, T4-3943 1009, www.hanoigourmet.com. 0830-2100. Not a restaurant but a delicatessen with a couple of tables at the back. For lovers of fine wine, cheese and cold cuts, **Hanoi Gourmet** is a great discovery. Find a free afternoon, go short on breakfast, then go for a long leisurely lunch. Freshly restocked from France every few weeks.

Ỷ **Quan An Ngon**, 18 Phan Boi Chau St, T4-3942 8162, ngonhanoi@vnn.vn. Daily 0700-2130. This place is insanely popular at lunch and dinner time. In a massive open-air courtyard setting with enormous umbrellas shading wooden tables you can wander around looking at all the street stalls with signage in Vietnamese. The menu is in English and you order from a waitress. All the food is delicious and you'll be keen to return again to sample the huge array on display.

Cafés

252 Hang Bong, actually in what is now Cua Nam St. Pastries, yoghurt and crème caramel, very popular for breakfast.

Cong Café, 152D Trieu Viet Vuong St. A communist parody in a city which, in the main, doesn't view such a sense of humour favourably. Music here is generally excellent and coffee a cut above the rest. Trieu Viet Vuong St is the café quarter of Hanoi.

Ho Chi Minh's Mausoleum complex and around *p35, map p24*

ỶỶ-Ỷ **Seasons of Hanoi**, 95B Quan Thanh St, T4-3843 5444, seasonsofhanoi@fpt.vn. 1100-1400, 1800-2200. Bookings recommended. This admirable restaurant has, inevitably, become very well known and is one of the most agreeable dining experiences in Hanoi. The building is a finely restored and authentically furnished colonial villa, the Vietnamese food is fresh and delicious and service attentive.

Ỷ **KOTO**, 59 Van Mieu St, T4-3747 0337, www.koto.com.au. Mon 0730-1800, Tue-Sun 0730-2230. A training restaurant for underprivileged young people. Next to the **Temple of Literature**, in new premises, pop in for a good lunch after a morning's sightseeing. The food is international, filling and delicious but avoid the fatty pork. Upstairs is the **Temple Bar** with Wi-Fi. Recommended.

North of the Old City *p40, map p53*

ỶỶỶ-ỶỶ **Bobby Chinn**, 77 Xuan Dieu, T4-3719 2640, www.bobbychinn.com. Bobby has been in Vietnam for many years having ventured out on his culinary career in HCMC. The restaurant is arguably one of Hanoi's most famous restaurants thanks to its TV star chef. Though now moved from its central Hoan Kiem Lake location, the food and decor remain the same: rich reds, comfortable tables and the same intricate fusion that made Bobby famous.

ỶỶỶ-ỶỶ **Daluva**, 33 To Ngoc Van St, T4-3718 5831. A wine bar with tapas and some main meals, Daluva is located in Hanoi's posher Tay Ho district. Though with prices beginning at 100,000d per glass it might seem expensive, keep in mind that all wine is exorbitantly priced in Vietnam.

ỶỶỶ-ỶỶ **Vine Wine Boutique Bar & Café**, 1A Xuan Dieu, T4-3719 8000, www.vine-group.com. 0800-2330. One of the most extensive cellars in town, housed in one of the more expensive restaurant's in Hanoi. Vine has been a fixture for years. It's fine dining with excellent food and service and many Western and Vietnamese dishes. Surrounds and service alone justifies the tab. Drinks selection is excellent. Make sure to stop in at **Vine Cellar Door** a few doors down as well.

ỶỶ **Don's Bistro**, 16/27 Xuan Dieu, T4-3719 2828, www.donviet.vn. A new venture from one of the founding chefs of both the **Press Club** and **Vine**, Don's is a multi-level restaurant, café and cocktail bar on the shores of West Lake. Though expensive, it has a lovely view and the pizzas are some of the best in the city. Cocktails are also excellent though the spirits list tends towards overpriced. Snatch the day-bed on top-floor cocktail bar for the best view.

ỶỶ **Hanoi Cooking Centre**, 44 Chau Long St, T4-3715 0088, http://hanoicookingcentre.com. A restaurant, café and cooking centre housed in a restored colonial villa near Truc Bach Lake, it has quickly become popular with expats and tourists. Past the excellent cooking classes, which provide a useful overview of street food dishes and others, the cooking centre serves things rarely seen in Hanoi, such as a seasonal Sunday Roast.

ΨΨ-Ψ Chien Beo, 192 Nghi Tam St, T4-3716 1461. A Vietnamese steakhouse serving huge platters of beef cooked in various ways and sometimes stuffed with cheese. It's rumoured the chef trained in some of the city's 5-star hotel kitchens before opening his own joint. The setting may be basic but it's worth it. Don't expect to linger, it's all about fast turnaround.

ΨΨ Pho Yen, 66 Cua Bac St, T4-3715 0269. This down-at-heel tables and chair joint does tasty *pho cuon*. Popular with locals.

Ψ Foodshop 45, 59 Truc Bach St. A Vietnamese-run Indian restaurant facing Truc Bach Lake. Offers the city's cheapest Indian meals. The menu is compact but good and vegetarian dishes begin at a bit over US$1.75. Also very popular for delivery. Traditional Vietnamese rice wines are also on the menu.

Ψ Kitchen, Lane 40, 7A Xuan Dieu, T4-3719 2679. 0700-2130. Down an alley with a small courtyard, a cheap and cheerful very popular hang-out serving great Mexican, sandwiches and salads and healthy juices. Greg's chicken shawarma pita is hugely filling.

Ψ Le Cooperative, 46 An Duong St, T4-3716 6401. A French-run restaurant and bar from the same people behind famous Vietnamese restaurant **Chim Sao**. **Le Cooperative** has a compact but good French menu of classics and the best-value steak in the city. The cold cuts are recommended. The Vietnamese menu is large but receives mixed reviews. Upstairs is done up like an ethnic minority stilt house and there's also a selection of rice wines; some are even drinkable.

Cafés

Duy Tri, 43A Yen Phu St, T4-3829 1386. Considered the best coffee in Hanoi. This tiny tube café is full on atmosphere and the smell of beans. The coffee with yoghurt (*ca phe sua chua*) is the signature drink.

Mau House & Ceramic, 17a Truc Bach, T4-3829 3744. A cute balcony café amid a clutter of interesting sculptures and handicrafts for sale overlooking the lake.

Outer Hanoi *p40, map p54*

ΨΨΨ Edo, **Daewoo Hotel**, 360 Kim Ma St, T4-3831 5000. Japanese restaurant in a Korean hotel, considered some of the finest Japanese food in town.

Bars and clubs

Hanoi's main bar street is Ta Hien, heading towards Hang Buom after it has cut across the famous Bia Hoi Corner (at Luong Ngoc Quyen). There are some 5 bars on this small strip and several around the corner. Though officially all bars are supposed to close at midnight, it's a rule sporadically enforced and one that often leads to a convivial, speakeasy atmosphere – as long as you know which closed roller door to knock on.

The Cheeky Quarter, 1A Ta Hien St, T9 0403 2829 (mob). Owned by the same family as **Tet bar**, and spitting distance away, **Cheeky** packs a lot into what space it has. A fussball table, bar stools, and an upstairs area with airplane-esque toilet are all part of the charm – as is the dodgy flock wallpaper and Old Master's style paintings of friends of the bar. Late night food here is arguably better.

Dragonfly, 15 Hang Buon St, T4-3926 2177. An all-red, 2-storey Hanoi bar popular for drinks specials and its Arabian Nights shisha pipe room, with many flavours of tobacco. Apple is the most popular but you can also opt for chocolate or cappuccino.

Finnegan's Irish Pub, 16A Duong Thanh St, T4-3828 9065. Longstanding Irish pub that manages to be far less tacky than the average. Food, especially stews, is good and the range of whisky reasonable. Despite the backpacker scrawl all over the walls of the back, with the inevitable shonkily drawn phalluses, it's popular with expats too.

Funky Buddha, 2 Ta Hien St, T4-3926 7615. A lounge/club bar that is something of an anomaly in Hanoi: equally popular with foreigners and Vietnam's rapidly growing middle class. Though it looks plenty glitzy, spirit prices are only a shade above anything else on the street and staff are extremely competent. Bottle service is on offer.

Golden Cock, 5A Bao Khanh St, T4-3825 0499. A popular 'gay friendly' bar a few doors away from Polite Pub, the Golden Cock has been around a long time and is still crowded years on.

Half Man/Half Noodle, 64 Dao Duy Tu St, T4-3926 1943. This oddly named bar is basic, but comfortable. Think beer, bamboo and a play list you can choose yourself. Of late they've begun doing late night food, including heartier meals such as schnitzels and chips. Planning a big night out? Ask for the alcoholic coconuts, which are exactly as they sound.

Hoa Vien, 1 Tang Bat Ho St, T4-3972 5088. Possibly the biggest and best-known of Hanoi's European-style beer halls, Hoa Vien is a multi-level behemoth serving beer in glasses ranging from standard to 1 litre steins. Pilsner and dark beer are both on offer as well as heart-clogging wonders such as fried cheese and pork cutlets.

Ho Guom Xanh, 32 Le Thai To St, T4-3828 8806. Few people passing by just yards away outside could imagine the colour and operatic spectacle of the stage shows this nightclub puts on. Performers, often dressed like something out of Miami Vice, arrive on stage via a pneumatic pole. It's loud, packed and popular with a mainly local crowd but a real visual treat. Drinks are fairly expensive, which is par for the course in most nightclubs aimed at rich Vietnamese.

The House of Son Tinh, 31 Xuan Dieu, T4-3718 6377, www.houseofsonthinh.com. Tapas dining and a liquor lounge for multiple rice wine tastings. This new kid on the block is already a hit in this expat quarter.

JoJo's, 23C Hai Ba Trung St, T4-3824 1028. Owned by the same company as Al Fresco's, Jaspa's and Pepperoni's, this dark, sleek and shiny wine bar has a good cocktail list and menu. Bottles and wines by the glass don't come cheap but it's a good list and weekend specials, such as Sun brunches, make up for it.

Legends, 1-5 Dinh Tien Hoang St, T4-3936 0345, www.legendsbeer.com.vn. Daily 0800-2300. Another of Hanoi's popular microbreweries. The German *helles bier* (light) and the *dunkels bier* (dark) are strong and tasty. This café bar has views over Hoan Kiem Lake. An extensive food menu too and good for snacks and ice cream.

Le Pub, 25 Hang Be St, T4-3926 2104, www.lepub.org. One of Hanoi's best pubs, now with a 2nd location on the shores of West Lake. Popular with tourists and expats, prices remain reasonable, beer is some of the coldest in the city and nightly drinks specials keep the wallet intact. Food is reasonably priced and competent but, excepting the breakfasts and Vietnamese, largely uninspiring. Le Pub has outdoor seating on one of the Old Quarter's busiest streets.

Library Bar, Press Club, 59A Ly Thai To St. Tranquil setting in which to tipple a few malts while smoking a fine Havana.

Mao's Red Lounge, 7 Ta Hien St, T4-3926 3104. A hugely popular hole-in-the-wall bar mostly frequented by young English teachers. Music is good though dependent on whomever of the publican's friends has control of the iPod. Some of the cheapest beers in town with famously honest staff.

Phuc Tan Bar, 51 Phuc Tan St. An out and out dive bar, and proud of it. Come the weekend there are precious few places open late at night where you can both drink and dance. Though basic, and with nightmare toilets, Phuc Tan Bar has a gorgeous view over the Red River, large outdoor seating area and often stays open late. Be very wary of catching any cabs from outside the bar on your way home. Ask staff to phone for one instead.

Polite Pub, 5 Bao Khanh St, T4-3825 0959. Good bar snacks and cocktails and a pool table at this popular expat haunt, which despite being supplanted by more popular bars on the other side of the Old Quarter has retained its high standards.

R & R Tavern, 10 Tho Nhuom St, T4-6295 8215. One of Hanoi's oldest bars, this new location outside the Old Quarter has everything its predecessor had, right down to the crowd. A mostly American bar, with reasonably priced Tex-Mex meals and one of Vietnam's best beers – the hard-to-find Huda.

Rock Billy, corner of Luong Van Can and Hang Gai streets. Climb up to the tiny balcony and look out on the adjacent shops and road junction for one of the best bird's eye views of the Old Quarter.

Roots, 2 Luong Ngoc Quyen St. A French-run reggae bar serving rums from the Francophile Caribbean and local rums infused with fruits and spices. Roots gets busy on weekends but tends to be quiet until mid-week. The bamboo and rattan add to the atmosphere but be prepared: the drinks pack a punch.

Solace, end of Chung Duong Do St. Expats might try their hand at word play and call this bar on a boat 'soul less' but you can bet come the weekend they'll wash up on the dance floor. A place to keep your hand on your dong, to be sure, but one of the few viable late-night clubs around and interesting for the most diverse clientele in the whole city, from foreign executives to overworked chefs to stumbling English teachers to loaded expat brats to backpackers to the local gay mafia.

Tadioto, 113 Trieu Viet Vuong St, T4-2218 7200, www.tadioto.com. Tadioto has no precedent in the city or other neighbours in the area. An art gallery-cum-bar, it's one of the few places to host poetry readings, play Tom Waits albums or play local to the local art community. Far from the centre of town it might be, but it's always worth the trip.

Tet bar, 2A Ta Hien St, T4-3926 3050. One of the city's late night mainstays and formerly known as 'Le Marquis', Tet closes when the last customers go home, pretty much. For some reason better known to fate, the toasted sandwiches here – a Croque Monsieur – are considered the best after hours snack in the city.

Entertainment

Cinema

See Vietnam News, the New Hanoian (http://newhanoian.xemzi.com) and *Hanoi Grapevine* (http://hanoigrapevine.com) for current listings.

Hanoi Cinematique, 22A Hai Ba Trung St, T4-3936 2648, info2@hanoicinema.org. This small club shows films in the original version. Membership is 100,000d; a 1-off visit costs 50,000d. Plenty of more unusual films, film festivals and a nice courtyard to enjoy a drink in.

Megastar Cineplex, Vincom City Towers, 191 Ba Trieu St, T4-3974 3333, www.megastarmedia.met. Western films with Vietnamese subtitles 50,000d; Wed is cheaper. Popcorn, snacks and beer available.

Dance and theatre

Opera House, T4-3933 0113, nthavinh@hn.vn, box office 0800-1700. A French-era building at the east end of Trang Tien St (see page 56) staging a variety of Vietnamese and Western concerts, operas and plays. Check *Vietnam News* or at the box office.

Water Puppet Theatre, 57b Dinh Tien Hoang St, at the northeast corner of Hoan Kiem Lake, T4-3936 4335, www.thanglongwaterpuppet.org. In recent years the troupe has performed in Japan, Australia and Europe. Entrance 60,000d (1st class), 40,000d (2nd class). Children half price on Sun 0930. Fabulous performances with exciting live music and beautiful comedy daily at 1530, 1700, 1830 and 2000 and 2130; an additional matinee on Sun at 0930. This is not to be missed. Very popular so advanced booking is required at the box office.

Music

Jazz Club (CLB Jazz), 31 Luong Van Can St, T4-3828 7890. Vietnamese jazz saxophonist, Quyen Van Minh, plays here. Open 1000-2400; live jazz every night 2100-2400.

❁ Festivals and events

Jan/Feb Dong Da Hill festival (5th day of Tet). Celebrates the battle of Dong Da in which Nguyen Hue routed 200,000 Chinese troops. Processions of dancers carry a flaming dragon of straw.

Perfume Pagoda Festival, 6th day of the 1st lunar month-end of the 3rd lunar month. This focuses on the worship of Quan Am. There are dragon dances and a royal barge sails on the river.

Hai Ba Trung Festival, 3rd-6th day of the 2nd lunar month. The festival commemorates the Trung sisters, see page 41. On the 3rd day the temple is opened; on the 4th, a funeral ceremony begins; on the 5th the sisters' statues are bathed in a ceremony; on the 6th day a ritual ceremony is held.

Hung Kings' festival, 10th day of the 3rd lunar month. A 2-week celebration when the temple site comes alive as visitors from all over Vietnam descend on the area, as Ho Chi Minh encouraged them to. The place seethes with vendors, food stalls and fairground activities spring up. There are racing swan boats on one of the lakes.

2 Sep National Day, featuring parades in Ba Dinh Sq and boat races on Hoan Kiem Lake.

Shopping

The city is a shopper's paradise with cheap silk and good tailors, handicrafts and antiques and some good designer shops. Hang Gai St is well geared to souvenir hunters and stocks an excellent range of clothes, fabrics and lacquerware. It's rather like the small-time Silk Road of Hanoi. Hats of all descriptions abound. You will not be disappointed.

Antiques

Along Hang Khay and Trang Tien streets, south edge of Hoan Kiem Lake. Shops sell silver ornaments, porcelain, jewellery and carvings – much is not antique, not all is silver; bargain hard.

Art galleries

Hanoi has always been known as the 'artistic' city compared to Saigon's powerhouse economy. Though many galleries do the typical Beautiful Hanoi paintings, more galleries stocking the work of serious artists are popping up. If you decide to get a painting commissioned, treat it much like an experience at the tailors': give it plenty of time and don't always expect perfection first time round. Galleries abound near Hoan Kiem Lake, especially Trang Tien St and on Dinh Tien Hoang St at northeast corner.

Apricot Gallery, 40B Hang Bong St, T4-3828 8965, www.apricot-artvietnam.com. High prices but spectacular exhibits.

Art Vietnam Gallery, 7 Nguyen Khac Nhu St, T4-3927 2349, www.artvietnamgallery.com. Mon-Sat 1000-1800. Art director Suzanne Lecht has created a cool interior in a chic space to display delectable works of art by Vietnamese and Vietnam-based artists. This is Hanoi's premier art space.

Dien Dam Gallery, 4b Dinh Liet St, T4-3825 9881, www.diendam-gallery.com. Beautiful photographic images in black and white and colour.

Hanoi Gallery, 17 Nha Chung St, T4-3928 7943, propaganda_175@yahoo.com. Sells propaganda posters. Original posters cost US$200 upwards; US$8 for a rice paper copy. Some of the reproductions aren't faithful to the colours of the originals; choose carefully.

Propaganda Art, 8 Nha Chung St, T4-3928 6588. More propaganda posters and other propaganda items like mugs and keyrings.

Bicycles

At the second-hand bike market at the intersection of Thinh Yen St and Pho 332, south of the city centre and on Ba Trieu St south of junction with Nguyen Du St.

Books and maps

Private booksellers operate on Trang Tien St and have pavement stalls in the evening; be sure to bargain (maps also available here and outside the post office. On Sun book stalls appear on Dinh Le St, parallel with Trang Tien St. Many travel cafés operate book exchanges. Some travel companies, such as **Love Planet** on Hang Bac St also sell books. Expect the typical travel fare interspersed with a few gems. Make sure to bargain.

Bookworm, 4b Yen The St, Ba Dinh District, T4-3747 8778, bookworm@fpt.vn. Tue-Sun 1000-1900. A couple of thousand books in stock. Unlike other bookshops in town imports new releases and harder-to-find things, though these aren't cheap. Also specializes in books about Vietnam and Southeast Asia. Stocks translations of famous Vietnamese stories. *Dumb Luck,* written about the rising Vietnamese petit bourgeousie in 1930s Hanoi, is worth buying.

Ethnic Travel, 35 Hang Giay St, T4-3928 3186. Books sold, exchanged (2 for 1).

Foreign Language Bookshop, 61 Trang Tien St. Also the alley by the side of this **bookshop** sells copies of books otherwise out of stock.

Xunhasaba, 32 Hai Ba Trung St. The state book distributor's shop. Many books in English,including books about Vietnam.

Camera shops

Processing and film is available all around Hoan Kiem Lake. Several shops also have download and printing services for digital cameras. Ma May street has a number and also do cheap passport photos. Quality may not be perfect.

Clothes, fashions, silk and accessories

Vietnam has produced some exciting fashion designers in the past couple of years (see box, page 60) and there is a growing number of stylish boutiques in the fashionable cathedral shopping cluster and a new 'designer' outlet in southern Hai Ba Trung district stocking labels like Mango and FCUK. Few can walk past the glittering displays of jackets, dresses, handbags, scarves and shoes without feeling some temptation to go in and buy. This is all the more remarkable considering how dowdy the dress sense of most Hanoians was just a few short years ago and how relatively uninviting the shop displays were. The greatest concentration is in the Hoan Kiem Lake area particularly on Nha Tho, Nha Chung, Hang Trong and Hang Gai streets. Outer suburbs arteries are home to endless shops selling cheap, Chinese-made t-shirts and outfits.

Bo Sua, beside skate shop Boo on Ta Hien St. Owned by the same people as **Boo, Bo Sua** is revolutionary for a Hanoian label. Plastic bags have been banned, t-shirts carry environmental awareness cartoons, and designs are mainly done by young Hanoians. If you want a sartorial souvenir that goes beyond the standard Captain Vietnam shirt – the Vietnamese flag shirt – shop here. Day-to-day objects, such as coal briquettes, plastic sandals or foamy glasses of *bia hoi* have been turned into stylish t-shirt icons.

Co, 18 Nha Tho St, T4-328 9925, conhatho@yahoo.com. 0830-1900. This tiny clothes tailor shop has a very narrow entrance on this popular street. It has some unusual prints and the craftsmanship is recommended.

Grace, 5 Nha Tho St and 72 Hang Trong St, T4-3928 7456, grace.vn@vn.vn. Jewellery and lovely flouncy dresses.

Ipa Nima, 34 Han Thuyen St, T4-3933 4000, www.ipa-nima.com. Enter the glittering and sparkling world of **Ipa Nima**. Shiny shoes, bags, clothes and jewellery boxes. Hong Kong Chinese Christina Yu is the creative force behind the designer label. Not cheap, but well made, unlike her legion of copycats.

Kien Boutique, 1B To Tich St, T4-3928 6835, kiensilk40@yahoo.com. Recommended tailors for good-quality clothes.

Song, 27 Nha Tho St, T4-3928 8733, www.asiasongdesign.com, 0900-2000. Its sister shop is in HCMC. Here the **Song** shop is on

Asian fusion fashion

The new entrepreneurial streak in Vietnam has proved a catalyst for fabulous design and ingenuity in the fashion world. Although known for the beautiful *ao dai*, the classic-cut trouser tunic of local women, Vietnam was not known for its haute-couture. Nowadays, fashionistas flock for the latest in desirable clothes, bags, shoes and other accessories from the country's designers who have come so far in just a few short years. From the inception of ideas to fabrication to the clothes rails, this has been fashion development on speed. Just 15 years ago, dour communist wear was the nation's lot but since economic liberalization national and international designers have gained fame at home and abroad with some selling to halls of sartorial fame such as **Harrods** and **Harvey Nichols** in London, and **Henri Bendel** in New York. Hollywood actress Cate Blanchett, Shakira Caine, wife of Oscar-winner Sir Michael, and US Senator Hillary Rodham Clinton are all followers of one such designer working under the **Ipa-Nima** label. Christina Yu, a Hong-Kong lawyer, now based in Vietnam, set up glitzy label **Ipa-Nima**. Her bags, clothes and shoes now decorate two shops in Hanoi. Valerie Gregori-McKenzie, a native Frenchwoman who lives in Vietnam, releases beautiful, ethereal clothes, embroidered cushions and bags under the label **Song**. She has two shops gracing Hanoi and Ho Chi Minh City. Sylvie Tran Ha, who is Viet Kieu, set up **SXS** in Ho Chi Minh City, which uses suede, among other materials. Many of these women have combined local materials with ideas, methods and motifs from the ethnic minority clothing of Vietnam. Mai Lam Mai, a Viet Kieu from Australia, has a boutique – Mai's – underneath the Continental Hotel. She sells cutting-edge fashions including a wonderful modern brightly coloured take and twist on the *ao-dai*.

Most of the fashion designers using Vietnam as their creative hub are women. The exception to this rule is the elegantly dressed Hoang Khai of the ubiquitous **Khaisilk** empire. **Khaisilk** began as a workshop in Hanoi in 1980. Since then the empire has expanded with shops in Hanoi, Ho Chi Minh City and Hoi An. Now entrepreneurial owner Mr Khai has combined silk with food to create a series of stylish restaurants that are some of the most chic and glamorous in Vietnam. In the hotel domain, he has established the Hoi An Riverside Resort, a peaceful haven just outside Hoi An where attention to detail combined with the setting has produced one of the most exquisite hotels in the country. Mr Khai, who always dresses in black, wins award after award for his silk output and **Khaisilk**, with a winning marketing thrust, has ensured its place as the number one boutique shop in the country.

the fashionable Nha Tho and run by friendly staff. Clothes and gorgeous homeware. The French designer is well known in Vietnam and her clothes are designed for the heat: natural fibres and airy looseness.

Things of Substance, 5 Nha Tho St, T4-3828 6965, contrabanddesign@hn.vnn.vn. 0900-2000. Selling swimwear, silk jewellery bags and attractive jewellery, this small shop, with excellent service in the shadow of the cathedral, offers something a bit different. An Australian designer is in charge and everything is made with the motto 'Western sizes at Asian prices' in mind. Popular enough that you're likely to run into someone else sporting your outfit, at some stage.

Tina Sparkle, 17 Nha Tho St, T4-3928 7616. 0900-2000. Funky boutique that sells mostly bags in a glittering array of colours – from tropical prints to big sequinned flower bags. Also stocks items by Spanish design team Chula. A good option if you want an Ipa Nima bag without a taxi ride to the next district.

Vincom City Towers, 191 Na Trieu St. Large mall in the city's south. Though the range of things stocked isn't amazing, the newly built 'high-end' addition behind, connected by a walkway, is home to plenty of well-known brands. Mango is marketed, and priced, as a high-end not high-street brand here.

Handicrafts and homeware

There has been a great upsurge in handicrafts on sale as the tourist industry develops. Many are also made for export. A wide range of interesting pieces is on sale all around the popular cathedral shopping cluster of Nha Tho, Ly Quoc Su and Nha Chung streets. Further shops can be found on Hang Khay St, on the southern shores of Hoan Kiem Lake, and Hai Gai St. A range of hand-woven fabrics and ethnographia from the hill tribes is also available.

Aloo Store, 37 Hang Manh St, T4-3928 9131, aloo181@yahoo.com. An abundance of well-priced ethnic goods from the north.

Chi Vang, 63 Hang Gai St, T4-3936 0601, chivang@fpt.vn. Chi Vang has moved to the centre of the Old Quarter – the Silk Road – and sells exquisitely embroidered cloths, baby's bed linen and clothing, cushion covers, table cloths and unusual-shaped cushions artfully arranged. All the goods displayed are embroidered by hand.

Craft Link, 43 Van Mieu St, T4-3843 7710, www.craftlink-vietnam.com.
Traditional handicrafts from a not-for-profit organization. Many are made by ethnic minorities.

La Casa, 12 Nha Tho St, T4-3828 9616, www.lacasavietnam.com. Lovely individual homeware items.

Mosaique, 22 Nha Tho St, T4-3928 6181, mosaique@fpt.vn. 0830-2000. An Aladdin's cave of embroidered table runners, lamps and stands, silk flowers for accessorizing, silk curtains, silk cushions, ball lamps, pillow cushions and lotus flower-shaped lamps.

Nagu, 20 Nha Tho St, T4-3928 8020, www.zantoc.com. Japanese designed and catering to that market. Things have a more minimalist tinge but conform to Japanese sizing: small. The teddy bears are popular.

Ngoc Oanh, 34 Hang Da Market, T4-3928 5479. Does a lovely line in all the Bat Trang village ceramics. Hang Da Market is lined with ceramic stalls.

Phuc Loi, 2b Ta Hien St. A little shop run by a husband and wife making and selling hand-carved wooden chopsticks or stamps. They come in a variety of oriental signs of the zodiac, etc. Cheap, fun and make excellent lightweight gifts.

Musical instruments

For unusual souvenirs visit the shop at 76 Hang Bong St, where they make wooden percussion instruments.

Shoes

Walking boots, trainers, flip flops and sandals, many in Western sizes, are sold in the shops around the northeast corner of Hoan Kiem Lake. Most are genuine brand name items and, having 'fallen off the back of a lorry', are remarkably inexpensive – but do bargain.

Supermarkets

Hapromart, 35 Hang Bong St. 0800-1200, 1230-2200. Stocks Western items.

Fivimart, 27a Ly Thai To St. Large-ish supermarket stocking all the necessities.

Activities and tours

Cookery classes

Hanoi Cooking Centre, 44 Chau Long St, T4-3715 0088, http://hanoicookingcentre.com. A large kitchen in a spacious building. Cooking classes for kids and adults. Western and Vietnamese.

Hidden Hanoi, 137 Nghi Tam, Tay Ho, T91-225 4045 (mob), www.hiddenhanoi.com.vn. A recommended outfit offering insightful

Vietnamese cultural and culinary tours. Walking tours of the Old Quarter, French Quarter, excellent and fascinating street food tours and walking tours US$20 min 2 people; cooking classes from US$40 per person and language classes from US$20.
Highway 4, 7 Truc Bach, T4-3715 0577. Visit the markets then head to the kitchen to learn how to cook some of the restaurant's best-loved signature items as well as simpler fare, such as fried rice.
Sofitel Metropole Hotel, 15 Ngo Quyen St, T4-3826 6919 ext 8110, concierge@sofitelhanoi.vnn.vn. Offers 3 programmes. You visit the market to buy ingredients, return to the **Metropole** kitchens for a cooking demonstration and then eat at the **Spices Restaurant** in the hotel.

Health clubs

All the big hotels provide fitness facilities, pool and gyms. Open usually free of charge to residents and to non-residents for a fee or subscription. **Sofitel Metropole** and the **Daewoo** boast the best facilities (see Sleeping, above). **Van Phuc Diplomatic Compound** (1 Pho Kim Ma, Ba Dinh District) and **Trung Tu Diplomatic Compound** (Dang Van Ngu, Dong Da District) give priority to diplomats but their facilities are available to the public.

Therapies

A Top Spot, 52 Au Trieu, T4-3828 8344. The top spot for pampering, hair and superior pedi and manicures.
Le Spa du Metropole, Sofitel Metropole, 15 Ngo Quyen St. A truly luscious and deliciously designed spa in the grounds of the hotel. Themed rooms provide the ambience for the ultimate spa rituals. Expensive but worth it.

Walking tours

Douglas Jardine, dougjardine76@gmail.com. Adjunct Professor, History and Humanity Studies at Hanoi University. Runs excellent, insightful and informative tours covering various subjects in the city.

Tour operators

The most popular option for travellers are the budget cafés that offer reasonably priced tours and an opportunity to meet fellow travellers. While an excellent way to make friends, these tours do tend to isolate visitors from local people. Operators match their rival's prices and itineraries closely and indeed many operate a clearing system to consolidate passenger numbers to more profitable levels.

Make sure to use only recommended tour operators. Also keep in mind that you get what you pay for and if something is too cheap to be true, it probably is. Many trips to Ha Long, for example, may seem cheap but once aboard the boat, you'll discover beer is expensive. Examples of tour prices include: **Perfume Pagoda**, US$18; **Hoa Lu and Tam Coc**, US$16; **Hanoi city tour**, US$16; 1 night on **Halong Bay** from US$29; **Halong Bay and Cat Ba Island** from US$70; **Cuc Phuong National Park**, US$30; overnight in **Mai Chau** from US$32.
Asian Trails, 24 Hang Than St, Ba Dinh District, T4-3716 2736, www.asiantrails.travel. Offers various package tours across Asia.
Asia Pacific Travel, 66 Hang Than St, Ba Dinh District, T4-3836 4212, www.asiapacifictravel.vn. Affordable small-group adventure travel and a wide selection of tours.
Asiatica Travel, A1203, building M3-M4, 91 Nguyen Chi Thanh St, T4-6266 2816 ext 114, www.asiatica-travel.com. Ask for Pham Duc Quynh as your guide; he is very knowledgeable and speaks fluent English and French.
Blue Star Hotel, 21 Bat Dan St, T4-3923 1585, www.bluestar-hotels.com. Recommended for its budget Halong Bay excursions which are good value.
Buffalo Tours, 94 Ma May St, Hoan Kiem, T4-3828 0702, www.buffalotours.com. Well-established and well-regarded organization. It has its own boat for Halong Bay trips and offers tours around the north as well as day trips around Hanoi. Cross-country and cross-border tours and tailor-made trips too. Staff are friendly and the guides are informative and knowledgeable.

Discovery Indochina, 63A Cua Bac St, T4-3716 4132, www.discoveryindochina.com. Organizes private and customized tours throughout Vietnam, Cambodia and Laos.

Ethnic Travel, 35 Hang Giay St, T4-3926 1951, www.ethnictravel.com.vn. Owner, Mr Khanh, runs individual tours to Bai Tu Long Bay – next to Halong Bay – and to Ninh Binh, the Red River Delta and trekking in the Black River area around Mai Chau. Always offers homestays and always, in a non-gimicky way, tries to ensure that travellers see the 'real' Vietnam. Book exchange inside.

ET-Pumpkin, 89 Ma May St, T4-3926 0739, www.et-pumpkin.com. Very professional in attitude, offering a good selection of travel services, particularly for visitors to the northwest. Now also offering motorbike tours of the north. Good and reasonably priced place for jeep hire and visa extensions too. Also has its own very comfortable train carriage which goes to Sapa. Footprint received reports that it has not been as helpful as it used to be.

Exotissimo, 26 Tran Nhat Duat St, T4-3828 2150, www.exotissimo.com. Specializes in more upmarket tours, good nationwide service.

Explorer Tours, 85 Hang Bo St, T4-3923 0713, www.explorer.com.vn. Useful for both individual travel needs and small groups.

Green Bamboo, 97/19 Van Cao St, Ba Dinh district, T4-3761 8638, www.greenbambootravel.com. Another well-established leader in the budget market, organizes tours of Halong Bay and Sapa.

Halong Travel, 10 Hang Be St, T4-3926 3606, www.halongtravel.com. A countrywide operator with friendly staff.

Handspan Adventure Travel, 80 Ma May St, T4-3926 2828, www.handspan.com. A reputable and well-organized business. Specializes in adventure tours, trekking in the north and kayaking in Halong Bay. It has its own junk in Halong Bay and kayaks. Booking office in Sapa also.

Hanoi Toserco, 8 To Hien Thang St, T4-3976 0066, www.tosercohanoi.com. It runs an efficient Open Tour service.

Kangaroo Café, 18 Pho Bao Khanh, Quan Hoan Kiem, T4-3828 9931, www.kangaroocafe.com. Specializes in small group and tailor-made tours.

Love Planet, 25 Hang Bac St, T4-3828 4864, www.loveplanettravel.com. Individual and small group tours; also organizes visas. Very helpful and patient service; good book exchange too.

Luxury Travel, 5 Nguyen Truong To St, Ba Dinh District, T4-3927 4120, www.luxurytravelvietnam.com. A newer tour operator offering countrywide tours and alternative excursions.

Real Darling Café, 33 Hang Quat St, T4-3826 9386, darling_café@hotmail.com. Long-established and efficient, this café concentrates on tours of the north and has a visa service. Motorbike hire US$5 per day; car hire US$50 minimum per day.

Sinh Tourist (formerly Sinh Cafe), 40 Luong Ngoc Quyen St, T4-3926 1568. This is the one and only official branch of Sinh in Hanoi. It is only listed here so that you know it is the official office. However, it is not recommended. There are dozens of far superior, switched on and efficient tour operators in the city far more deserving of your patronage. It is, however, good in other parts of the country.

Topas, 52 To Ngoc Van St, Tay Ho, T4-3715 1005, www.topasvietnam.com. Good, well-run tour operator offering cross-country tours as well as those in the north. Also has an office in Sapa using local guides. It also organizes treks to Pu Luong Nature Reserve. Draw card is its eco-lodge in Sapa, with 3-star villas overlooking spectacular scenery. See Sapa Sleeping, page 62.

Vega (formerly Fansipan Tours), 24A Hang Bac St, T4-3926 2092, www.vega-travel.com. Small operator organizing tours of Sapa and the north.

Voyage Vietnam Co, Mototours Asia, 1-2 Luong Ngoc Quyen St, T4-3926 2616, www.

voyagevietnam.net. Well-organized, reliable and great fun motorbiking, trekking and kayaking tours, especially of the north. The super-friendly and knowledgeable Tuan will take professional bikers to China, Laos, and the Golden Triangle. Trips include all protective gear and nights are spent in homestays and hotels. 4WD car hire also available. This is the only company permitted to import your bike into Vietnam and to organize trips from Vietnam through to China and Tibet.

Transport

The traffic in Hanoi is becoming more frantic – and lethal – as each month goes by. Bicycles, cyclos, mopeds, cars, lorries and buses fight for space with little apparent sense of order, let alone a highway code. At night, with few street lamps and some vehicles without lights, it can seem positively dangerous. Pedestrians should watch out.

Air

Airport information

There are an increasing number of direct international air connections with Hanoi's **Noi Bai Airport**, north of the city. (Cat Bi Airport, at Haiphong, has been identified as a replacement international airport for Noi Bai in the future.) See pages 63 and 63.

The airport has the **Aero Café**, post office, exchange facilities and **Pacific Travel** (www.pacifhotelsgroup-travel.com) has a tour desk offering hotel reservations. Lost and found, T4-3884 0008/3866 5013.

The official **Noi Bai Taxi**, 2A Quang Trung St, T4-3873 3333, charges a price of US$12-15 to and from the airport. Journey time is approximately 45-60 mins. When leaving the airport go out to the official taxi line and pay at the kiosk/with the seller there.

If you get any other kind of cab do set the price before leaving. Taxi scams have become problems in both Ho Chi Minh City and Hanoi and agreeing a price beforehand is very important.

You can also catch a minibus from the airport to various locations around the city, where you will likely be beset by more cab drivers and *xe ôms*; 30,000d. **Jet Star** passengers get their bus free.

Minibuses leave for the airport from opposite the **Vietnam Airlines** office, 2A Quang Trung St, US$2, running a service at regular intervals from 0500-1800, 50 mins.

There's also an a/c **city bus** that leaves the airport every 20 mins, 5000d.

Chartering a taxi from a hotel to the airport should cost no more than around US$10. Meter taxis may cost over US$20 and will charge an additional road toll of 10,000d.

Airline offices

Air Asia, 30 Le Thai To St, www.airasia.com. **Air France**, 1 Ba Trieu St, T4-3825 3484, www.airfrance.com. **American Airlines**, 99 Ba Trieu St, T4-3933 0330, www.aa.com. **Asiana Airlines**, 604, 4 Da Tuong St, Hoan Kiem District, T4-3822 2671. **Cathay Pacific**, 49 Hai Ba Trung St, T4-3826 7298, www.cathaypacific.com/vn. **China Airlines**, 6B Trang Tien St, T4-3936 6364, www.china-airlines.com. **China Southern Airlines**, 27 Ly Thai To St, T4-3826 9233, www.cs-air.com. **Japan Airlines**, 5th floor, 63 Ly Thai To St, T4-3826 6693, www.vn.jal.com. **Jetstar**, 204 Tran Quang Khai St, Hoan Kiem District, www.jetstar.com/vn. **Korean Air**, 330 Ba Trieu St, Hai Ba Trung District, T4-3974 0240, www.koreanair.com. **Lao Airlines**, 46 Tho Nhuom St, Hoan Kiem District, T4-3822 9951, www.laoairlines.com. **Malaysia Airlines**, 49 Hai Ba Trung St, T4-3826 8820, www.malaysiaairlines.com. **Singapore Airlines**, 17 Ngo Quyen St, T4-3826 8888, www.singaporeair.com. **Thai**, 44B Ly Thuong Kiet St, T4-3826 7921, www.thaiair.com. **Tiger Airways**, T120-60114, www.tigerairways.com. **Vietnam Airlines**, 1 Quang Trung St, T4-3832 0320, www.vietnamairlines.com. Mon-Fri 0700-1830, Sat and Sun 0800-1130, 1330-1700 for both domestic and international bookings. Telephone sales are

Mon-Fri 0700-1900, Sat and Sun 0730-1700. Branch offices: 25 Trang Thi St, T4-3832 0320; 221B Tran Ding Ninh St, T4-73930 0507; 231 Nguyen Trai St, T4-3558 7341; Noi Bai International Airport, T4-3884 3389.

Bicycle

This is the most popular form of local mass transport and it is an excellent way to get around the city. Bikes can be hired from the little shops at 29-33 Ta Hien St and from most tourist cafés and hotels; expect to pay about US$2 per day. For those staying longer, it might be worth buying a bicycle (see Shopping, page 58).

Bus

Local

The Hanoi city bus service, www.hanoibus.com.vn, is still lacking in some ways – routes may be re-routed and drivers continue to drive colourfully. Though to be fair the system is weighted against them – any late returns incur fines so they tend to speed at breakneck pace and sometimes don't stop for passengers.

Buses go all over but you'll want to catch them from around Hoan Kiem Lake, the new bus station on the dyke road at the top of the Old Quarter. Further afield is the Cau Giay bus station, also a relatively new transport hub in the west. Most journeys are 3000-5000d.

Long distance

Hanoi has a number of bus stations. The Kim Ma bus station is closed.

The Southern bus terminal (Giap Bat, T4-3864 1467) is out of town, but linking buses run from the northern shore of Hoan Kiem Lake. The terminal serves destinations south of Hanoi: **HCMC**, **Buon Ma Thuot**, **Vinh**, **Danang**, **Thanh Hoa**, **Nha Trang**, **Dalat**, **Qui Nhon**, **Ninh Binh**, **Nam Dinh** and **Nho Quan** for **Cuc Phuong National Park**.

Express buses usually leave at 0500; advance booking is recommended.

Luong Yen bus station, 1 Nguyen Khoai St. The Hoang Long bus company, T4-3928 2828, https://hoanglongasia.com, runs deluxe buses to **HCMC** with comfortable beds, 690,000d one way, including all meals and drinks, 36 hrs, 12 a day 0500-2300. Hoang Long, also leaves for **Haiphong** from here; 7 daily from 0415-1645 and on to **Cat Ba Island** by ferry. Hoang Long also runs to other desinations. Other bus companies run to, **Haiphong** 0450-1920, 42 daily.

Other buses leave for **Haiphong** and **Halong** from the Gia Lam bus station, Nguyen Van Cu, Gia Lam District, T4-3827 1529, over Chuong Duong Bridge.

From Ha Dong bus station Tran Phu Rd, Ha Tay Province, T4-3825 209, buses leave for **Mai Chau**, **Hoa Binh**, **Son La** and **Dien Bien Phu**. Take a local bus or *xe ôm* to the bus station.

From My Dinh station, T4-3768 5549, there are buses to **Halong**, every 20 mins, 3 hrs 15 mins, US$2.80. Other destinations in the north are also served from here such as **Thai Nguyen**, **Tuyen Quang** and **Ha Giang**.

International

To **Vientiane** via Cau Treo. Several travellers have contacted Footprint to complain of this journey. Complaints usually centre around the fact that there always appears to be a delay at or just before the border meaning a 20-hr journey takes nearly 24 hrs. The lesson is be prepared for this to happen, or take alternative transport. For visa info, see page 38 and under Embassies and consulates, page 67. Tickets can be booked through tour operators for straight through services or those where you change buses or direct with one of the bus companies that runs a straight through service such as the International Passenger Transportation Co Viet-Laos, 3A Nguyen Gia Thieu St, T4-3942 0554, phongvelao@yahoo.com.vn, daily 0700-1900. This agency runs a direct bus service to **Vientiane** (Laos), daily 1900, 20 hrs, US$17-22. Book ahead. It dissuades passengers from buying Lao visas at the border as it alleges the bus won't wait. This is a ploy to get you to buy the visa through them at US$40 for 1 month.

Cyclo

Hanoi's cyclo drivers have obviously heard through the cyclo grapevine that foreigners pay more than locals, but have taken this to extremes; prices quoted are usually 500% more than they should be. Drivers also tend to forget the agreed fare and ask for more: be firm; some ask that the price be written down. A trip from the railway station to Hoan Kiem Lake should not cost more than 30,000d. The same trip on a *xe ôm* would be 15,000d.

Motorbike

Hiring a motorbike is a good way of getting to some of the more remote places. Tourist cafés and hotels rent a variety of machines for US$5-40 per day. Honda scooter 100/110, US$5 per day; Minsk Russian 125, US$7 per day; Honda scooter 125cc, US$10 per day; off-road bike Honda Baja 250 (old), US$25 per day and US$40 per day for a new one. **Voyage Vietnam**, see Tour operators, above, will rent you a Minsk including riding pans, jacket, helmet and saddle-bags, or an off-road Yamaha XT 250 including riding pans, jacket, helmet and saddle-bags and 3rd-party insurance. Note that hire shops insist on keeping the renter's passport.

Taxi and private car

Watch out for taxi scams in Hanoi. There are rogue taxis waiting for the early morning train arrivals; drivers have been known to almost triple the fare to the Old Quarter. Some rogue drivers have been known to lock customers in the car during a fare dispute. Be careful. Make enquiries at hotels about reasonable fares. Small cabs, not saloon cars, can be dodgy. Also be careful catching cabs at night from bars. Agree on a fare first in these situations. It is unlikely you will be hurt but it has happened.

The following are recommended:

Noi Bai Taxi, T4-3873 3333; **Mai Linh Taxi**, T4-3822 2666.

Private cars can be chartered from most hotels and from many tour operators, see page 62.

Train

The **central station** (**Ga Hanoi**) is at 120 Le Duan St, at the end of Tran Hung Dao St (a 10-min taxi ride from the centre of town), T4-3747 0666. There's an information desk at the entrance, T4-3942 3697, 0700-2300 but minimal English is spoken, and luggage lockers at the end of the ticket hall. The **Thong Nhat** (north-south train) booking office is on the left; northern trains office, on the right. Train times and prices can be found at www.vr.com.vn. The train station remains old-fashioned but fast-food joints – such as the Korean-owned Lotteria – have opened up near the premises if you need a last minute snack before boarding. There's a **VNR** ticket agency at 41 Ma May St, T4-3210 9775, daily 0900-2100. There's a US$1 commission and the ticket can be brought to your hotel.

For trains to **HCMC** and the south, enter the station from Le Duan St. For trains to **Haiphong** and **Lao Cai,** enter the station from Tran Quy Cap St, T4-3747 0308 (take care arriving here at night). It is possible to walk through corridors to get to these platforms from the main entrance if you go to the wrong part.

5 daily connections with **HCMC**, approx 30-40 mins. Advance booking is required. There are daily trains to **Haiphong**, 1 from the the central station, 3 from Long Bien station, T4-3747 0308. There are 3 trains daily to **Ninh Binh**. **Long Bien Station** is at the western end of Long Bien Bridge near the Red River. Get there by taxi or *xe ôm*.

Trains to **Lao Cai** (Sapa). For the full timetable, see page 65. **ET-Pumpkin**, www.et-pumpkin.com and **Ratraco**, www.ratraco.com.vn, run standard comfortable a/c 4-berth cabins in its carriages with complimentary water, bedside lights and space for luggage. For luxury, the **Victoria Hotel** carriages (http://www.victoriahotels-asia.com/eng/hotels-in-vietnam/sapa-resort-spa/victoria-express-train) run Sun-Fri at 2150 to **Sapa** arriving 0630. The dining carriage is only available Mon, Wed and Fri.

Places are only available to **Victoria Sapa** hotel guests. The a/c carriages, wood-panelled and with comfortable mattresses and reading lights are very attractive and comfortable; the train caters for 52 people in 2-4 berth cabins. All carriages have a loo and washbasin at one end. The dining carriage is a real treat with big cushions to pad the seats and everything from plum wine to snacks to meals served.

For details of the train from Hanoi to **Beijing** see Dong Dang and the Chinese border, page 65.

Directory

Banks

Commission is charged on cashing TCs into US dollars but not if cashing directly into dong. It is better to withdraw dong from the bank and pay for everything in dong. Most hotels will change dollars, often at quite fair rates. ATMs are increasingly common and most Vietnamese banks these days are linked into the large international networks such as Visa and Maestro. You will be charged a fee but it's generally not exorbitant. These days banks aren't as free with the US dollar so if you need some head to Hang Bac or Ha Trung streets. Both black-market changers will give you more favourable rates on your US dollar-dong exchanges. **ANZ Bank**, 14 Le Thai To St, T4-3825 8190, Mon-Fri 0830-1600. Provides full banking services including cash advances on credit cards, 2% commission on TCs, 24-hr ATMs. **Citibank**, 17 Ngo Quyen St, T4-3825 1950. Only cashes TCs into dong. **Vietinbank**, 37 Hang Bo St, T4-3825 4276. Dollar TCs can be changed here. Deals with Amex, Visa, MasterCard and Citicorp. **Foreign Exchange Centre**, 2 Le Lai St. **National Bank**, 10 Le Lai St, T4-3824 9042, 0800-1100 and 1300-1600. **Sacombank**, 87 Hang Bac St, has a 24-hr Visa and MasterCard ATM. **VID Public Bank**, 2 Ngo Quyen St, T4-3826 6953. Charges 1.5% on TCs. **Vietcombank**, 198 Tran Quang Khai St, T4-3824 3108.

Embassies and consulates

Australia, 8 Dao Tan St, T4-3831 7755. **Belgium**, 49 Hai Ba Trung St, T4-3934 6179. **Burma**, 289 Kim Ma St, T4-3845 3369. **Cambodia**, 71A Tran Hung Dao St, T4-3942 7646. **Canada**, 31 Hung Vuong St, T4-3734 5000. **China**, 46 Hoang Dieu St, T4-3845 3736. For Chinese visa information, see page 66. **Denmark**, 19 Dien Bien Phu St, T4-3823 1888. **France**, 57 Tran Hung Dao St, T4-3944 5700. **Germany**, 29 Tran Phu St, T4-3845 3836. **Israel**, 68 Nguyen Thai Hoc St, T4-3843 3140. **Italy**, 9 Le Phung Hieu St, T4-3825 6256. **Japan**, 27 Lieu Giai St, T4-3846 3000. **Laos**, 22 Tran Binh Trong St, T4-3942 4576. A 1-month Lao visa costs US$32-40; visas are available at all international crossings from Vietnam. **Malaysia**, 43-45 Dien Bien Phu St, T4-3734 3836. **Netherlands**, 360 Kim Ma, T4-3831 5650. **New Zealand**, 5th floor, 63 Ly Thai To St, T4-3824 1481.**Russia**, 191 de La Thanh St, T4-3833 6991. **Singapore**, 41-43 Tran Phu St, T4--3944 5700. **Sweden**, 2 Nui Truc St, T4-3726 0400. **Switzerland**, 44B Ly Thuong Kiet St, T4-3934 6589. **Thailand**, 63-65 Hoang Dieu St, T4-3823 5092. **UK**, Central Building, 31 Hai Ba Trung St, T4-3936 0500. **USA**, 7 Lang Ha St T4-772 1500; Consulate: 1st floor, Rose Garden Tower, 170 Ngoc Khanh St, T4-3850 5000.

Hospitals

Eye Hospital, 85 Ba Trieu St, T4-3826 3966. **Family Medical Practice Hanoi**, Building A1, Van Phuc Compound, 298 Kim Ma Rd, Ba Dinh, T4-3843 0748, www.vietnammedicalpractice.com. 24-hr medical service, including intensive care, also dental care. **Hospital Bach Mai**, Giai Phong St, T4-3869 3731. English-speaking doctors. Also dental service. **International Hospital**, Giai Phong St, T4-3574 0740. **International SOS**, Central Building, 31 Hai Ba Trung St, T4-3934 0555, www.internationalsos.com. 24-hr, emergencies and medical evacuation. Dental service too. **L'Hôpital Français de Hanoi**, 1 Phuong Mai St, Dong Da, T4-3577 1100, www.hfh.com.vn. **Vietnamese-German**

Hospital, 40 Trang Thi St, T4-3825 5934. Dental treatment also available.

Pharmacies are as common as *pho* stands in Hanoi and basic drugs, such as painkillers, are generally reliable. Most pharmacy proprietors aren't trained and some of the drugs are fake and/or expired. The **Nha Thuoc Pharmacy** is at 47 Hang Bo St.

Immigration

Immigration Department, 40A Hang Bai St, T4-3826 6200.

Internet

Internet access and emailing is cheap and easy in Hanoi. Many hotels now have free internet use. Failing that, all the travel cafés have internet services. Wi-Fi is everywhere and even outer suburban cafés with no sit-down toilet will have Wi-Fi.

Post office, courier and telephone

GPO, 75 Dinh Tien Hoang St. **DHL** at the GPO. **Express Mail Service** at the GPO and at 778 Duong Lang St, T4-3775 0144 and 49 Nguyen Thai Hoc St, T4-3733 2086. International telephone, telex and fax services also available at the PO at 66-68 Trang Tien St and at 66 Luong Van Can St and at the PO on Le Duan next to the railway station. **TNT** International Express, 25D-25E Lang Ha St, T4-3514 2575. **UPS**, 4C Dinh Le St, T4-3824 6483.

Contents

Footprint features

Northwest

The geology of much of Northwest Vietnam is limestone; the effect on this soft rock of the humid tropical climate and the resulting numerous streams and rivers is remarkable. Large cones and towers (hence tower karst), sometimes with vertical walls and overhangs, rise dramatically from the flat alluvial plains. Dotted with bamboo thickets, this landscape is one of the most evocative in Vietnam; its hazy images seem to linger deep in the collective Vietnamese psyche and perhaps symbolize a sort of primeval Garden of Eden, an irretrievable age when life was simpler and more innocent.

Interwoven into this landscape are the houses of the ethnic minorities, beautiful tiled houses in the main. Passing through you will see people tending paddies in traditional clothing and boys on the backs of buffalo. In the far-flung northwest corner is Dien Bien Phu, the site of the overwhelming defeat of the French in Vietnam in 1954 and now home to the largest monument in Vietnam, erected in 2004 to commemorate the 50th anniversary of the Vietnamese victory. » *For listings, see pages 84-86.*

Ins and outs

Getting there and around There are three points of entry for the Northwest circuit: the south around Hoa Binh (reached by road); the north around Lao Cai/Sapa (reached by road or by train) and in the middle Dien Bien Phu reached by plane or road. Which option you pick will depend upon how much time you have available and how much flexibility you require. It is possible to hire a jeep in Hanoi to do the clockwise circuit via Hoa Binh and Dien Bien Phu and pay off your driver at Sapa leaving you free to return by train. Most people arrive by train or by luxury bus, the cheapest option, to Sapa.

Another option for those so inclined is to do the whole thing by motorbike. The rugged terrain and relatively quiet roads make this quite a popular choice for many people. It has the particular advantage of enabling you to to make countless side trips and get to remote and untouched tribal areas. It is not advisable to attempt the whole circuit using public transport as this would involve fairly intolerable levels of discomfort and a frustrating lack of flexibility and would be very time-consuming. » *For further details, see Transport, page 86, and Hanoi tour operators, page 70.*

Best time to visit The region is wet from May to September, making travel quite unpleasant at this time. Owing to the altitude of much of the area winter can be quite cool, especially around Sapa, so make sure you go well prepared.

Tourist information The Northwest is not a single administrative area so see the province and town tourist authorities for local information. Otherwise tour operators in Hanoi are the best source of information, see page 70.

Hanoi to Sapa via Dien Bien Phu → *For listings, see pages 84-86.*

The road from Hanoi to Dien Bien Phu winds its way for 420 km into the Annamite Mountains that mark the frontier with the Lao People's Democratic Republic. The round trip from Hanoi and back via Dien Bien Phu and Sapa is about 1200 km and offers some of the most spectacular scenery anywhere in Vietnam. There are, of course, opportunities to meet some of Vietnam's ethnic minorities and learn something about their lives and customs (see page 70). The loop can be taken in a clockwise or anti-clockwise direction; the advantage of following the clock is that you'll have the opportunity to recover from the rigours of the journey in Sapa.

Highway 6, which has been thoroughly rebuilt along almost the entire route from Hanoi to Son La, leads southwest out of Hanoi to Hoa Binh. Setting off in the early morning the important arterial function of this road is evident. Ducks, chickens, pigs, bamboo and charcoal (the energy and building materials of the capital) all pour in to Hanoi – a remarkable volume of it transported by bicycle. Beyond the city limit the fields are highly productive, with bounteous market gardens and intensive rice production.

Hoa Binh

Hoa Binh, on the banks of the Da (Black) River, marks the southern limit of the interior highlands. It is 75 km from Hanoi, a journey of about 2½ hours. Major excavation sites of the Hoabinhian prehistoric civilization (10,000 BC) were found in the province, which is its main claim to international fame. In 1979, with Russian technical and financial assistance, work began on the **Hoa Binh Dam** and hydroelectric power station; it was complete 15 years later. The reservoir has a volume of nine billion cubic metres: it provides two functions, to prevent flooding on the lower reaches of the Red River (that is Hanoi) and to generate power. Architecture buffs may want to swing by to see the Russian-influenced industrial architecture. Vietnam is so dependent on Hoa Binh for its electricity that when water levels fall below critical thresholds in the dry season large areas of the country are blacked out. More than 4000 households had to be moved from the valley floor to rugged, infertile hillsides where ironically they are too poor to afford electricity.

The **Hoa Binh Province Museum** ⓘ *0800-1030, 1400-1700, 10,000d*, contains items of archaeological, historical and ethnographical importance. Relics of the First Indochina War, including a French amphibious landing craft, remain from the bitterly fought campaign of 1951-1952 that saw Viet Minh forces successfully dislodge the French.

Muong and **Dao minority villages** are accessible from Hoa Binh. **Xom Mo** is around 8 km from Hoa Binh and is a village of the Muong minority. There are around 10 stilt houses, where overnight stays are possible through **Hoa Binh Tourism** ⓘ *next to the Hoa Binh 1 Hotel, T18-385 4374, www.hoabinhtourism.com*, and there are nearby caves to visit. **Duong** and **Phu** are villages of the **Dao Tien** (Money Dao), located 25 km upriver. A permit is required for an overnight stay. Permits and boat hire are available from **Hoa Binh**

People of the north

Ethnic groups belonging to the Sino-Tibetan language family such as the Hmong and Dao, or the Ha Nhi and Phula of the Tibeto-Burman language group are relatively recent arrivals. Migrating south from China only within the past 250-300 years, these people have lived almost exclusively on the upper mountain slopes, practising slash-and-burn agriculture and posing little threat to their more numerous lowland-dwelling neighbours, notably the Thai.

Thus was established the pattern of human and political settlement that would persist in North Vietnam right up until the colonial period – a centralized Viet state based in the Red River Delta area, with powerful Thai vassal lordships dominating the Northwest. Occupying lands located in some cases almost equidistant from Hanoi, Luang Prabang and Kunming, the Thai, Lao, Lu and Tay lords were obliged during the pre-colonial period to pay tribute to the royal courts of Nam Viet, Lang Xang (Laos) and China, though in times of upheaval they could – and frequently did – play one power off against the other for their own political gain. Considerable effort was thus required by successive Viet kings in Thang Long (Hanoi) and later in Hué to ensure that their writ and their writ alone ruled in the far north. To this end there was ultimately no substitute for the occasional display of military force, but the enormous cost of mounting a campaign into the northern mountains obliged most Viet kings simply to endorse the prevailing balance of power there by investing the most powerful local lords as their local government mandarins, resorting to arms only when separatist tendencies became too strong. Such was the political situation inherited by the French colonial government following its conquest of Indochina in the latter half of the 19th century. Its subsequent policy towards the ethnic minority chieftains of North Vietnam was to mirror that of the Vietnamese monarchy whose authority it assumed; throughout the colonial period responsibility for colonial administration at both local and provincial level was placed in the hands of seigneurial families of the dominant local ethnicity, a policy which culminated during the 1940s in the establishment of a series of ethnic minority 'autonomous zones' ruled over by the most powerful seigneurial families.

Tourism, which can also organize homestays and trekking tours to Thanh Hoa and Mai Chau. So many foreign travellers are bypassing Hoa Binh for the stunning Mai Chau Valley that a homestay may be a more authentic and less touristy experience.

Mai Chau → *For listings, see pages 84-86.*

After leaving Hoa Binh, Highway 6 heads in a south-southwest direction as far as the Chu River. Thereafter it climbs through some spectacular mountain scenery before descending into the beautiful Mai Chau Valley. During the first half of this journey, the turtle-shaped roofs of the Muong houses predominate, but after passing Man Duc the road enters the territory of the Thai, northwest Vietnam's most prolific minority group, heralding a subtle change in the style of stilted-house architecture. While members of the Thai will be encountered frequently on this circuit, it is their Black Thai sub-ethnic group which will be seen most often. What makes the Mai Chau area interesting is that it is one of the few places en route where travellers can encounter their White Thai cousins.

An isolated farming community until 1993, Mai Chau has undergone significant change in just a few short years. Its tranquil valley setting, engaging White Thai inhabitants and superb rice wine make Mai Chau a very worthwhile stop.

Background

The growing number of foreign and domestic tourists visiting the area in recent years has had a significant impact on the economy of Mai Chau and the lifestyles of its inhabitants. Some foreign visitors complain that the valley has already gone a long way down the same road as Chiang Mai in northern Thailand, offering a manicured hill-tribe village experience to the less adventurous tourist who wants to sample the quaint lifestyle of the ethnic people without too much discomfort. There may be some truth in this allegation, but there is another side to the coin. Since the region first opened its doors to foreign tourists in 1993, the Mai Chau People's Committee has attempted to control the impact of tourism in the valley. **Lac** is the official tourist village to which tour groups are led (there are some 108 guesthouses), and although it is possible to visit and even stay in the others, by 'sacrificing' one village to tourism it is hoped the impact will be limited. Income generated from tourism by the villagers of Lac has brought about a significant enhancement of lifestyles, not just in Lac but also throughout the entire valley, enabling many villagers to tile their roofs and purchase consumer products such as television sets, refrigerators and motorbikes. Of course, for some foreign visitors the sight of a television aerial or a T-shirt is enough to prove that an ethnic village has already lost its traditional culture, but in Lac they are wily enough to conceal their aerials in the roof space.

Lac (White Thai village)

ⓘ *Lac is easily accessible from the main road. From the direction of Hoa Binh take the track to the right, immediately before the ostentatious, red-roofed People's Committee Guesthouse. This leads directly into the village of Lac.*

This village is popular with day-trippers and overnight visitors from Hanoi. Turning into the village one's heart may sink: minibuses are drawn up and stilt houses in the centre of the village all sport stickers of Hanoi tour operators. But before you turn and flee take a stroll around the village, find a non-stickered house and by means of gestures, signs, broken English and the odd word of Vietnamese ask whether you can spend the night.

Rent a bicycle from your hosts and wobble across narrow bunds to the neighbouring hamlets, enjoying the ducks, buffaloes, children and lush rice fields as you go. It is a most delightful experience. If you are lucky you will be offered a particularly refreshing tea made from the bark of a tree.

Grottoes

About 5 km south of Mai Chau on Route 15A is the Naon River on which, in the dry season, a boat can be taken to visit a number of large and impressive grottoes. Others can be reached on foot. Ask your hosts for details.

Around Mai Chau

A number of interesting and picturesque walks and treks can be made in the countryside surrounding Mai Chau. These cover a wide range of itineraries and durations, from short circular walks around Mai Chau, to longer treks to minority villages in the mountains beyond. One such challenging trek covers the 20 km to the village of **Xa Linh**, just off Highway 6. This usually takes between two and three days, with accommodation provided in small villages along the way. Genial host Mr Gia in the Hmong village of **Hung Kia** will warmly welcome you for a couple of dollars per night, copious amounts of rice wine included. Be forewarned that this route can become dangerously slippery in the wet and a guide is required; ask at the People's Committee Guesthouse or in Lac. Expect to pay US$15-20 for two days and arrange for transport to collect you in Xa Linh.

Pu Luong Nature Reserve

ⓘ *Ba Thuoc Project Office, Trang Village, Lam Xa Commune, Ba Thuoc District, Thanh Hoa, T37-388 0494/671, ffiplcpbto@hn.vnn.vn.*

Pu Luong Nature Reserve is a newly protected area of limestone forest southeast of Mai Chau that harbours the endangered Delacour's langur, clouded leopard, Owston's civet and bear. Bird watching is best from October to March. From Ban Sai, 22 km south of Mai Chau, trekkers can visit caves and local Thai and Muong communities. From the south, near the reserve headquarters close to Canh Nang, there is the Le Han ferry crossing. From here visitors can see the traditional water wheels at Ban Cong, trek deep east to Ban Son and then, after overnighting, trek up north back to Highway 6. Also from Le Han, trekkers can overnight in Kim Giao forest in the west of the reserve before visiting an old French airbase, Pu Luong mountain (1700 m) and trekking north back to the Mai Chau area. Biking and boat in and around the reserve is also possible. Contact the reserve office or Hanoi tour operators, see page 74, for details.

Moc Chau and Chieng Yen

North of Mai Chau on the road to Son La is Chieng Yen. Home to 14 villages of Thai, Dao, Muong and Kinh, there are new homestay options with trekking and biking opportunities as well as tea farm visits at Moc Chau. A highlight is the weekly Tuesday market.

Son La → *For listings, see pages 84-86.*

The road to Son La is characterized by wonderful scenery and superb Black Thai and Muong villages. The road passes close to several attractive villages each with a suspension footbridge and fascinating hydraulic works. Mini hydroelectric generators on the river supply houses with enough power to run a light or television and water power is also used to husk and mill rice. The succession of little villages located just across the river to the left-hand side of the road between 85 km and 78 km from Son La, affords an excellent opportunity to view Black Thai stilt-house architecture. **Cuc Dua** village at the 84-km mark is photogenic. Typically there is a suspension bridge over the incised river in which you can see fish traps and swimming children as clouds of butterflies flutter by on the breeze.

History

It was not until the 18th century, under the patronage of the Black Thai seigneurial family of Ha, that Son La began to develop as a town. During the late 1870s the region was invaded by renegade Chinese Yellow Flag bands taking refuge after the failed Taiping Uprising. Allying himself to Lin Yung-fu, commander of the pursuing Black Flag forces, Deo Van Tri, Black Thai chieftain, led a substantial army against the Yellow Flags in 1880, decisively defeating and expelling them from the country. Thus Tri established hegemony over all the Black and White Thai lords in the Son La area, enabling him to rely on their military support in his subsequent struggle against the French – indeed, the chieftains of Son La were to take an active role in the resistance effort between 1880 and 1888.

As the French moved their forces up the Da River valley during the campaign of 1888, the chieftains of the area were one by one obliged to surrender. A French garrison was quickly established at Son La. As elsewhere in the Northwest, the French chose to reward the chieftains of Son La district for their new-found loyalty by reconfirming their authority as local government mandarins, now on behalf of a colonial rather than a royal master.

While large-scale resistance to French rule in the Northwest effectively ceased after 1890, sporadic uprisings continued to create problems for the colonial administration. The French responded by establishing detention centres throughout the area, known to the Thai as *huon mut* (dark houses). The culmination of this policy came in 1908 with the construction of a large penitentiary designed to incarcerate resistance leaders from the Northwest and other regions of Vietnam. Just one year after the opening of the new Son La Penitentiary, prisoners staged a mass breakout, causing substantial damage to the prison itself before fleeing across the border into Laos.

During the final days of colonial rule Son La became an important French military outpost, and accordingly an air base was built at Na San, 20 km from the town. Both Na San air base and the colonial government headquarters in Son La town were abandoned to the Viet Minh in November 1953, on the eve of the Battle of Dien Bien Phu.

Sights

There is little to see other than the **Son La Provincial Museum** ⓘ *on Youth Hill, just off Highway 6 and near the centre of town, daily 0700-1100, 1330-1730, 10,000d.* The museum building is in fact the town's old French Penitentiary, constructed in 1908, damaged in 1909, bombed in 1952 and now partially rebuilt for tourists. The original 3-m-deep dungeon and tiny cells complete with food-serving hatches and leg-irons, can be seen together with an exhibition illustrating the history of the place and the key individuals who were incarcerated here.

Around Son La

To reach **Tham Coong** (Coong Caves), walk or drive to the north end of town (Hoa Ban Street); after a few hundred metres (roughly opposite a petrol station) are the tanks of the Son La Water Company; turn left off the road and follow the track gently uphill towards a small group of houses, turning left again just before it forks. Follow the stream or take the path and yomp across the bunds of the rice fields. There are two caves, the wet cave is now fenced off but a scramble up the limestone face brings you to a **dry cave** ⓘ *5000d*, from which the views are lovely. As you have probably come to expect by now in Vietnam, the caves are rather unremarkable, the walk a never-ending joy – with wet feet. The fields, ponds and streams below the caves are a miracle of inventiveness and beauty: stilt houses, gardens, hibiscus hedgerows, poinsettia plants and a range of colours and smells that are particularly appealing in the late-afternoon sunlight. Fish are bred in the ponds covered with watercress (*salad soong*) and what looks like a red algal bloom, but it actually a small floating weed (*beo hoa dau*) fed to ducks and pigs.

Ban Co is a Black Thai village and a visit here can be combined with a trip to Tham Coong. Returning from the caves, rejoin the road then turn left and take a track across the fields and over a small bridge to the village of Co. The village is a largish and fairly ordinary Black Thai settlement but a diverting twilight hour can be spent watching its inhabitants returning from the fields with a fish or duck for the pot and a basket of greens, washing away the day's grime in the stream and settling down to a relaxing evening routine that has changed little in the last few hundred years.

West to Dien Bien Phu or north to Muong Lay from Son La

The scenery on leaving Son La is breathtaking. Reds and greens predominate – the red of the soil, the costumes and the newly tiled roofs, and the green of the trees, the swaying fronds of bamboo and the wet-season rice. Early morning light brings out the colours in their finest and freshest hues, and as the sun rises colours transmute from orange to pink to ochre.

Around every bend in the road is a new visual treat. Most stunning are the valley floors, blessed with water throughout the year. Here generations of ceaseless human activity have engineered a land to man's design. Using nothing more than bamboo technology and human muscle, terraces have been sculpted from the hills: little channels feed water from field to field illustrating a high level of social order and common purpose. Water powers devices of great ingenuity: water wheels for raising water from river level to field level, rice mills and huskers and mini electrical turbines. And, in addition, these people, who for centuries have been isolated from outside perceptions of beauty, have produced a fusion of natural and human landscape that cannot fail to please the eye. Shape, form, scale and colour blend and contrast in a pattern of sympathy and understanding wholly lost to the modern world. Then the road climbs away from the river to a village dependent on rain for its water: the grey and red dust and the meagre little houses indicate great poverty and make one realize the importance of a constant water supply.

There is a small and colourful market village 25 km from Son La and 10 km further on is **Thuan Chau**, another little market town where, in the early morning, people of different minorities in traditional dress can be seen bartering and trading. Thuan Chau is a good spot for breakfast and for buying headscarves. The settlements along this route nicely illustrate the law that describes the inverse relationship between the size of a place and the proportion of the population traditionally garbed. The road is remarkably good with crash barriers, mirrors positioned strategically on hair-pin bends and warning signs, which, considering the precipitous nature of the terrain from Thuan Chau to Tuan Giao, and that visibility is often obscured by cloud and fog, is just as well.

Tuan Giao is 75 km and approximately three hours from Son La (accommodation is available). From Tuan Giao travellers have the choice of either going north across the mountains direct to Muong Lay (formerly Lai Chau), or taking the longer route via Dien Bien Phu.

Highway 6 from Tuan Giao heads north across the Hoang Lien Son Range direct to Muong Lay. From Tuan Giao, the road climbs up through some spectacular scenery reaching altitudes of around 1800-1900 m. Red and White Hmong villages are passed en route.

The journey from Tuan Giao to Dien Bien Phu on Highway 279 is 80 km (about four hours) and tends to be chosen by those with a strong sense of Vietnamese history.

Dien Bien Phu → *For listings, see pages 84-86.*

Situated in a region where even today ethnic Vietnamese still represent less than one-third of the total population, Dien Bien Phu lies in the Muong Thanh valley, a heart-shaped basin 19 km long and 13 km wide, crossed by the Nam Yum River.

For such a remote and apparently insignificant little town to have earned itself such an important place in the history books is a considerable achievement. And yet the Battle of Dien Bien Phu in 1954 was a turning point in colonial history (see box, page 78). It marked the end of French involvement in Indochina and heralded the collapse of its North African empire. Had the Americans, who shunned French appeals for help, taken more careful note of what happened at Dien Bien Phu they might have avoided their own calamitous involvement just a decade later.

Ins and outs

Getting there Dien Bien Phu is deep in the highlands of Northwest Vietnam, close to the border with Laos and 420 km from Hanoi (although it feels much further). The airport is 2 km north of town. Buses snake their way up from Hanoi via Hoa Binh and Son La, and there are also connections onward with Muong Lay, Sapa and Lao Cai. Expect overland journeys to be slow and sometimes arduous in this mountainous region but the discomfort is compensated for by the sheer majesty of the landscapes. It is also possible to reach the town via the border with Laos at Tay Trang (Sop Hun border gate in Phongsaly Province).

Getting around The town of Dien Bien Phu with its neat streets is quite easy to negotiate on foot. The battlefield sites, most of which lie to the west of the Nam Yum River, are, however, a bit spread out and best visited by car or by motorbike. Since the majority of visitors arrive in Dien Bien Phu using their own transport, this is not normally a problem.

History

Modern Dien Bien Phu is a growing town. This reflects the decision to make it the provincial capital of the newly created Dien Bien Phu Province and attempts to develop it as a tourist destination.

Settled from an early date, Muong Thanh valley has been an important trading post on the caravan route between China and Burma for 2000 years. Over the years numerous fortifications were constructed in and around Muong Thanh, the best known being the fabled Citadel of the Thirty Thousand (Thanh Tam Van) built by the Lu during the 15th century. Remnants of this citadel can still be seen today, near Xam Mun.

The early years of the 18th century were a period of acute political instability throughout Vietnam. During this time the Northwest was overrun by armies of the Phe from China's southern Yunnan Province who committed unspeakable acts of barbarism against the inhabitants of the area. In 1751, however, a Vietnamese peasant leader from the Red River Delta named Hoang Cong Chat, whose army had retreated into the region to escape from

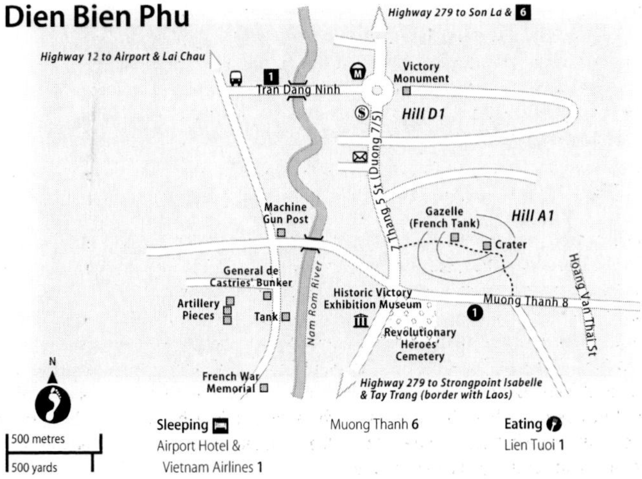

Battle of Dien Bien Phu

On 20 November 1953, after a series of French successes, Colonel Christian de Castries and six battalions of French and French-colonial troops were parachuted into Dien Bien Phu. The location, in a narrow valley surrounded by steep, wooded peaks, was chosen specifically because it was thought by the French strategists to be impregnable. From there, they believed, their forces could begin to harry the Viet Minh close to their bases as well as protect Laos from Viet Minh incursions. At the centre of the valley was the all-important airstrip – Colonel de Castries' only link with the outside world.

In his history of Vietnam, Stanley Karnow describes de Castries thus: "Irresistible to women and ridden with gambling debts, he had been a champion horseman, dare-devil pilot and courageous commando, his body scarred by three wounds earned during the Second World War and earlier in Indochina."

In response, the famous Vietnamese General Giap moved his forces, some 55,000 men, into the surrounding area, manhandling heavy guns (with the help, it is said, of 200,000 porters) up the impossibly steep mountainsides until they had a view over the French forces. The French commander still believed, however, that his forces would have the upper hand in any set-piece confrontation and set about strengthening his position. He created a series of heavily fortified strongholds, giving them women's names (said to be those of his numerous mistresses): Anne-Marie, Françoise, Huguette, Béatrice, Gabrielle, Dominique, Claudine, Isabelle and Eliane.

As it turned out, de Castries was not luring the Viet Minh into a trap, but creating one for himself and his men. From the surrounding highlands, Giap had the French at his mercy. The shelling started in the middle of March, and the strongholds fell one by one; Béatrice first and then Gabrielle and Anne-Marie by mid-March until de Castries' forces were concentrated around the airstrip. Poor weather, which prevented the French from using their air power, and human-wave attacks gradually wore the French troops down. By this time, de Castries had withdrawn to his bunker and command had effectively been taken over by his junior officers. A furious bombardment by the heavy guns of the Viet Minh from 1 May led to the final massed assault five days later. On the final night, the Viet Minh taunted the French defenders by playing the *Song of the Partisans*, the theme of the French Resistance, over the garrison's radio frequencies. The colonel's HQ fell on 7 May at 1730 when 9500 French and French-colonial troops surrendered.A small force of paratroopers at the isolated southern position, Isabelle, continued to resist for a further 24 hours. The humiliation at Dien Bien Phu led the French to sue for peace at a conference in Geneva. On 20 July 1954 it was agreed that Vietnam should be divided in two along the 17th parallel: a communist north and a capitalist south. In total, 20,000 Viet Minh and over 3000 French troops were killed at Dien Bien Phu. The Geneva agreement set terms so that the dead from both sides would be honoured in a massive ossuary. But when Ngo Dinh Diem, the President of the Republic of South Vietnam, symbolically urinated over Viet Minh dead in the South rather than bury them with honour, Giap and Ho Chi Minh decided to leave the French dead to lie where they had fallen. Over the nine years of war between the Viet Minh and the French, the dead numbered between a quarter of a million and one million civilians, 200,000-300,000 Viet Minh and 95,000 French-colonial troops. Who was to guess another 20 years of warfare lay ahead.

royal troops, rallied local Lu, Lao and Thai chieftains to his cause and expelled the Phe back across the border to China. Building a new fortress at Ban Phu, Chat set himself up as lord of a large area including most of modern Son La and Lai Chau provinces, winning the hearts of the local people by carrying out important land and taxation reforms.

The town of Dien Bien Phu itself only came into existence in 1841 when, in response to continued Lao, Siamese and Chinese banditry in the area, the Nguyen dynasty ordered the establishment of a royal district governed from a fortified settlement at Muong Thanh.

Occupied by French forces during the course of their major Northwest campaign of 1888-1889, Dien Bien Phu was subsequently maintained as a garrison town. The town fell briefly to Thai insurgents during the latter stages of the 1908 Son La Penitentiary uprising (prompting the suicide of Dien Bien Phu's French commander) and again during the course of the 1914-1916 uprising of Son La chieftains, but perhaps the most serious threat to French rule in the region came in 1918 when the Hmong rebelled against the harsh fiscal policies of the new Governor General Paul Doumer, by refusing to pay taxes in silver coins or to supply opium to the French and taking up arms against the garrison. The insurrection quickly spread east to Son La and south across the Lao border into Samneua, and although the French responded ruthlessly by devastating rebel areas, destroying food crops to provoke famine and setting a high price on the heads of prominent rebels, the revolt persisted until March 1921.

In Vietnam, as elsewhere in Asia, the defeat of the European Allies during the early years of the Second World War utterly shattered the image of Western colonial supremacy, fuelling the forces of incipient nationalism. French attempts to resume their authority in the region in 1945 thus encountered stiff resistance from Viet Minh forces, and in the nine years of fighting which followed, the Northwest became a cradle of national resistance against French colonialism.

Following the French defeat at Hoa Binh in 1952 the Vietnamese Army went on the offensive all over the Northwest, forcing the French to regroup at their two remaining strongholds of Na San (Son La) and Lai Chau. Early the following year, acting in conjunction with Pathet Lao forces, the Viet Minh overran Samneua in upper Laos and proceeded to sweep north, threatening the Lao capital of Luang Prabang. By November 1953 the French colonial government headquarters at Lai Chau (now Muong Lay), just 110 km north of Dien Bien Phu, had also come under siege.

Dien Bien Phu was the site of the last calamitous battle between the French and the forces of Ho Chi Minh's Viet Minh, and was waged from March to May 1954. The French, who under Vichy rule had accepted the authority of the Japanese during the Second World War, attempted to regain control after the Japanese had surrendered. Ho, following his Declaration of Independence on 2 September 1945, thought otherwise, heralding nearly a decade of war before the French finally gave up the fight after their catastrophic defeat here. The lessons of the battle were numerous, but most of all it was a victory of determination over technology. In the aftermath, the French people, much like the Americans two decades later, had no stomach left for a war in a distant, tropical and alien land.

Sights

On the sight of the battlefield **General de Castries' bunker** ⓘ *daily 0700-1100, 1330-1700, 5000d*, has been rebuilt and eight of the 10 French tanks (known as bisons) are scattered over the valley, along with numerous US-made artillery pieces.

On **Hill A1** (known as Eliane 2 to the French) ⓘ *daily 0700-1800*, scene of the fiercest fighting, is a bunker, the bison named Gazelle, a war memorial dedicated to the Vietnamese who died on the hill and around at the back is the entrance to a tunnel dug by coal miners from Hon Gai. Their tunnel ran several hundred metres to beneath French positions and was filled with 1000 kg of high explosives. It was detonated at 2300 on 6 May 1954 as a signal for the final assault. The huge crater is still there. The hill is a peaceful spot and a good place from which to watch the sun setting on the historic valley. After dark there are fireflies. Hill A1 was extensively renovated in readiness for Dien Bien Phu's 50th anniversary of the French defeat in 2004.

The **Historic Victory Exhibition Museum** (Nha Trung Bay Thang Lich Su Dien Bien Phu) ⓘ *daily 0700-1100, 1330-1800, 5000d*, has a good collection of assorted Chinese, American and French weapons and artillery in its grounds. It has been renovated and there are photographs and other memorabilia together with a large illuminated model of the valley illustrating the course of the campaign and an accompanying video. It's interesting to note that, while every last piece of Vietnamese junk is carefully catalogued, displayed and described, French relics are heaped into tangled piles.

The **Revolutionary Heroes' Cemetery** ⓘ *opposite the Exhibition Museum adjacent to Hill A1, 0700-1100, 1330-1800*, contains the graves of some 15,000 Vietnamese soldiers killed during the course of the Dien Bien Phu campaign.

Located close to the sight of de Castries' command bunker is the **French War Memorial** (Nghia Trang Phap). It consists of a white obelisk surrounded by a grey concrete wall and black iron gates sitting on a bluff overlooking the Nam Yum River.

Dien Bien Phu's newest sight towers over the town. Erected on Hill D1 at a cost of US$2.27 million, the **Victory Monument** (Tuong Dai Chien Dien Bien Phu) ⓘ *entrance next to the TV station on 6 Pho Muong Thanh (look for the tower and large, gated pond)*, is an enormous, 120-tonne bronze sculpture and is, as such, the largest monument in Vietnam. It was sculpted by former soldier Nguyen Hai and depicts three Vietnamese soldiers standing on top of de Castries' bunker. Engraved on the flag is the motto *Quyet Chien, Quyet Thang* (Determined to Fight, Determined to Win). One of the soldiers is carrying a Thai child. It was commissioned to mark the 50th anniversary of the Vietnamese defeat over the French in 1954.

Dien Bien Phu to Muong Lay

It is 104 km on Highway 12 from Dien Bien Phu to Muong Lay (formerly Lai Chau). The road was originally built by an energetic French district governor, Auguste Pavie, and was used by soldiers fleeing the French garrison at Lai Chau to the supposed safety of the garrison at Dien Bien Phu in 1953. Viet Minh ambushes along the Pavie Track meant that the French were forced to hack their way through the jungle and those few who made it to Dien Bien Phu found themselves almost immediately under siege again.

The five-hour journey is scenically interesting and there are a few minority villages – Kho-mú and Thai on the valley floors and Hmong higher up on the way.

The scenery is different from any you will have encountered so far. What is amazing around Son La is the exquisite human landscape. From Dien Bien Phu to Muong Lay what impresses is the scenery in its natural state. It is unfriendly but spectacular. The agents at work here are rivers, rain, heat and gravity, and the raw materials are rock and trees. There are no rice terraces but forested hills in which slash-and-burn farming takes place. This is the land of rockslide and flood. It is geologically young and dangerous; the steep slopes of thinly bedded shales collapse after heavy rain, in contrast to the more solid limestone bands of Son La. The density of population is low and evidence abounds that the living here is harsh. A less romantic side to minority-village life is evident:

tiny four-year-old children stagger along with a baby strapped to their back, there is no colourful dress or elaborate costume, just ragged kids in filthy T-shirts.

Pu Ka village, 46 km from Muong Lay, is a White Hmong settlement newly established by the authorities to transplant the Hmong away from their opium fields.

Muong Lay (formerly Lai Chau) → *For listings, see pages 84-86.*

If Son La is notable for the colour of its minorities (Red, Black and White Thai) and Dien Bien Phu for its history, then Muong Lay, should be noted for the splendour of its trees. The town occupies a majestic setting in a deep and wide valley which is cloaked in dense tiers of forest. For various reasons the trees have not been felled and the beauty they confer on Muong Lay presumably extended over a much wider reach of country in an age gone by.

Background

Much of the present town of Muong Lay dates from 1969-1972, when it was expanded to accommodate the large numbers of Chinese engineers posted here to upgrade the road from Dien Bien Phu to the Chinese border (the Friendship Road). In 1993 the status of capital of Lai Chau Province was transferred from Lai Chau town to Dien Bien Phu, partly in recognition of the latter's growing importance as a hub of economic and tourist activity and partly in deference to the side effects of the massive **Son La hydroelectric power scheme** being planned for the Da River valley in which Muong Lay rests. (Dien Bien Phu later became capital of its own eponymous province when this was created in 2004). The dam and reservoir will be three times bigger than the Hoa Binh complex, currently the biggest in Southeast Asia, and as many as 100,000 people could be displaced. For a rather paltry sum of money and a promise of a plot of land the government appears to have bought grudging acquiescence – at least from the people interviewed by *Vietnam News*. The damming of the Da River will drive the final nail into the coffin of this unhappy but lovely town. In 1996 floods killed 29, making 4000 homeless. Some 20,000 will have lost their homes as residents continue to be moved north to Tam Dung in preparation for the Son La project's anticipated completion date; it is expected to be fully operational by 2012.

History

The history of Lai Chau (present-day Muong Lay) is inextricably entwined with that of the Black Thai seigneurial family of Deo who had achieved ascendancy over the former White Thai lords of Muong Lay by the first half of the 15th century. In 1451 the Vietnamese King Le Thai To is recorded as having led a campaign against the Deo family of Muong Lay (then a village 13 km south of the town) for its disloyalty to the crown.

The Deo family in fact comprised a number of separate Black Thai lineages dotted around what is now Northwest Vietnam and the Yunnan Province of China, but it was the marriage during the 1850s of Deo Van Xeng, a wealthy merchant from Yunnan, to the daughter of a Muong Lay Deo chieftain, which established the most notorious line of the Deo family. When his father-in-law died, Xeng seized control of the Muong Lay dominions and, with the support of the royal court in Luang Prabang and the mandarinate of Yunnan, quickly established himself as one of the most powerful lords in the Northwest.

Deo Van Xeng's eldest son, the energetic Deo Van Tri, continued his father's expansionist policies. Allying himself with Chinese Black Flag commander Lin Yung-fu, Tri succeeded in expelling a Chinese Yellow Flag occupation force from Son La, instantly winning the respect and allegiance of the Black and White Thai chieftains of that area. Apart from a small number who stayed and were subsequently integrated into the Thai community, the Black Flags also left the country shortly after this, enabling Tri to assume suzerainty over a large area of Northwest Vietnam.

When French forces launched their campaign to pacify the Northwest, Tri initially took an active part in the resistance, leading a joint Black and White Thai force against the colonial army at the battle of Cau Giay in 1883. Consequently, king-in-exile Ham Nghi appointed Tri military governor of 16 districts. But the garrisoning of French troops at Lai Chau during the campaign of 1888-1889 marked a turning point in the war of resistance and Tri was ultimately obliged to surrender to the French at Lai Chau in 1890.

As elsewhere in the north, the French moved quickly to graft their colonial administrative systems onto those already established by the Nguyen court, and they ensured Deo Van Tri's future co-operation by awarding him the hereditary post of Supreme Thai Chieftain.

After his death in 1915, Tri was succeeded as Governor of Lai Chau by his son Deo Van Long who later took office as mandarin of the colonial government in 1940. However, as the Viet Minh war of resistance got under way in 1945, the colonial government sought to ensure the continued allegiance of ethnic minority leaders by offering them a measure of self-government. Accordingly, in 1947 Muong, Thai, Tay, Hmong and Nung Autonomous Regions were set up throughout the Northwest and, in Lai Chau, Deo Van Long was duly installed as king of the Thai.

King Deo Van Long is remembered with loathing by most older inhabitants of the Lai Chau area. By all accounts he was a tyrant who exercised absolute authority, striking fear into the hearts of the local people by occasionally having transgressors executed on the spot. The overgrown ruins of Long's mansion lie just across the river from Doi Cao (High Hill) and may be visited either by boat or by road (see below).

During the latter days of French rule, as the security situation began to deteriorate throughout the Northwest, Lai Chau became an important French military base; older citizens of the town remember clearly the large numbers of Moroccans, Algerians and Tunisians who were posted here between 1946 and 1953. The French were finally forced to abandon Lai Chau during the winter of 1953 on the eve of the momentous battle of Dien Bien Phu. Bereft of his colonial masters, a discredited Deo Van Long fled to Laos and then to Thailand, whence he is believed to have emigrated to France. A few remaining relatives still live in the area, but have wisely changed their family name to Dieu.

Sights

Former French Colonial Government Headquarters are used as offices and house the local hospital. To get there walk up High Hill past the hospital and fork left up a track leading to the crest of the hill, 500 m further along. Also, on a terrace above the river, is a former airfield (Sang Bay Phap). A very pleasant couple of hours can be whiled away pottering around the largely overgrown and derelict French remains. In trying to identify French areas any budding Indiana Jones can put botanical archaeology to good use. The French were fond of ornamental trees and planted many exotic types: straight rows of huge century-old trees (*muong*) fringe what may have been a former parade ground or playing field; the vivid colours of the flame trees (*phuong*) flag the nascent archaeologist up flights of decaying steps and balustrades towards what looks to have been the sanitorium.

The ruins of **Deo Van Long's House**, originally a plush colonial mansion, lie on Road 127 to Muong Te on the opposite bank of the Da River from High Hill (Doi Cao). The remains are wonderfully overgrown with creeper and strangling figs. Older inhabitants of the six or seven remaining houses recall that for many years Deo Van Long and his family lived in great luxury with a large retinue of servants. Some say that before fleeing the country in 1953, Long had all his servants poisoned so they could not inform the advancing Viet Minh forces of his whereabouts. Beware of piles of loose masonry and deep vaults (dungeons or wine cellars, who can be sure?) covered with only a matting of creeper. You can get to the house by boat from below High Hill (not when river levels are too high or too low); otherwise, it's a circuitous 8-km road trip, crossing one especially rickety suspension bridge

Around Muong Lay → *For listings, see pages 84-86.*

Phi Hay (White Hmong village)

ⓘ *Take Highway 6 in the direction of Tuan Giao until just beyond the 10 km way marker from Muong Lay. Stop next to a group of small shops as the road begins to level out, and walk either steeply down left from the road between two shops, or up the path also to the left of the road, but in the direction of a small school building. Continue for a further 2 km.*

This makes an interesting morning's excursion for those who made the detour via Dien Bien Phu. It offers a snapshot of the stunning scenery along the more direct Muong Lay-Tuan Giao mountain route. Phi Hay village is very old and comprises some 50 houses spread out over a considerable area.

Sin Ho

Driving to Sin Ho is hazardous as you need to negotiate the hairpin bends and precipitous drops that characterize the road. If the weather is clear you would be strongly advised to walk some stretches to appreciate the full majesty of the scenery. It will also give you a chance to absorb the delicious cool air, the forest sounds and smells and the wayside flowers. You will also have the opportunity to witness the extraordinary perpendicular fields and to wonder how it is that local farmers can actually harvest slopes on which most people could not even stand.

The first 20 km towards Sin Ho off the main highway is possibly the most spectacular and terrifying drive in Vietnam. After 20 km the road levels off and meanders over the Sin Ho plateau passing hamlets of Red, White and Flower Hmong and Dao minorities. Sin Ho provides little that won't have been seen already, although the Sunday morning market is worthy of note. As with other markets in the region, the Sunday market is an important social occasion.

Lai Chau (formerly Tam Duong)

There are some interesting walks to **Na Bo**, a Pu Na (Giay sub-group) minority village, **Giang** (Nhang minority) and **Hon** minority villages. Pu Na and Nhang people are similar in culture and clothes. Na Bo is 7 km from Lai Chau from which Giang is a further 1.5 km and Hon a further 5 km still. Alternatively a motorbike and driver can be hired.

About 35 km southeast of Lai Chau, Highway 4D swings sharply to the northeast and the altitude climbs abruptly into the Hoang Lien Son range. Here is harsh mountain scenery on a scale previously unencountered on this circuit of Northwest Vietnam. The geology is hard and crystalline as is the skyline, with sharp jagged peaks punching upwards into the sky. Vertical cliffs drop below and soar above; friendly rolling scenery has been replaced by 3000-m-high mountains. There are buses from Lai Chau to Sapa.

Northwest listings

For sleeping and eating price codes and other relevant information, see page 10-13.

Sleeping

Hoa Binh *p71*

$$ Hoa Binh 1, 54 Phuong Lam, T18-385 2051. On Highway 6, 1 km out of Hoa Binh towards Mai Chau. Clean rooms with a/c and TV; some rooms built in ethnic style. There's also an 'ethnic dining experience' complete with rice drunk through bamboo straws. The gift shop stocks local produce.

Mai Chau *p72*

$$$$-$$$ Mai Chau Lodge, a short walking distance southwest of Lac village, T18-386 8959, www.maichaulodge.com. Owned and operated by Buffalo Tours and staffed by locals, there are 16 warmly furnished rooms with modern facilities. The attractive lodge has 2 restaurants, a bar, swimming pool, sauna and jacuzzi. Bicycling, kayaking and trekking tours are offered. Room prices include round-trip transfer from Hanoi.

$ Ethnic Houses, Lac village. Visitors can spend the night in a White Thai house on stilts. Mat, pillow, duvet, mosquito net, communal washing facilities (some hot showers) and sometimes fan provided. This is particularly recommended as the hospitality and easy manner of the people is a highlight of many visitors' stay in Vietnam. Food and local rice wine provided. Avoid the large houses in the centre if possible. Guesthouse No 6, T18-386 7168, is popular with plentiful food and rice wine. Minimal English is spoken.

Moc Chau and Chieng Yen *p74*

$ Homestays with meals are possible. Contact Son La Province, T22-385 5714 or tour operator Handspan in Hanoi. Breakfasts are 12,000-15,000d; lunch and dinner 40,000-50,000d each.

Son La *p74*

$ Hoa Ban 2, Hoa Ban St, T22-385 2395. All rooms have a/c and hot water; it's clean and fairly comfortable.

$ Nha Khach Cong Doan (Trade Union Guesthouse), Chieng Le St, T22-385 2804. A short distance off the main road, located behind a large, white exhibition building, beyond the red façade sports department. A/c, fan rooms, basic, some English spoken. Breakfast included in more expensive rooms.

$ Nha Khach Uy Ban Nhan Dan (People's Committee Guesthouse), Highway 6, T22-385 2080. Signed Nha Khach just off Highway 6. This hotel has upgraded and expanded to 40 rooms with a/c and fans. It's in a lovely setting overlooking hillsides and villages; breakfast included.

$ Phong Lan 1, Chu Van Thinh St, T22-385 3515. Opposite Central Market. A/c, clean and ordinary.

Dien Bien Phu *p76, map p77*

$$ Muong Thanh Hotel, 25 Him Lam, T230-381 0043. Breakfast included with the more expensive rooms. 62 rooms with TV, a/c, minibar and fan. Internet service, swimming pool (open to non-guests), karaoke, Thai massage and airport transfer free for guests. Souvenir shop and bikes for rent.

$ Airport, Tran Dang Ninh, near the bus station, T230-382 5052. Fairly basic, 20 rooms, a/c, hot water.

Muong Lay (formerly Lai Chau) *p81*

$$-$ Lan Anh Hotel, 9 Phuong Song Da, T23-385 2682, www.lananhhotel.com. Clean fan and a/c rooms in the main part of town with restaurant, not far from the treacherous Da River; a new block has been built on stilts. The hotel organizes transport and tours, hotel, bus and airline reservations. It has also opened a hotel in Pa So. Tours to the weekend markets. Ring in advance as this place will no longer be open once the Son La hydropower scheme is fully operational.

Sin Ho *p83*
$ People's Committee Guesthouse, on the right as you enter the town, T23-387 0168. The long, low building is very basic.

Lai Chau (formerly Tam Duong) *p83*
$$ Phuong Thanh, T23-387 5235, phuongthanhotel@yahoo.com. 21 fan rooms, hot water, clean, comfortable, lovely views.

Eating

Hoa Binh *p71*
The **Hoa Binh hotel** (see Sleeping, above) is open for breakfast, lunch and dinner.
Thanh Toi, 22a Cu Chinh Lan St, T18-385 3951. Local specialities, wild boar and stir-fried aubergine.

Mai Chau *p72*
Most people will eat with their hosts. Mai Chau town itself has a couple of simple *com pho* places near the market. The rice wine in Mai Chau is excellent, particularly when mixed with local honey. The **Mai Chau Lodge**, see Sleeping, has 2 restaurants.

Son La *p74*
Hai Phi, 189 Dien Bien St, just down from the turning for the Provincial Museum, T22-385 2394. Goat specialities.

Dien Bien Phu *p76, map p77*
Lien Tuoi, 27 Muong Thanh 8 St, next to the Vietnamese cemetery and Hill A1, T230-382 4919. Daily 0700-2200. Delicious local fare in a family-run restaurant.
Muong Thanh Hotel Restaurant, 25 Him Lam, T230-381 0043. Daily 0600-2200. Breakfasts, plenty of Vietnamese dishes, a few spaghettis and pastas. Also duck, boar, pork, frog, curry and some tofu dishes and quite a bit of seafood.

Muong Lay (formerly Lai Chau) *p81*
Lan Anh Hotel (see Sleeping, above).

Sin Ho *p83*
Eat early at one of the cafés around the market. They may only have instant noodles at night and eggs for breakfast. But, washed down with the local rice wine, it tastes like a feast. Wine costs less than US$0.50 a bottle.

Entertainment

Hoa Binh *p71*
Hoa Binh Ethnic Minority Culture Troupe, 1-hr shows featuring dance and music of the Muong, Thai, Hmong and Dao in the **Hoa Binh 1** hotel.

Mai Chau *p72*
Mai Chau Ethnic Minority Dance Troupe, Thai dancing culminating in the communal drinking of sweet, sticky rice wine through straws from a large pot. This troupe performs most nights in Lac in one of the large stilt houses; admission is included as part of the package for people on tours; otherwise you'll need to make a small contribution.

Shopping

Mai Chau *p72*
Villagers offer a range of woven goods and fabrics on which they are becoming dependent for a living. There are also local paintings and well-made wicker baskets, pots, traps and pouches.

Activities and tours

Hoa Binh *p71*
Hoa Binh Tourism, next to the Hoa Binh 1 hotel, T18-385 4374, www.hoabinhtourism.com. Daily 0730-1100, 1330-1700. Can arrange boat hire as well as visits to minority villages, trekking and transport.

Mai Chau *p72*
Hanoi tour operators, see page 85, run overnight tours to the area.

Transport

Hoa Binh *p70*
Bus
Bus station on Tran Hung Dao St. Morning departures to **Hanoi**, 2 hrs.

Mai Chau *p72*
Bus
Connections with **Hoa Binh**, 2 hrs, **Hanoi**, 4hrs, and onward buses northwest to **Son La**. While it is easy and cheap to get here by bus most people visit on an organized tour.

Son La *p74*
Bus
Connections with **Hanoi**, 8 hrs, 5 services daily between 0400 and 0900. En route to Hanoi, services also to **Mai Chau** and **Hoa Binh**. Onward services to **Dien Bien Phu**, 5½ hrs.

Dien Bien Phu *p76, map p77*
Air
The airport (T230-382 4416) is 2 km north of town, off Highway 12; there are daily flights to **Hanoi**.

Airline offices Vietnam Airlines, Nguyen Huu Tho Rd, T230-382 4948.

Bus
Note that public transport in the mountains can be time-consuming and arduous. The bus station is close to the centre of town, on Highway 12. It's an easy walk to the hotels. There are daily direct bus connections with **Hanoi**, 13 hrs; daily connections to **Son La**, 5½ hrs; to **Muong Lay**, 3 hrs and some buses to **Sapa**. It is also possible to reach **Mai Chau** via Thai Binh and to **Hoa Binh** en route to Hanoi. There's a bus to the Laos border crossing at Tay Trang to **Muang Khua** (Laos) every other day leaving at 0500. A Laos visa is available at the border; Vietnamese visas are not available at land borders.

Car
The main roads in the Northwest have been improved in the last few years, but a 4WD is still recommended. The price of hiring a jeep has come down, and many tour operators in Hanoi (see page 86) rent them out for the 5- or 6-day round trip (1200 km via Sapa). A cheaper option is to leave the jeep in Sapa and catch the train to Hanoi from Lao Cai.

Muong Lay (formerly Lai Chau) *p81*

Bus
Connections south with **Dien Bien Phu**, 4 hrs (and from there to **Hanoi** via **Son La**) and north and east with **Sapa**, 7 hrs. The bus station is south of town, on the road to Dien Bien Phu; try to get dropped off by the bridge in the centre.

Sin Ho *p83*
Bus
Sin Ho is a 40-km detour off Highway 12. Connections with **Dien Bien Phu** via **Muong Lay**, daily from the market.

Lai Chau (formerly Tam Duong) *p83*
From Muong Lay, Highway 12 heads almost due north following the Na river valley towards the Chinese border. At Pa So, 10 km from China (border crossing closed), take Highway 4D, southeast. Lai Chau is in fact a collection of 3 settlements, all new.

Bus
Connections with **Hanoi** via **Sapa**; connections with **Lao Cai** also via **Sapa**, and south with **Dien Bien Phu** via **Muong Lay**.

Directory

Hoa Binh *p71*
Post office Tran Hung Dao St.

Son La *p74*
Bank Vietcombank, 57 To Hieu St.
Post office 43 To Hieu St.

Dien Bien Phu *p76, map p77*
Banks Vietcombank and Agribank.
Internet Muong Thanh Hotel, 25 Him Lam St.

Sapa and around

Despite the countless thousands of tourists who have poured in every year for the past decade Sapa retains great charm. Its beauty derives from the impressive natural setting high on a valley side with Fan Si Pan, Vietnam's tallest mountain, either clearly visible or brooding in the mist.

Sapa's access point is Lao Cai, which is also the Chinese border crossing. The markets of the region are popular one-day or overnight trips for visitors. One such local market is Bac Ha.

» *For listings, see pages 94-98.*

Sapa → *For listings, see pages 94-98.*

The beauty of the town is a little compromised by the new hotels sprouting up everywhere. Certainly none of the new ones can compare with the lovely old French buildings – pitched roofs, window shutters and chimneys each with their own neat little garden of temperate flora, foxgloves, roses, apricot and plum trees, carefully nurtured by generations of gardeners. Weekends are peak tourist time but during the week the few visitors who remain will have the town to themselves.

Ins and outs

Getting there You get to Sapa either by road as part of the Northwest loop or by overnight train from Hanoi, via Lao Cai. A fleet of minibuses ferries passengers from Lao Cai railway station to Sapa. There are numerous classes of seat or berth on the trains and some hotels have their own private carriages (see Sleeping, page 94, for details). It is quite easy to make the travel arrangements yourself, but booking with an operator removes the hassle. A railway office in Sapa also sells tickets for the journey back to Hanoi. Tour operators in Hanoi sell tours and packages that include treks of various lengths. New comfortable buses now also run the Hanoi–Sapa route. » *See Transport, page 97, and Hanoi tour operators, page 87.*

Getting around Sapa is small enough to walk around easily. From Sapa there are a great many walks and treks and the tracks and paths are fun to explore on a Minsk.

Best time to visit At 1650 m Sapa enjoys warm days and cool evenings in the summer but gets very cold in winter. Snow falls on average every couple of years and settles on the surrounding peaks of the Hoang Lien Son Mountains. Rain and cloud can occur at any time of year but the wettest months are May to September with nearly 1000 mm of rain in July and August alone, the busiest months for Vietnamese tourists. December and January can be pretty miserable with mist, low cloud and low temperatures. Spring blossom is lovely but even in March and April a fire or heater may be necessary in the evening.

Tourist information **Sapa Tourist Information Center** ⓘ *2 Phan Si Pang St, T20-387 1975, www.sapa-tourism.com, daily 0800-1130, 1330-1730*. Free tourist information, tours with local guides offered including Fan Si Pan, markets and homestays in local villages; tickets booked; border questions helpfully answered.

Background

Originally a Black Hmong settlement, Sapa was first discovered by Europeans when a Jesuit missionary visited the area in 1918. By 1932 news of the quasi-European climate and beautiful scenery of the Tonkinese Alps had spread throughout French Indochina. Like Dalat in the south it served as a retreat for French administrators when the heat of the plains became unbearable. By the 1940s an estimated 300 French buildings, including a sizeable prison and the summer residence of the Governor of French Indochina, had sprung up. Until 1947 there were more French than Vietnamese in the town, which became renowned for its many parks and flower gardens. However, as the security situation began to worsen during the latter days of French rule, the expatriate community

Sapa

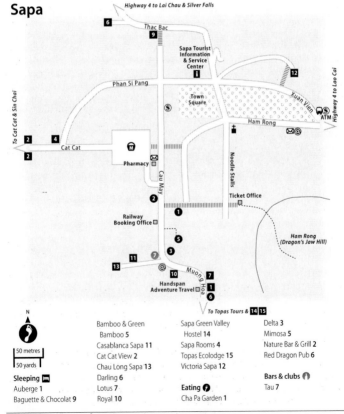

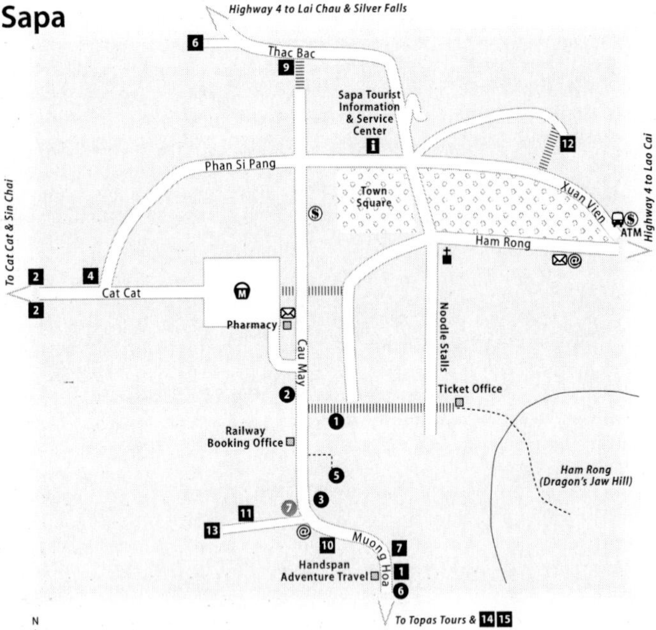

N

50 metres

50 yards

Sleeping
Auberge **1**
Baguette & Chocolat **9**
Bamboo & Green Bamboo **5**
Casablanca Sapa **11**
Cat Cat View **2**
Chau Long Sapa **13**
Darling **6**
Lotus **7**
Royal **10**
Sapa Green Valley Hostel **14**
Sapa Rooms **4**
Topas Ecolodge **15**
Victoria Sapa **12**

Eating
Cha Pa Garden **1**
Delta **3**
Mimosa **5**
Nature Bar & Grill **2**
Red Dragon Pub **6**

Bars & clubs
Tau **7**

steadily dwindled, and by 1953 virtually all had gone. Immediately following the French defeat at Dien Bien Phu in 1954, victorious Vietnamese forces razed a large number of Sapa's French buildings to the ground.

Sapa was also one of the places to be invaded by the Chinese in the 1979 border skirmish. Chinese soldiers found and destroyed the holiday retreat of the Vietnamese Communist Party Secretary-General, Le Duan, no doubt infuriated by such uncomradely display of bourgeois tendencies.

The huge scale of the Fan Si Pan range gives Sapa an Alpine feel and this impression is reinforced by *haute savoie* vernacular architecture with steep-pitched roofs, window shutters and chimneys. But, with an alluring blend of European and Vietnamese vegetation, the gardeners of Sapa cultivate their foxgloves and apricot trees alongside thickets of bamboo and delicate orchids, just yards above the paddy fields.

People

Distinctly oriental but un-Vietnamese in manner and appearance are the Hmong, Dao and other minorities who come to Sapa to trade. Interestingly, the Hmong (normally so reticent) have been the first to seize the commercial opportunities presented by tourism; they are engaging but very persistent vendors of hand-loomed indigo shirts, trousers and skull caps and other handicrafts. Of the craftwork, the little brass and bamboo Jew's-harp is particularly notable. The Dao women, their hands stained purple by the dye, sell clothing on street corners, stitching while they wait for a customer. The girls roam in groups, bracelets, earrings and necklaces jingling as they walk. "*Jolie, jolie*" they say as they push bracelets into your hand and it is hard to disagree. '*Mua mot cai di, mua mot cai di*' (buy one, buy one), the little ones sing, and most people do.

Saturday night is always a big occasion for Black Hmong and Red Dao teenagers in the Sapa area, as youngsters from miles around come to the so-called Love Market to find a partner. The market proved so popular with tourists that the teenagers now arrange their trysts and liaisons in private.The regular market is at its busiest and best on Sunday morning when most tourists scoot off to Bac Ha.

Sights

Sapa is a pleasant place to relax in and unwind, particularly after the arduous journey from Dien Bien Phu. Being comparatively new it has no important sights but several French buildings in and around are worth visiting.

The small church, built in 1930, dominates the centre of Sapa. Recently rebuilt, the church was wrecked in 1952 by French artillerymen shelling the adjacent building in which Viet Minh troops were billeted. In the churchyard are the tombs of two former priests, including that of Father Jean Thinh, who was brutally murdered. In the autumn of 1948, Father Thinh confronted a monk named Giao Linh who had been discovered having an affair with a nun at the Ta Phin seminary. Giao Linh obviously took great exception to the priest's interference, for shortly after this, when Father Thinh's congregation arrived at Sapa church for mass one foggy November morning, they discovered his decapitated body lying next to the altar.

Ham Rong (Dragon's Jaw Hill) ⓘ *0600-1800, 30,000d, free for children under 5,* on which the district's TV transmitter is stuck, is located immediately above Sapa town centre. Apart from offering excellent views of the town, the path winds its way through a number of interesting limestone outcrops and miniature grottoes as it nears the summit. Traditional dance performances take place on the mountain, see Entertainment, page 97.

Treks around Sapa → *For listings, see pages 94-98.*

The derelict French seminary is near the village of Ta Phin. The names of the bishop who consecrated it and the presiding Governor of Indochina can be seen engraved on stones at the west end. Built in 1942 under the ecclesiastical jurisdiction of the Parish of Sapa, the building was destroyed 10 years later by militant Vietnamese hostile to the intentions of the order.

To get there from Sapa, take the road 8 km east towards Lao Cai then follow a track left up towards Ta Phin; it's 3 km to the monastery and a further 4 km to Ta Phin.

Beyond the seminary, the path descends into a valley of beautifully sculpted rice terraces and past Black Hmong settlements toTa Phin.

Note – You should never just turn up in a village for homestay opportunities; book with a tour operator.

Mount Fan Si Pan

At a height of 3143 m, Vietnam's highest mountain is a three-day trek from Sapa. It lies on a bearing of 240 degrees from Sapa; as the crow flies it is 9 km but by track it is 14 km and involves dropping to 1200 m and crossing a rickety bamboo bridge before ascending. The climb involves some steep scrambles which are quite nasty in wet conditions. Only the very fit will make it to the summit. A three-day expedition is recommended. There are few suitable spots for camping other than at the altitudes suggested here: **Day 1**: depart Sapa (1650 m) 0800. Lunch at 1400 m, 1200. Camp at 2285 m; **Day 2**: reach summit late afternoon. Return to camp at 2800 m; **Day 3**: descend to Sapa. A good tour operator, either in Sapa or Hanoi, will provide camping equipment and porters.

Lau Chai (Black Hmong) village and Ta Van (Giáy) village

This is a round trip of 20 km taking in minority villages and beautiful scenery. Heading southeast out of Sapa (see map, page 91), past the **Auberge** guesthouse, Lao Chai is 6 km away on the far valley side. Follow the track leading from the right-hand side of the road down to the valley floor, cross the river by the footbridge (*cau may*) and then walk up through the rice fields into Lao Chai village. You will find Ta Van 2 km further on.

A leisurely stroll through these villages could well be the highlight of a trip to Vietnam. It is a chance to observe rural life led in reasonable prosperity. Wet rice forms the staple income; weaving for the tourist market puts a bit of meat on the table. Here nature is kind, there is rich soil and no shortage of water. Again it's possible to see how the landscape has been engineered to suit human needs. The terracing is on an awesome scale (in places more than 100 steps), the result of centuries of labour to convert steep slopes into level fields which can be flooded to grow rice. Technologically, and in no sense pejoratively, the villages might be described as belonging to a bamboo age. Bamboo trunks carry water huge distances from spring to village; water flows across barriers and tracks in bamboo aqueducts; mechanical rice huskers made of bamboo are driven by water requiring no human effort; houses are held up with bamboo; bottoms are parked on bamboo chairs; and tobacco and other substances are inhaled through bamboo pipes. Any path chosen will lead to some hamlet or other; the Hmong in villages further from Sapa tend to be more reserved and suspicious; their fields and houses are often securely fenced off.

Cross back to the north side of the river by the suspension bridge. A dip in the deep pools of the Muong Hoa river is refreshingly invigorating. Engraved stones are a further 2 km southeast (away from Sapa, that is) by the side of road; they are believed to be inscribed in ancient Hmong. The return walk to Sapa from the inscribed stones is a steady 10-km uphill climb. It's exhausting work but, stimulated by the views and the air and fuelled by hard-boiled eggs and warm Lao Cai beer from roadside shacks, and the prospect of cold beer at home, it is a pleasure, not an ordeal. In the late afternoon sun the rice glows with more shades of green than you would have thought possible and the lengthening shadows cast the entire landscape into vivid three-dimensional relief – even through a camera lens.

Cat Cat and Sin Chai villages

ⓘ *15,000d fee for taking the track.*

The track heading west from Sapa through the market area offers either a short 5-km round-trip walk to Cat Cat Black Hmong village or a longer 10-km round-trip walk to Sin Chai Black Hmong village; both options take in some beautiful scenery. The path to Cat Cat leads off to the left of the Sin Chai track after about 1 km, following the line of pylons

Around Sapa

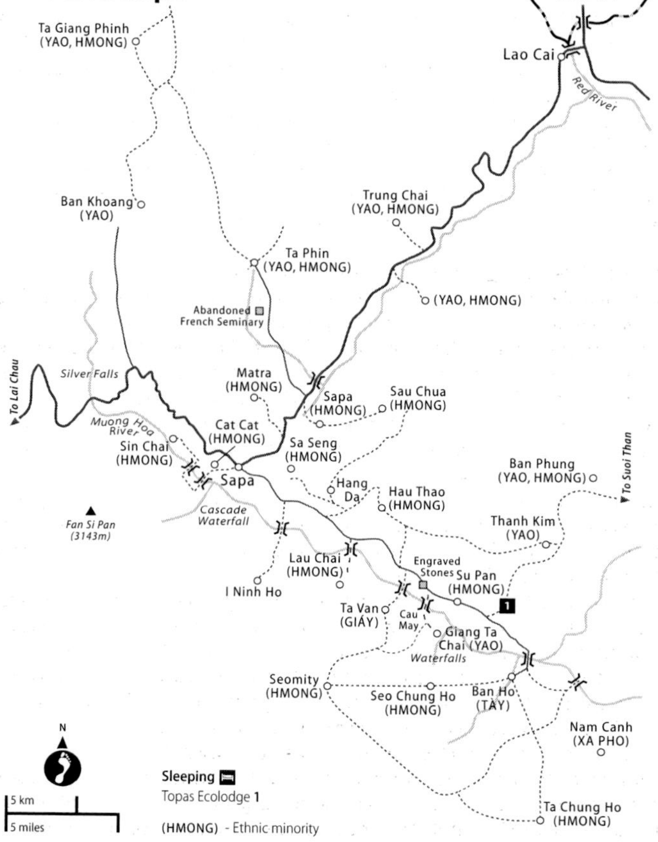

down through the rice paddies to Cat Cat village; beyond the village over the river bridge you can visit the **Cascade Waterfall** (from which the village takes its name) and an old French hydroelectric power station that still produces electricity. Sin Chai village is 4 km northwest of here.

The **Silver Falls** are 12 km west of Sapa on the Muong Lay road and are spectacular following rain. They are hardly worth a special visit but if passing it's quite nice to stop for a paddle in the cold pools.

Other market villages

In the region it's possible to visit Can Cau (Saturday market), Muong Hum (Sunday market), Muong Khuong (Sunday market), Coc Ly (Tuesday market), Lung Khau Nhin (Thursday market), Tam Duong (Thursday market).

Nam Sai and Nam Cam

Some 40 km south and southeast of Sapa are the communities of Nam Sai and Nam Cam that are being developed for local tourism with the help of NGOs. The area is inhabited by Tay, Xa Pho, Red Dao and Hmong ethnic minorities. Village way of life (including cardamom, mushroom and soybean crop growing) can be explored and homestays are possible; see Sleeping, page 123. Treks can be arranged to the area or you can travel by car and explore the area from there.

Lao Cai → *For listings, see pages 94-98.*

Lao Cai is the most important border crossing with China. A two-way flow of people and trade cross through the city each day. But whereas the balance of human traffic is roughly equal, the value of traded goods is highly one-sided: an endless flow of products from China's modern factories wreaks havoc on Vietnam's own hapless state-owned enterprises struggling to fill quotas of shoddy goods that no one wants to buy.

If you travel from Lao Cai back to Hanoi, the road begins in a beautiful valley where rice, cinnamon (in places the air is scented) and tea are grown. By Viet Tri it has become a drab industrial landscape and remains so all the way back.

Background

An important north-south transit stop for traders with caravans of pack oxen or horses since time immemorial, Lao Cai has changed hands many times over the past thousand years as rival Chinese, Vietnamese and ethnic minority chieftains fought for ascendancy in the region. The town itself dates back at least to 1463, when the Viet kings established it as the capital of their northernmost province of Hung Hoa.

Lao Cai fell to the French in 1889 and thereafter served as an important administrative centre and garrison town. The direct rail link to Hanoi was built during the first decade of the last century, a project notable for the 25,000 Vietnamese conscripted labourers who died during its seven-year construction period.

Following the Vietnamese invasion of Cambodia in late 1978, China, Cambodia's ally, responded in February 1979 by launching a massive invasion of North Vietnam, 'to teach the Vietnamese a lesson'. More than 600,000 Chinese troops were deployed occupying territory from Pa So (formerly Phong Tho) in the Northwest to Cao Bang and Lang Son in the Northeast. From the start of the campaign, however, the poorly trained Chinese forces encountered stiff resistance from local militia and, as the Vietnamese Army got into gear, the Chinese invasion force ground to a halt. After two weeks Chinese troops had penetrated no further than 30 km into Vietnamese territory and, with an estimated 20,000 casualties already incurred by the People's Army, the Chinese government withdrew its troops, declaring the operation "a great success".

Trade with China, much of it illegal, has turned this former small town into a rich community of (dong if not dollar) millionaires and Lao Cai is experiencing something of a construction boom. Huge boulevards flanked by some enormous local government buildings are sprouting up in the main part of town, west of the Red River. In 2006 Lao Cai became a city; by 2020 it looks set to get an airport. Other than for border-crossers Lao Cai holds little appeal.

There is a branch of **Sapa Tourism Center** ⓘ *306 Khanh Yen St, T20-362 52506, www.sapa-tourism.com,* very close to the train station.

International border crossing

The border is open to pedestrians (0700-2200) with the correct exit and entry visas for both countries. Travellers must report to the International Border Gate Administration Center south of the bridge and near the level crossing for passport stamping and customs clearance. Visas into Vietnam must be obtained in Hong Kong or Beijing and must specify the Lao Cai crossing; they normally take a week to process and are not obtainable at the border. Visas for China must be obtained in Hanoi and must also specify the Lao Cai crossing. The Chinese visa costs US$30 but US citizens need to pay US$100; the visa takes four days to be issued. An express 24-hour service costs a further US$20; a two-hour service, a further US$30. **Binh Minh Travel** ⓘ *39 Nguyen Hue, T20-383 6666, www.binhminhtravel.com.vn,* can arrange visas and foreign currency. It costs 10,000d from the train station to the border on a *xe ôm.* ⏩ *See Transport, page 97.*

Bac Ha → *For listings, see pages 94-98.*

ⓘ *If you have your own transport, arrive early. If you don't, nearly all the hotels and all the tour operators in Sapa organize trips.*

Bac Ha is really only notable for one thing and that is its Sunday market. That 'one thing', however, is very special. Hundreds of local minority people flock in from the surrounding districts to shop and socialize, while tourists from all corners of the earth pour in to watch them do it. Otherwise there is very little of interest and neither the appeal nor comforts of Sapa.

Bac Ha now has a branch of **Sapa Tourism Center** ⓘ *Hoang A Tuong's Palace, T20-378 0662, www.sapa-tourism.com.*

Around 18 km before Bac Ha the scenery is wonderful; huge expanses of mountains, pine trees and terracing engraved by the winding road as it climbs skywards towards Bac Ha.

The **Sunday market** ⓘ *0600-1400*, draws in the Flower Hmong, Phula, Dao Tuyen, La Chi and Tay – the Tay being Vietnam's largest ethnic minority. It is a riot of colour and fun: the Flower Hmong wear pink and green headscarves; children wear hats with snail motifs and tassles. While the women trade and gossip, the men consume quantities of rice wine and cook dog and other animal innards in small cauldrons. By late morning they can no longer walk so are heaved onto donkeys by their wives and led home.

There are a number of walks to outlying villages. **Pho** village of the Flower Hmong is around 4 km north; **Thai Giang Pho** village of the Tay is 4 km east; and **Na Hoi** and **Na Ang** villages, also of the Tay, are 2km and 4 km west respectively.

Sapa and around listings

For sleeping and eating price codes and other relevant information, see page 10-13.

Sleeping

Sapa *p87, map p88*

Prices tend to rise at weekends and Jun-Oct to coincide with northern hemisphere university vacations. Hoteliers are accustomed to bargaining; healthy competition ensures fare rates in Sapa.

$$$$ Victoria Sapa, T20-387 1522, www.victoriahotels-asia.com. Opened in 1998, the hotel has 77 rooms with heating, fans and TVs and comfortable furnishings. It has a nice position above the town and a pleasant aspect: this hotel is easily the best in town and is a lovely place in which to relax and enjoy the peace. In winter there are lovely open fires in the bar and dining rooms. The food is excellent and the set buffets are superb value. The health centre offers everything from traditional massage to reflexology. The centre, pool, tennis courts and sauna are open to non-guests. Packages are available. The hotel has private sleeper carriages on the train from Hanoi to Lao Cai.

$$$$-$$$ Chau Long Sapa Hotel, 24 Dong Loi St, T20-387 1245, www.chaulonghotel.com. 2 buildings – the old wing and new wing (opposite each other) – in faux castle style make up this hotel with a restaurant boasting great views of the valley. However, the prices in the new wing are unjustified. The old wing represents excellent value although it is looking a little unloved. There's a health centre and indoor pool on site.

$$$-$$ Bamboo and Green Bamboo, Cay Mau St, T20-387 1075, www.sapatravel.com. A lovely valley-side location. All 26 rooms in this nice old building have wonderful views and have electric heaters in winter. Breakfast is included in the price. However, rooms are damp and shabby compared with those in the new hotel next door, where the 20 nice rooms have good views and bathtubs.

$$$-$$ Cat Cat View, 46 Phan Xi Pang St, on the Cat Cat side of town through the market. T20-387 1946, www.catcathotel.com. The guesthouse has expanded up the hillside, with new terraces and small bungalows with balconies all with views down the valley. A friendly and popular place, its 40 rooms span the price range but all represent good value for money. Some of its rooms enjoy the best views in Sapa. The hotel has a good restaurant and, like most others, arranges tours and provides useful information. More expensive rooms come with breakfast.

$$$-$$ Sapa Rooms, 18 Phan Xi Pang St, T20-387 2130, www.saparooms.com. Brand new and popular hotel in town with smart rooms and heaps of facilities including recommended restaurant, see Eating. Supports the local ethnic minority community.

$$ Casablanca Sapa Hotel, 26 Dong Loi St, T20-387 2667, http://casablancasapahotel.com. This is a new popular spot so book in advance. Rooms are standard but attractively furnished.

$$ Darling, Thac Bac St, T20-387 1349, www.tulico-sapa.com.vn. It's a short walk from town to this secluded building but for those seeking peace it's worth every step of the way: simple and clean with a warm welcome, stunning views and a colourful garden. There are 45 rooms, most with fabulous views. The top terrace bedroom has the best view in all of Sapa. Swimming pool, gym and pool table.

$$-$ Auberge, Muong Ha St, T20-387 1243, www.sapanowadays.com. Mr Dang Trung, the French-speaking owner, shows guests his wonderful informal garden with pride: sweet peas, honeysuckle, snapdragons, foxgloves, roses and irises – all familiar to visitors from temperate climes – grow alongside sub-Alpine flora and a fantastic collection of orchids. The rooms are simply furnished but clean and boast bathtubs, and log fires in winter. Restaurant on a lovely terrace. Tours also offered. More expensive rooms enjoy views and a breakfast included in the price.

$$-$ Royal, Cay Mau St, T20-387 1313, royalhotel_sapa@hotmail.com. A not particularly attractive and quite large (28-room) hotel that spoils some views, although it is friendly enough and quite popular. Cheaper rooms overlook the town, more expensive rooms are rewarded with magnificent views of the valley. The hotel has a special train carriage for the Hanoi to Lao Cai route. Changes money and TCs; cash withdrawn on credit cards attracts a 6% fee.

$ Baguette & Chocolat, Thac Bac St, T20-387 1766, www.hoasuaschool.com. From the same company that brought you **Hoa Sua** training restaurant in Hanoi, this tastefully decorated training hotel offers year-long placements in Hanoi for local ethnic minority girls. With only 4 rooms it is small, well run and extremely clean and comfortable. The downstairs comprises a stylish restaurant and café, with small boulangerie attached. Highly recommended.

$ Lotus, Muong Ha St, next to **Auberge**, T20-387 1308. A small guesthouse with a nice terrace. Rooms have open fire and TV, etc. Those with a view cost more.

$ Sapa Green Valley Hostel, 45 Muong Hoa Rd, T20-387 1449, www.hihostels.com. A very friendly place on the road out of Sapa, a 10-min walk from the centre. There are 14 private rooms and 1 dorm of 4 beds (US$3 per person in dorm) with mosquito nets and an en suite bathroom. One private room has its own terrace. Breakfast is included if you book through the internet. Free internet.

Treks around Sapa *p90, map p91*

$$$ Topas Ecolodge, 18 km southeast from Sapa, www.topasecolodge.com (Sapa office: 24 Muong Hoa St, T20-387 1331). 25 bungalows with balconies built from white granite are built around a hill over- looking Ban Ho village in the stunning valley. Bungalows are simply furnished and powered by solar energy. The food is good and abundant. Butterflies, flowers and fire flies abound. Treks organized from the lodge can take you to less touristy Red Dao areas. Unfortunately a hydroelectric power station is being built in the valley, near Seo Trung Ho, spoiling the view. However, for peace and quiet in a natural setting this eco-lodge is unique in Vietnam.

$ Nha San Dan Toc (**Ethnic Houses**). It is possible to spend the night in one of the ethnic houses in the Sapa district. Those of the Black Hmong are probably the best bet, though facilities are more basic than in the Muong and Thai stilted houses of Hoa Binh, Mai Chau and Son La. This can only be arranged through tour operators.

Nam Sai and Nam Cam *p92*

$ Homestays. Contact Sapa-based operators, **Sapa Tourism Center** or the tourism department of Lao Cao province, T30-384 6586, svhttdllaocai@gmail.com, for homestays in this newly opened up area.

Lao Cai *p92*

$$$ Lao Cai International Hotel, 88 Thuy Hoa St, T20-382 6668. This grand-looking hotel faces the border gate across the river and has 34 rooms with all facilities. There's a restaurant, health centre and staff can help with obtaining visas if necessary.

$ Binh Minh, 39 Nguyen Hue St, T20-383 0085. A/c, hot water, fridge and TV in top-end rooms.

$ Hoa Lan, 82 Nguyen Hue St, T20-383 0126. One of the more clean and comfortable of the hotels listed. 12 rooms, all with a/c, fridge and TV. No English spoken but nevertheless friendly and helpful.

Bac Ha *p93*

$$ Sao Mai, a short walk north of the centre, T20-388 0288, saomaibh@vnn.vn. Quiet, clean and with a restaurant and free internet. The new building has 25 rooms with a/c and TV; the old wooden building incorporates 15 rooms with fan.

The hotel also offers trekking, motorbike hire, jeep tours and can book train tickets for you. There's an ethnic song and dance performance every Sat night.

$ Anh Duong, opposite the original market site, T20-388 0329. A family-run place. 12 rooms with toilet, shower, fan and TV. Nice courtyard in which to sit. No English spoken.

$ Dang Khoa, northwest of the market, T20-388 0290. Hotel with 20 clean rooms with TV, but overpriced.

Eating

Sapa *p87, map p88*

There are rice and noodle stalls in the market and along the path by the church.

ΨΨΨ Ta Van, in **Victoria Sapa**, see Sleeping, above, T20-387 1522. The food served in this large restaurant is 1st class and the service is exceptional. Choose from à la carte or buffet dinners; the latter are excellent value. The soups are particularly tasty; you'll want to eat here at least twice to savour the full range of haute cuisine. The large dining room is dominated by an open fire that is hugely warming during those chilly days and nights.

ΨΨ Delta, Cay Mau St, T20-387 1799. Open 0730-2200. Sapa's Italian restaurant serves good portions of pasta and pizzas as well as tasty seafood. It's great for people-watching from its big windows as it's on the main bend on the main road. There's a good wine list too.

ΨΨ-Ψ Cha Pa Garden, 23b Cau May St, T20-387 2907, www.chapagarden.com. A peaceful little oasis where you can hide from the street vendors during a romantic meal. Try to ignore the bizarre lounge area with flatscreen TV right off the main dining room while you watch the staff prepare roasted red peppers in a wood fire beside you for a tasty sandwich. The staff are kind and the wine selection is extensive.

ΨΨ-Ψ Sapa Rooms, 18 Phan Xi Pang St, T20-387 2130, www.saparooms.com. If you can't manage to snag a room at this boutique hotel, stop in for a meal at its delightful restaurant. An Aussie owner and an Hanoian artist have worked together to decorate this establishment with whimsical, hilltribe-inspired works, while the KOTO-trained chefs (see page 79) whip up delicious meals, though the portions are on the smaller side. Try the home-made cookie and ice-cream dessert. Across the street, check out Sapa Rooms' small gallery and cooking school.

Ψ Auberge, see Sleeping, above. Popular terrace with partial views of the valley and overlooking the town; it's a lovely breakfast setting. The full menu includes vegetarian food and several types of rice wine.

Ψ Baguette & Chocolat, see Sleeping, above, T20-387 1766. Open 0700-2100. The ground floor of the guesthouse comprises a stylish restaurant and café, with small boulangerie attached; lovely home-made cakes for exhausted trekkers go down a treat.

Ψ Mimosa, up a small path off Cau May St, T20-387 1377. Open 0700-2300. This small family-run restaurant is in an old house. Sit cosy indoors or in the fresh air on a small terrace. Long menu of good Western and Asian dishes and a reasonably good vegetarian menu.

Ψ Nature Bar & Grill, Cau May St, T20-387 2091. This place is great for cosy evenings with an open fire in a cauldron close to the bar. It has nice comfy seats by the window overlooking the main street. There's a decent selection of soups and juices, meat and fish.

Ψ Red Dragon Pub, 21 Muong Hoa St, T20-387 2085, reddragonpub@hn.vnn.vn. Open 0800-2230. Done out like an English tearoom with mock Tudor beams and red and white checked table cloths with nosh to match – teas, cornflakes and a mean shepherd's pie. There is a pub upstairs with a tiny balcony that is great for people-watching. Run by a British expat and his Vietnamese wife.

Lao Cai *p92*

Ψ Hiep Van, 342 Nguyen Hue St, opposite the station, T20-383 5470. This place with tables spilling out onto the street serves up reasonable Vietnamese and Western food at slightly inflated prices. Its real attraction lies in the fact that you can store luggage and take a shower for 20,000d (towel, soap and shampoo lent) while you wait the odd hour or 2 for the train back to Hanoi.

Bac Ha *p93*

Cong Phu, on the right-hand side of the road walking towards the traditional market site, T20-388 0254. Caters for the tourist trade with pancakes and Vietnamese dishes and a large range of drinks.

Ngan Nga, just north of **Dang Khoa Hotel**, T20-388 0251. This restaurant, used by tour groups, serves up abundant and reasonable fare. The set lunch menu is very good value. There's good service and a clean WC despite the numbers passing through.

Bars and clubs

Sapa *p87, map p88*

Red Dragon Pub, see Eating, above.

Tau Bar, 42 Cau May St, T912-927756. Open 1500-late. Beneath the **Tau Hotel**. It must have the longest bar made of a single tree trunk in the world and worth a beer just to see it. There's a darts board and pool table and a large range of beers and spirits.

Entertainment

Sapa *p87, map p88*

Ethnic minority dancing, Dragon's Jaw Hill, daily at 0930 and 1500, 10,000d. Also at the **Bamboo Hotel**, 2030-2200; free as long as you support the bar and at the **Victoria Sapa** every Sat at 2030.

Shopping

Sapa *p87, map p88*

Sapa is the place for buying ethnic clothes. Nowhere in Vietnam has the range of shirts, baggy trousers, caps, bags and other garments of Sapa. Sold by vendors or in shops, a lot is second-hand but all the more authentic for that. Note that it is not possible to buy walking shoes or decent climbing equipment in Sapa. Quite a good range is available in Hanoi. Temperate fruit, plums and apricots and delicious baby pineapples are sold in the market.

Activities and tours

Sapa *p87, map p88*

Therapies

Victoria Sapa, see Sleeping, above. Massage and other treatments are available. The hotel also has an indoor swimming pool.

Tour operators

Handspan, 7 Cau May St, T20-387 1214, www.handspan.com. Tours in the vicinity of Sapa, including treks, mountain bike excursions, homestays and jeep expeditions. This is a booking office for the **Handspan Adventure Travel** group with offices in Hanoi.

Topas, 24 Muong Hoa St, T20-387 1331, http://topastravel.vn. A combined Danish and Vietnamese operator offering numerous treks varying from fairly leisurely 1-day walks to an arduous 4-day assault on Mount Fan Si Pan. It also organizes bicycling tours and family tours. Well-run operation employing hundreds of local people and providing equipment where necessary. It has an office in Hanoi.

Transport

Sapa *p87, map p88*

Roads to Sapa have been improved but heavy rain and trucks can destroy a good surface very quickly. For train information, see Transport, Lao Cai, below.

Bus

Frequent connections from the bus station, T20-387 1006, with **Lao Cai**, US$2, 1½ hrs; minibuses also congregate on the corner next to the church. To **Hanoi** on more comfortable buses, several departures daily, 150,000-160,000d, T167-412 6412, or contact them at Lao Cai Railway station. Bus to **Kunming**, China, passing through Lao Cai, US$25, 10 hrs.

Lao Cai *p92*

Bus

Minibuses to **Sapa** from the train station, US$2 or some hotels have their own pickup.

Town bus station on Hong Ha St. Bus to **Dien Bien Phu**, 0730, 250,000d, 12 hrs. To **Hanoi**, 3 a day 0300-0500, 10 hrs, 100,000d. To **Bac Ha**, 0530, 0730, 30,000d.

Train

The station is about 2 km south of the hotel area. Trains run to and from **Hanoi** daily. See below for timetable. Tickets from Lao Cai can be booked for a small charge at the railway booking office in Sapa.

Tour operators in Hanoi (see page 98) can also book your ticket for you for a small fee from the top of the class – the Victoria Sapa carriage – downwards. It is often less hassle than organizing it yourself and, if you are in a hurry, it's a great time saver.

The train service into China is suspended. Enquire locally before travel.

To take a motorbike on the train you need a ticket, luggage ticket, registration papers, and the petrol tank must be empty. You must be on the platform at least 30 mins before departure and pay an uploading fee of 20,000d-25,000d. If the machine is larger than 150 cc, you will require a special permit.

Hanoi – Lao Cai

Train	Depart	Arrive
LC3	0610	1540
SP1	2115	0615
LC5	2040	0435
SP3	2155	0600
LC1	2005	0710
SP5	0820	1705

Lao Cai – Hanoi

Train	Depart	Arrive
LC4	0915	2015
LC2	1845	0400
SP2	2015	0430
LC6	1930	0415
LC8	1930	0415
SP4	2100	0505

The **Victoria carriages** (www.victoriahotels-asia.com/eng/hotels-in-vietnam/sapa-resort-spa/victoria-express-train) run Sun-Fri at 2045 to **Hanoi** and 2150 from Hanoi. See Hanoi, page 98, for further information.

Bac Ha *p93*

The drive from Sapa to Hanoi is very long. Those wanting a detour to Bac Ha on the way home face a gruelling day; **Sapa** to Bac Ha is 3 hrs, Bac Ha to **Hanoi** around 10 hrs.

Bus

Bus to **Lao Cai** departs 0500; 2 buses daily to **Pho Lu**, 0900 and 1100, 15,000-20,000d.

Train

From Lao Cai or Hanoi (10 hrs) to **Pho Lu**, then bus up to Bac Ha.

Directory

Sapa *p87, map p88*

Banks Agribank, 1 Pho Cau May St, T20-387 1206, Mon-Fri and Sat morning, will change US dollars, euro, Australian dollar, Chinese yuan and Canadian dollar cash, as will most hotels but at poor rates. It will also change US dollar and euro TCs. **BIDV**, Ngu Chi Son St, T20-387 2569, has a Visa ATM and will change cash and TCs. Convert before you travel. **Internet** There are now a dozen internet places in town. **Post office** 2 in Sapa from where international calls can be made. The main post office offers internet.

Lao Cai *p92*

Banks Agribank, Nguyen Hue St, T20-383 0013, has a Visa and MasterCard ATM. Techombank, 19 Nguyen Hue St, T20-383 0655, accepts Visa, MasterCard and Amex. **Internet** Lao Cai Internet opposite the shopping centre. **Post office** Opposite railway station and just south of border at 13 Nguyen Hue St.

Bac Ha *p93*

Internet Opposite the Ngan Nga restaurant.

Far North

The Far North of Vietnam is a beautiful, mainly mountainous region that skirts the Chinese border. Its steep slopes have been carved into curved rice terracing with paddies shimmering in the strong sun; further north where the steepness increases, majestic limestone mountain peaks will enthrall. The sparse populations that live here are predominantly indigenous groups and, thankfully, they have not yet been corrupted by commercialization to the same extent as their cousins in the Northwest. The way of life in the traditional villages remains just that, traditional; it is not a show put on for the entertainment of tourists. The far north is still one of the least-visited areas of the country and, as such, it offers the chance to see Vietnamese life as it really is. » *For listings, see pages 104-105.*

Ins and outs

Getting there and around Unlike Northwest Vietnam, which has so conveniently aligned its attractions along one road circuit, the far north is somewhat fragmented although through road links have improved. For much of the area a **permit** is required to visit. Dutch NGO **SNV** is trying to encourage tourism in this area as the Northern Highlands Trail and is seeking to ease restrictions in the area » *See Ha Giang Ins and outs, page 100, and Transport, page 105.*

Best time to visit The best time to visit this area is from October until March. Although this is winter and spring, the weather is milder than if you were to visit later in the year.

The road to Ha Giang

For much of its length the well-maintained Highway 2 follows the Lo River northwards from Hanoi through some delightful scenery. During the early stages of the journey as the road passes the eastern shores of the **Thac Ba Lake**, tea plantations may be seen everywhere, but northwards from Ham Yen, 41 km beyond Tuyen Quang, it is orange groves which carpet the hillsides. At Thac Ba it's possible to stay in White Trouser Dao communities and take boats out onto the lake.

Tuyen Quang Province has a large ethnic minority population and, not long after leaving the provincial capital, travellers will begin to see people from the two main groups of this province, the Tay and the Dao. The delightful little town of **Vinh Tuy**, near the banks of the Lo River, is a possible lunch stop. Boats can be seen on the river most days, dredging the bed for gold.

Detouring to **Xin Man** in the far east of Ha Giang province is worth the hike. This ethnic minority town mostly draws Hmong, Nung, Tay and Dao minorities, and Sunday market time is busy and hectic.

From Xin Man, a road twists and turns towards Hoang Su Phi passing Heaven's Gate II and the Hoang Su Phi Pass.

Tan Quang is a sizeable market town located some 60 km before Ha Giang at the junction with Highway 279, the mountain road west to Bao Yen in Lao Cai Province.

Ha Giang → *For listings, see pages 104-105.*

The provincial capital of Ha Giang lies on the banks of the Lo River just south of its confluence with the River Mien, perched picturesquely between the beautiful Cam and Mo Neo mountains. Like Cao Bang and Lang Son, Ha Giang was badly damaged during the border war with China in 1979 and has since undergone extensive reconstruction.

Ins and outs

Getting there and around From Hanoi Highway 2 goes directly to Ha Giang. The journey should take between six and seven hours. Ha Giang can be reached comfortably in a day from Sapa. Within the town, there are a few taxis and also the ubiqitous *xe ôm*.

Best time to visit There are four distinct seasons in the north (spring, summer, autumn and winter). The best time to visit would be either during autumn or spring.

Tourist information Ha Giang Tourist company ⓘ *5 Nguyen Trai St, T219-387 5288/ T219-386 7054, dulichhagiang@gmail.com, Mon-Fri 0800-1130, 1330-1700*. To visit the surrounding area you will need a special **permit** which the company can obtain for you; 250,000d for up to a group of five and you must hire a local guide.

History

Archaeological evidence unearthed at Doi Thong (Pine Hill) in Ha Giang town indicates there was human settlement in the region at least 30,000 years ago. It was during the Bronze Age, however, that the most important flowering of early culture took place under the Tay Vu. This was one of the most significant tribes of the Hung kingdom of Van Lang, whose centre of power was in the Ha Giang region. Some of the most beautiful Dong Son bronze drums were found in Ha Giang Province, most notably in the Meo Vac region, where the tradition of making bronze drums for ceremonial purposes continues even to this day among the Lolo and Pu Peo communities.

The original settlement in Ha Giang lay on the east bank of the Lo River and it was here that the French established themselves following the conquest of the area in 1886. The town subsequently became an important military base, a development confirmed in 1905 when Ha Giang was formally established as one of four North Vietnamese military territories of French Indochina.

The Ha Giang area saw a number of important ethnic rebellions against the French during the early years of the colonial period, the most important being that of the Dao who rose up in 1901 under the leadership of Trieu Tien Kien and Trieu Tai Loc. The revolt was quickly put down and Trieu Tien Kien was killed during the fighting, but in 1913 Trieu Tai Loc rose up again, this time supported by another family member known as Trieu Tien Tien, marching under the slogans: "No corvées, no taxes for the French; Drive out the French to recover our country; Liberty for the Dao".

Carrying white flags embroidered with the four ideograms *To Quoc Bach Ky* (White Flag of the Fatherland) and wearing white conical hats (hence the French name 'The White

Hat Revolt'), the rebels launched attacks against Tuyen Quang, Lao Cai and Yen Bai and managed to keep French troops at bay until 1915 when the revolt was savagely repressed. Hundreds of the insurgents were subsequently deported and 67 were condemned to death by the colonial courts.

Sights

The **Ha Giang Museum** ⓘ *next to Yen Bien Bridge in the centre of town, daily 0800-1130, 1330-1700, free*, contains important archaeological, historical and ethnological artefacts from in and around the region, including a very helpful display of ethnic costumes.

Located close to the east bank of the River Lo in the old quarter of the town, Ha Giang Market is a daily affair although it is busiest on Sunday. Tay, Nung and Red Dao people are always in evidence here, as are members of northern Ha Giang Province's prolific White Hmong.

Doi Thong (Pine Hill) lies just behind the main Ha Giang Market. The pine trees are newly planted but the hill itself is an area of ancient human settlement believed to date back some 30,000 years to the Son Vi period. Many ancient axe-heads and other primitive weapons were discovered on the hill during land clearance; these are now in the local museum and in the History Museum in Hanoi.

Dong Van-Meo Vac Region

→ *For listings, see pages 104-105.*

This is the northernmost tip of Vietnam, close to the Chinese border and just 30 km south of the Tropic of Cancer. It's an impressive natural setting high on a valley side with Fan Si Pan, Vietnam's tallest mountain, either clearly visible or brooding in the mist.

Ins and outs

Getting there All foreign visitors are required to obtain a special permit and take a licensed guide before proceeding beyond Ha Giang into the remote Dong Van-Meo Vac area on the Chinese border including the districts of Quan Ba and Yen Minh. This can be obtained either directly from the local police or alternatively through the **Ha Giang Tourist Company** (see page 105). One possible advantage of booking a tour in Hanoi is that they do it for you, although the permit arrangement must be completed in the Ha Giang tourist office.

Getting around Local bus services are infrequent and slow. The roads north of Ha Giang have now been sealed and are in good condition but the roads are narrow and windy with high mountain slopes. A 4WD vehicle or sturdy motorbike is highly advisable. Ha Giang to Dong Van via Yen Minh is 148 km, five hours; Dong Van to Meo Vac, 22 km, one hour. Returning from Meo Vac to Ha Giang head straight to Yen Minh via Highways 176 and 180 bypassing Dong Van and cutting off 22 km. It is a straight small and windy 50-km road in good condition but the most superb scenery is the Dong Van-Meo Vac road. Note that since both Dong Van and Meo Vac are located very close to the Chinese border, hill-walking by foreigners around both towns is forbidden, making the number of things to do in Dong Van and Meo Vac somewhat limited although Hanoi tour operators (see page 101) can organize four- to seven-day trekking tours in the area.

Quan Ba

Quan Ba is 45 km from Ha Giang. The road climbs up the Quan Ba Pass to 'Heaven's Gate' – identifiable by the TV transmitter mast to the left of the summit – from where there are wonderful views of the Quan Ba Valley with its extraordinary row of uniformly shaped hills.

Quan Ba has a Sunday market, one of the largest in the region, which attracts not only White Hmong, Red Dao, Dao Ao Dai and Tay people but also members of the Bo Y ethnic minority who live in the mountains around the town.

Yen Minh and Pho Bang

Yen Minh is located 98 km northwest of Ha Giang and is a convenient place to stop for lunch on the way to Dong Van and Meo Vac – a possible overnight stop for those planning to spend longer in the region. It has a Sunday market where, in addition to the groups mentioned above, you'll see Giay, Pu Peo, Co lao, Lolo and the local branch of Red Dao.

Northwest of Yen Minh right on the Chinese border lies the town of Pho Bang. Time seems to have stood still here with mud construction homes with a second galley floor to house firewood. This is remote but worth the hike for the ambience in the town.

Sa Phin

Crossing the old border into the former demesne of the White Hmong kings the very distinctive architecture of the White Hmong houses of the area becomes apparent; it is quite unlike the small wooden huts characteristic of Hmong settlements elsewhere in North Vietnam. These are big, two-storey buildings, constructed using large bricks fashioned from the characteristic yellow earth of the region and invariably roofed in Chinese style. But it is not only the Hmong who construct their houses in this way – the dwellings of other people of the area such as the Co lao and the Pu Péo are of similar design, no doubt a result of their having lived for generations within the borders of the former Hmong kingdom.

The remote Sa Phin valley is just 2 km from the Chinese border. Below the road surrounded by conical peaks lies the village of Sa Phin, a small White Hmong settlement of no more than 20 buildings from which loom the twin, white towers of the Hmong royal house, at one time the seat of government in the Dong Van-Meo Vac region, see box, left. The **Sa Phin tourist office** ⓘ *T219-288290*, just below the house, provides a guide with a little English, 5000d. A visit to the royal house is fascinating. The Sa Phin market is a treat and is held every 12 days. Duck into the food market and drink beer with the locals from bowls.

Lung Cu

Lung Cu is the most northern point in Vietnam. It is marked by a hillock, flag pole and observation tower. From the top of the hill low mounds and China can be spied. There's an army post there so you'll need to register in the small town before walking up the steep steps.

Dong Van

This remote market town is itself nothing special (situated 16 km from Sa Phin) but is set in an attractive valley populated mainly by Tay people. However, it does have a street of ancient houses that is very attractive. One has been converted into a café. Dong Van has a Sunday market, but is very quiet at other times of the week. Since the town is only 3 km from the Chinese border, foreigners are not permitted to walk in the surrounding hills or visit villages in the vicinity. (Interestingly no two maps of this part of Vietnam tell the same story.)

Meo Vac

Passing through the **Ma Pi Leng Pass** around 1500 m above the Nho Que River, the scenery is simply awesome. Like Dong Van, Meo Vac is a restricted border area, and foreigners are not permitted to walk in the surrounding hills or visit villages outside the town. Phallic-shaped mountainous peaks and chasms of running rivers make up the scenery. A small

Hmong Kings of Sa Phin

While it is clear that Hmong people have lived in the Dong Van-Meo Vac border region for many centuries, the ascendancy of White Hmong in the area is believed to date from the late 18th century, when the powerful Vuong family established its seat of government near Dong Van. In later years the Vuong lords were endorsed as local government mandarins of Dong Van and Meo Vac by the Nguyen kings in Hué and later, following the French conquest of Indochina, by their colonial masters.

Keen to ensure the security of this key border region, the French authorities moved to further bolster the power of the Vuong family. Accordingly, in 1900 Vuong Chi Duc was recognized as king of the Hmong, and Chinese architects were brought in to design a residence befitting his newly elevated status. A site was chosen at Sa Phin, 16 km west of Dong Van; construction commenced in 1902 and was completed during the following year.

During the early years of his reign, Vuong Chi Duc remained loyal to his French patrons, participating in numerous campaigns to quell uprisings against the colonial government. In 1927 he was made a general in the French army; a photograph of him in full military uniform may be seen on the family altar in the innermost room of the house. But, as the struggle for Vietnamese independence got underway during the 1930s, Duc adopted an increasingly neutral stance. Following his death in 1944, Duc was succeeded as king of the Hmong by his son, Vuong Chi Sinh, who the following year met and pledged his support for President Ho Chi Minh.

Built between 1902 and 1903, the house of the former Hmong king faces south in accordance with the geomantic principles which traditionally govern the construction of Northeast Asian royal residences, comprising four, two-storey sections linked by three open courtyards. The building is surrounded by a moat, and various ornately carved tombs of members of the Vuong family lie outside the main gate. Both the outer and cross-sectional walls of the building are made of brick, but within that basic structure everything else is made of wood. The architecture, a development of late 19th-century Southern Chinese town-house style, features *mui luyen* or *yin-yang* roof tiles.

market is held every day in the town square, frequented mainly by White Hmong, Tay and Lolo people. Meo Vac is also the site of the famous Khau Vai 'Love Market' held once every year on the 27th day of the third month of the lunar calendar, which sees young people from all of the main ethnic groups of the region descending on the town to look for a partner. The Lolo people, with their highly colourful clothes, make up a large proportion of the town's population. A Lolo village is nearby, up the hill from the town centre.

If you are lucky to pass Lung Phin, 15 km after Meo Vac on the way back to Yen Minh on market day you will see the wildest market on the village hillside. It is the most colourful of the markets in the Ha Giang region. This market is held every six days.

East from Ha Giang → *For listings, see pages 104-105.*

Beyond Meo Vac the road used to be impassable to motorized vehicles but new bridges mean direct access to Bac Me, Bao Lac, and Tinh Túc and onward to Cao Bang and Lang Son. **Bao Lac** is a small town but visitors can be put up for the night at the People's Committee Guesthouse. There is a busy morning market but this is far from anywhere and food is limited. **Tinh Túc** is a tin mining town in a pretty valley. It has a simple but adequate hotel next to the post office; there's also a canteen-type diner with very cold beer. Tinh Túc to **Cho Ra** (for Ba Be Lake) is a scenic and rewarding trip.

Far North listings

For sleeping and eating price codes and other relevant information, see page 10-13.

Sleeping

The road to Ha Giang *p99*

$ Ethnic minority homestay at Thac Ba Lake. Mr Thuong and Miss Nhat offer homestay in the village of Ngoi Tu, Vu Linh, Yen Bai province, T9-7284 5982 (English not spoken). Dinner is US$4.50 and breakfast is US$1.20.

$ Gia Long Hotel, Xin Man, T219-383 6479, gialonghotel.2001@gmail.com. It's the only thing going in Xin Man with rooms with kitsch decor down to dorms.

$ Lavie Vu Linh Resort, a sustainable tourism project in Ngoi Tu village, Vu Linh commune, Yen Bai province, www.lavievulinh.com. Sleep in a longhouse on the floor or a private room with en suite. The shared bathroom has the most fabulous bathtub. Hot water is available. Trekking, rafting, fishing, boating, biking and badminton is possible. Dinner is with a local family and costs 110,000d. This is billed as a sustainable tourism project. It has a great lookout across the lake but there is some criticism of the project in the community. It may be better to stay with a local family in the nearby village.

Ha Giang *p100*

$$-$ Huy Hoan Hotel, 10 Nguyen Trai St, T219-386 1288. Follow the main road coming into the town centre and on the left-hand side, just 20 m after the junction of Yen Bien 2 bridge is the hotel. The best hotel in Ha Giang with 41 very comfortable a/c rooms with private bathroom. Very little English is spoken but they are fluent in Chinese. Wi-Fi available.

$ Hotel Hoang Anh, 5 Nguyen Trai St, T219-386 3559. 39 rooms in this town centre spot. Drawcard is the bathtubs.

$ Pan Hou Village, T219-383 3565, www.panhouvillage.hebergratuit.com, is some distance south of Ha Giang off the main road. You would need to have your own transport to get to this lodge in the mountains. It would be a good place from where to trek which is organized.

$ Phuong Dong Hotel, 5 Nguyen Trai St, T219-386 7979. A total of 17 a/c rooms all with en suite facilities. Helpful staff.

$ Thon Tha Hamlet (Lam Phuong cooperative), T219-386 0647, T123-852 2447 (mob). Mr Nguyen Van Quyen is in charge of the homestay rota at this picturesque Tay ethnic minority village amid paddy fields, 5 km west of Ha Giang.

The **Yen Bien**, 517 Nguyen Trai St, T219-386 8229. The biggest hotel in town was being rebuilt at the time of going to press.

Yen Minh and Pho Bang *p102*

$ Nha Nghi Noa Hong, T219-859557. There is 1 hotel in Pho Bang in a small courtyard. Rooms are spacious with comfortable beds and mosquito nets but bathrooms are tiny and running cold water may not even be available. Dinner is what's available.

$ People's Committee Guesthouse, Yen Minh Tinh Ha Giang, T219-385 2297. 12 rooms all equipped with a/c and hot water. The staff are friendly but speak no English.

Dong Van *p102*

$ Cao Nguyen Da (Rocky Plateau Hotel), T219-385 6868. Service is appalling but you've got to dig the orange suede and white retro furniture in the lobby and the clay pot sculpture in the stairwell. 14 overdecorated rooms with small bathrooms. Prices rise at weekends. Breakfast not included.

$ Khai Hoan Hotel, T219-385 6147. A 25-roomed hotel with large rooms; fan only. It's the biggest and cleanest hotel in town. Breakfast not included.

Meo Vac *p102*
$ Hoa Cuong Hotel, T219-387 1888. This new 26-roomed hotel is luxurious for these parts. Hot gushing showers and firm beds with crisp linens are most welcome up here.
$ Nho Que Guesthouse, T219-387 2322. A good guesthouse with 12 a/c rooms and hot water showers.

Eating

The road to Ha Giang *p99*
Nhat Thuy Com Binh Dan (Common Rice Restaurant), Xin Man, T219-383 6117. A basic restaurant serving tasty pork dishes, sardines, soups and fried spring rolls.

Ha Giang *p100*
Com Pho Bo, 200 m from the **Huy Hoan Hotel** on Nguyen Trai St serving simple dishes.
Com Vietnam, 1 Quang Trung St, T219-386 8034. Open daily. The menu's not in English but there's chicken, duck, beef, water buffalo, fish and spring rolls.
Tourist Company Quan Com Pho, 160 Tran Hung Dao St, corner of Nguyen Trai St. The most traveller-friendly place to eat in Ha Giang. Another restaurant next door. There are numerous other small places to eat down side streets off Tran Hung Dao and on the other side of town near the main market. The Pho Da café is nearby.

Yen Minh and Pho Bang *p102*
There are plenty of rice restaurants along Thi Tran Yen Minh St in Yen Minh.
Minh Hai, by the market, is a good place for food.

Dong Van *p102*
Pho Co Cafe. A charming café with an interior courtyard and wooden balustrading in an old building. Just drinks on offer.
Tien Nhi Restaurant, main road, Dong Van, T219-385 6217. Get yourself a slice of superb roasted pig from here. Failing that a coffee from this friendly restaurant.

Shopping

Tea is the speciality produce of the region, which grows many different varieties including green, yellow, black and flower-scented. Best known is Shan Tuyet tea, a flavoursome variety which is exported but will not be to everyone's taste.

Ha Giang *p81*
Minisupermarket, 143 Nguyen Trai St.

Activities and tours

Ha Giang *p100*
Ha Giang Tourist Company, see page 100. Permits for Dong Van-Meo Vac region are obtainable here, 250,000d for up to a group of 5; takes 1 hr.

Transport

Ha Giang *p100*
Bus
The bus station is at 13 Nguyen Trai St. Departures to **Hanoi**'s Gia Lam terminal, 6 hrs. 4WD vehicle recommended in the far north, whatever the season.

East from Ha Giang *p103*
Bus
Buses from Ha Giang to **Bao Lam** via Bac Me on Route 34. Direct to **Bac Me** also. From **Bao Lam** to **Bao Lac**, **Tinh Túc**, **Nguyen Binh** and **Cao Bang** daily; 7-8 hrs to **Cao Bang**.

Directory

Ha Giang *p100*
Banks Agribank, Tran Hung Dao St. BIDV with ATM, 159 Nguyen Trai St. **Post office** Nguyen Trai St.

Cao-Bac-Lang

The three provinces of Cao Bang, Bac Can and Lang Son – the famous Cao-Bac-Lang resistance zone of the 1947-1950 Frontier Campaign – form the heartland of the Viet Bac (literally North Vietnam). This a mountainous region, heavily populated by Tay and Nung people, became the cradle of the revolution during the twilight years of the French colonial period. » *For listings, see pages 114-116.*

Ins and outs

Getting there and around Tours are available from the plethora of tour operators in Hanoi. It is possible to tour this beautiful area by way of a circuit which leads north along Highway 3 from Thai Nguyen to Bac Can, making a small diversion to Ba Be National Park before continuing north to Cao Bang and the historic border district of Pac Bo. From here, Highway 4, scene of some of the most bitter fighting during the First Indochina War, leads south to the important frontier town of Lang Son. The return journey from Lang Son to Hanoi may then be made either directly along Highway 1A or across the mountains along Highway 1B. Although it is possible to reach the larger centres by bus from Hanoi, the going is tough and detours are not possible. A 4WD vehicle is recommended. » *See Transport, page 115.*

North from Hanoi → *For listings, see pages 114-116.*

Heading north from Hanoi you'll pass through the indutrial town of Thai Nguyen; the only reason to stop would be to visit the **Thai Nguyen Museum of Ethnology** ⓘ *Tue-Sun 0800-1630, 20,000d*. This notable museum houses a collection of artefacts relating to all of Vietnam's 54 ethnic groups. It includes clothes, agricultural and handicraft tools and textiles.

Bac Can

The market town and eponymous capital of Bac Can Province lies on the River Cau. Bac Can acquired enormous strategic significance during the First Indochina War as the westernmost stronghold of the Cao-Bac-Lang battle zone. The town was captured by the Viet Minh in 1944 and its recovery was considered crucial to the success of the 1947 French offensive against the Viet Bac resistance base. Although colonial troops did succeed in retaking Bac Can, and built military outposts along Highway 3 in the autumn of 1947, guerilla attacks on the town's garrison subequently became so frequent that the French were forced to abandon the town two years later.

Bac Can's daily market is frequented by all the main ethnic groups of the region, which include not only Tay but also local branches of the White Hmong and Red Dao, in addition to Coin Dao (*Dao Tien*) and Tight-Trousered Dao (*Dao Quan Chet*).

Ba Be National Park

ⓘ *44 km west of Na Phac on Highway 279, 1 hr from Cho Ra town, T281-389 4026, 10,000d plus 1000d insurance per person and 10,000d per car. The park centre is located on the eastern shore of Ba Be Lake. It runs many different tours led by English-speaking guides with an expert knowledge of the area and its wildlife. These tours range from 2-hr boat trips to 2-day mountain treks staying overnight in Tay or Dao villages and visiting caves, waterfalls and other local beauty spots.*

Ba Be National Park (Vuon Quoc Gia Ba Be) was established in 1992. It is Vietnam's eighth national park and comprises 23,340 ha of protected area plus an additional 8079 ha of buffer zone. It is centred on the very beautiful Ba Be Lake (*ba be* means 'three basins'), 200 m above sea level. The lake is surrounded by limestone hills carpeted in tropical evergreen forest. The park itself contains a very high diversity of flora and fauna, including an estimated 417 species of plant, 100 species of butterfly, 23 species of amphibian and reptile, 110 species of bird and 50 species of mammal. Among the latter are 10 seriously endangered species, including the Tonkinese snub-nosed langur (*Rhinopitecus avunculus*) and the black gibbon (*Hylobates concolor*). Within the park there are a number of villages inhabited by people of the Tay, Red Dao, Coin Dao and White Hmong minorities.

Cao Bang and around → *For listings, see pages 114-116.*

Cao Bang stands in a valley on a narrow peninsula between the Bang Giang and Hien rivers, which join just to the northwest of the town. Cao Bang was badly damaged during the 1979 border war with China and has since been extensively rebuilt. The market here is one of the largest in the country.

Ins and outs

Getting there and around Cao Bang is located on Highway 3 and is 270 km from Hanoi. Na Phac to Cao Bang is 83 km, 1½ hours along a well-metalled road. The Cao Bac Pass runs between 39 km and 29 km before Cao Bang, with stunning scenery all the way and breathtaking views at its summit. Arriving in Cao Bang, fork left over a bridge and keep going until the **Bang Giang Hotel** appears straight in front of you. Once in the town, there are plenty of taxis and *xe ôm*. Walking is an option as many of the sights in Cao Bang itself are easy reach. ▸▸ *See Transport, page 115.*

Best time to visit As Cao Bang is only 300 m above sea level, the climate is temperate all year round.

Tourist information Cao Bang Tourist ⓘ *1 Nguyen Du St, T26-385 2245*. As provincial travel agencies go, it is good and offers a selection of tours at reasonable prices. The staff are friendly and helpful.

History

Tay-Thai settlement in the area began at a very early date, leading to the emergence of the powerful Tay Au kingdom here during the Bronze Age. The Tay Au kings moved their capital south to Co Loa in the Red River Delta where, over the ensuing centuries, they gradually succumbed to the dominant Viet culture.

In the mid-10th century the Viet kings set about establishing fortifications in and around Cao Bang owing to its strategic position near the Chinese border, but the region continued to pose a significant security problem throughout the feudal era, as indicated by the revolts of Tay lords, Be Khac Thieu and Nung Dac Thai, against the Le Dynasty during the 1430s.

During the late 16th and early 17th centuries Cao Bang became a hotbed of revolt against royal authority. The essential background to the events of that period was the usurpation of the Le throne in 1527 by the Mac; although the Le kings were reinstated in 1592, members of the Mac family subsequently seized Cao Bang and proceeded to rule the region as an independent kingdom for a further 75 years. The ruins of a temple which once functioned as the palace of the Mac kings may still be seen today near the small market town of Cao Binh, 12 km northwest of Cao Bang town.

Before the arrival of the French, the market town of Cao Binh served as the administrative headquarters of Cao Bang Province. However, the Cao Bang Peninsula had also been settled from an early date and, following the French conquest of the area in 1884, the colonial authorities decided to transfer the provincial capital to the current site. A substantial fortress was subsequently constructed on the hill overlooking the town centre – the outer walls of this fortress still stand today, although what's left of the fortress itself currently serves as a base for the People's Army and is therefore off-limits to visitors.

From the late 1920s onwards Cao Bang became a cradle of the revolutionary movement in the north. The following years saw the establishment of many party cells through which a substantial programme of subversive activity against the colonial regime was organized. It was thus no accident that in 1940, when he returned to Vietnam after his long sojourn overseas, Ho Chi Minh chose to make remote Cao Bang Province his revolutionary headquarters during the crucial period from 1940 to 1945.

Sights

There is not a lot to see in the town. A few late-19th-century **French buildings** have survived the ravages of war and redevelopment in the old quarter of town which stretches down the hill from the fortress to the Hien River Bridge, making that area worth exploring on foot.

Cao Bang Exhibition Centre ⓘ *Hoang Nhu St, T26-385 2616, Wed and Sat 0800-1100, 1300-1700, free,* records the history of the revolutionary struggle in Cao Bang Province, with particular reference to the years leading up to the establishment of the Democratic Republic of Vietnam when Ho Chi Minh's headquarters were based at Pac Bo, 56 km north of Cao Bang. Pride of place in the exhibition hall is given to Ho's old staff car, registration number 'BAC 808'. Unfortunately all information is in Vietnamese only.

Ky Sam Temple

ⓘ *18 km north of Cao Bang town on Highway 203 to Pac Bo. It is located in the Nung village of Ngan, 200 m east of Highway 203.*

This temple honours the memory of Nung Tri Cao, Nung lord of Quang Uyen, who led one of the most important ethnic minority revolts against the Vietnamese monarchy during the 11th century.

The story of Nung Tri Cao began in 1039 when Nung Tri Cao's father Nung Ton Phuc and his elder brother Nung Tri Thong rose in rebellion against Le Thai Tong. An expeditionary force was swiftly assembled by the Viets and the rebels were caught and summarily executed. However, two years later Nung Tri Cao himself gathered an army, seizing neighbouring territories and declaring himself ruler of a Nung kingdom which he called Dai Lich. He too was quickly captured by Viet troops, but having put his father and elder brother to death two years earlier, King Le Thai Tong took pity on Nung Tri Cao and let him return to Quang

Uyen. For the next seven years peace returned to the area, but in 1048, Nung Tri Cao rose up in revolt yet again, this time declaring himself 'Emperor of Dai Nam' and seizing territories in southern China. For the next five years he managed to play the Viet and Chinese kings off against each other until Le Thai Tong finally captured and executed him in 1053.

There has been a temple in the village of Ngan for many centuries, but the one standing today dates from the 19th century. It comprises two buildings, the outer building housing an altar dedicated to one of Nung Tri Cao's generals, the inner sanctum originally containing statues of the king, his wife and his mother; unfortunately these statues were stolen many years ago. The poem etched onto the walls in the outer building talks of Nung Tri Cao's campaigns and declares that his spirit is ever ready to come to the aid of his country in times of need.

Ruins of Cao Binh Church

ⓘ *5 km north of Ky Sam Temple along Highway 203 to Pac Bo, fork left at a junction; the ruins are 500 m from the junction.*

Constructed in 1906, Cao Binh Church was one of three churches administered from Cao Bang during the French period, the others being those of Cao Bang and That Khe. There used to be many French houses in the vicinity of the church, but the majority of those that survived the French war were destroyed in 1979. However, the former vicar's house still stands relatively intact, adjacent to the ruins of the church. The family which currently occupies it runs one of the Cao Bang region's most famous apiaries.

Mac Kings' Temple

ⓘ *1.5 km beyond Lang Den (Temple village), located on the west bank of the Dau Genh River, opposite Cao Binh. Accessible either on foot or by 4WD capable of fording the river.*

Cao Binh is situated on the east bank of the Dau Genh River, a tributary of the Bang Giang River. On the opposite bank lies Lang Den (Temple village), which takes its name from the ruined 16th-century palace of the Mac Dynasty located on a hill just above the village.

This structure is believed to have been built during the early 1520s by Mac Dang Dung, a general of the Le army who in 1521-1522 seized control of the kingdom, forcing the 11-year-old King Le Chieu Tong into exile and setting up his younger brother Le Thung as king. Two years later Mac Dang Dung forced Le Thung to abdicate, declaring himself king of Dai Viet.

The Mac Dynasty retained control of Dai Viet for 65 years, during which period representatives of the deposed Le Dynasty mounted numerous military campaigns against the usurpers. The Le kings were finally restored to power in 1592 by the powerful Trinh family, but in that year a nephew of Mac Mau Hop, the last Mac king, seized Cao Bang and set up a small kingdom there. Over the next 75 years three successive generations of the Mac family managed to keep the royal armies at bay, even managing to launch two successful attacks on Thang Long (Hanoi) before Cao Bang was finally recaptured by Trinh armies in 1667.

It is apparent that this building was originally constructed as a small royal residence; the original cannon placements may still be seen on the hill in front of the main entrance.

Pac Bo

The road from Cao Bang to Pac Bo passes through 56 km of stunning scenery, 1½ hours. Despite its proximity to China, no special permit is needed, but walking outside the area is not permitted.

On 28 January 1941 Ho Chi Minh crossed the Sino-Vietnamese border, returning home to take charge of the resistance movement after 30 years overseas. In the days which followed, he and his colleagues set up their revolutionary headquarters in a cave in the Pac Bo valley. Of interest primarily to scholars of the fledgling Vietnamese Socialist Party, Pac Bo is the sort of pilgrimage spot that model carpet-weavers or revolutionary railwaymen might be brought to as a reward.

History

Taking advantage of the surrender of the French administration to the Japanese, Ho Chi Minh returned to Vietnam setting up his headquarters at Pac Bo, an area populated mainly by the Nung people. It was from here that Ho Chi Minh – dressed in the traditional Nung costume – guided the growing revolutionary movement, organizing training programmes for cadres, translating *The History of the Communist Party in the USSR* into Vietnamese and editing the revolutionary newspaper *Independent Vietnam*.

The eighth Congress of the Communist Party Central Committee, convened by Ho Chi Minh at Pac Bo from 10-19 March 1941, was an event of great historic importance which saw the establishment of the Vietnam Independence League (*Vietnam Doc Lap Dong Minh Hoi*), better known as the Viet Minh. This Congress also assisted preparations for the future armed uprising, establishing guerilla bases throughout the Viet Bac.

The years from 1941 to 1945 were a period of severe hardship for the Vietnamese people, as the colonial government colluded with Japanese demands to exploit the country's natural resources to the full in order to support the Japanese war effort. But, by 1945, the Vichy Government in France had fallen and the French colonial administration belatedly drew up plans to resist the Japanese. However, on 9 March 1945, their plans were foiled by the Japanese who set up a new government with King Bao Dai as head of state.

At this juncture, Viet Minh guerilla activity was intensified all over the country with the result that by June 1945, almost all of the six provinces north of the Red River Delta were under Communist control. On 13 August Japan surrendered to the Allied forces; three days later Ho Chi Minh headed south from Pac Bo to Tan Trao near Tuyen Quang to preside over a People's Congress which declared a general insurrection and established the Democratic Republic of Vietnam. The August Revolution that followed swept all in its wake; within a matter of weeks the three major cities of Hanoi, Hué and Saigon had fallen to the Viet Minh and King Bao Dai had abdicated. On 2 September 1945 President Ho Chi Minh made a historic address to the people in Hanoi's Ba Dinh Square, proclaiming the nation's independence.

Sights

The **Pac Bo Vestiges Area Exhibition Center** ⓘ *T26-385 2425, daily 0800-1700*, houses artefacts concerning the revolution and Ho Chi Minh's part in it. The centre is 2 km from the vestiges themselves and comprises two buildings: the **Ho Chi Minh House of Remembrance** contains an altar dedicated to Ho Chi Minh, while the **museum** has background information on the Pac Bo area and its historical role in the revolutionary struggle. It also contains information about Ho Chi Minh's long journey back to Vietnam between 1938 and 1941, culminating in his arrival at Pac Bo on 28 January 1941. There is a series of artefacts associated with the various periods between 1941 and 1945 during which Ho Chi Minh lived and worked at Pac Bo, including many of his private possessions. Then there are further exhibits surrounding the events leading up to Ho's journey south from Pac Bo to Tan Trao near Tuyen Quang, where a decision was taken in August 1945 to launch a general insurrection to seize power and found the Democratic Republic of Vietnam.

A further 2 km by road is a parking area located next to the Lenin Stream under the shade of Karl Marx Mountains; both names chosen by Ho Chi Minh (the place is festooned with commemorative plaques). From here, visitors can do two walks: one to **Coc Bo Cave** (500 m), where Ho lived and worked after his return from overseas, and the other to Khuoi Nam Jungle Hut (800 m).

Ban Doc (Ban Zop), Vietnam's most recently discovered waterfall, and apparently the highest, is about 80 km due north of Cao Bang. Views of the waterfall are incredible.

Northeast frontier

From Cao Bang to Lang Son along Highway 4 is a journey of 135 km; the road is in relatively poor condition and the going can be quite hard, taking 3½ hours, but it is not without its rewards. About 10 km south of Dong Khe, Highway 4 climbs up to the infamous **Lung Phay Pass**. From here to the village of Bong Lau the wonderful mountain scenery makes it difficult to imagine the carnage that took place between 1947 and 1950, when convoy after convoy of French supply trucks ran into carefully planned Viet Minh ambushes. The **War Heroes' Cemetery** at Bong Lau is sited on a hill where a French military outpost once stood and marks the border between Cao Bang and Lang Son provinces.

About 30 km south of That Khe the road passes through more towering limestone outcrops before commencing its climb up through another of the Frontier Campaign's infamous battle zones, the beautiful **Bo Cung Pass**.

The Frontier Campaign of 1947-1950

The government established by Ho Chi Minh in September 1945 soon found itself in a cleft stick. The terms of the Potsdam Conference had provided for the surrender of Japanese forces to be accepted south of the 16th parallel by British-Indian forces and north of that line by the Chinese Kuomintang (Nationalist Party) troops of Chiang Kai-shek. In the south, General Gracey promptly freed thousands of French troops detained in the wake of the Japanese coup.

Unable to confront both the French and the Chinese, Ho Chi Minh decided to negotiate with the French, concluding, as we have already seen, that they were the lesser of the two evils. In February 1946 the French signed a treaty with the Chinese Nationalists which secured their withdrawal from Vietnamese territory. The following month a Franco-Vietnamese agreement confirmed the status of Vietnam as a free state within the French Union and the Indochinese Federation.

After consolidating their positions in the Red River Delta, the French resolved to launch a major offensive against the Viet Bac in October 1947 with the objective of destroying the resistance leadership. Their plan involved a pincer movement of two armed columns – one under Colonel Communal moving by water up the Red and Lo rivers to attack and occupy Tuyen Quang and Chiem Hoa, the other under Colonel Beaufre travelling to Lang Son and then north along Highway 4 to That Khe, Dong Khe and Cao Bang before heading southwards to Bac Can. The offensive was intended to take the Viet Minh by surprise but, just six days after the attack had begun, an aircraft carrying the French chief of staff was shot down near Cao Bang, allowing the plans to fall into the hands of the Viet Minh High Command.

Sailing up the Lo River, Communal's column fell into a Viet Minh ambush suffering a humiliating defeat and losing some 38 gunboats before being forced to retreat to Tuyen Quang. Meanwhile, Beaufre's forces suffered repeated ambushes at the hands of Viet Minh before finally managing to recapture the fortresses of Cao Bang and Bac Can in late

October 1947. Having failed to achieve the objective of their offensive, the French were now obliged to dig-in for a long and costly war.

The position of the French became steadily more and more precarious. Supply convoys travelling from Lang Son to Cao Bang and Bac Can were ambushed repeatedly, particularly along Highway 4. Thousands of colonial troops lost their lives en route, on what French press dubbed the 'Road of Death', the most dangerous stretches of which were the Lung Phay Pass 10 km south of Dong Khe and the Bo Cung Pass 30 km south of That Khe.

Despite massive subsidy from the United States under the emerging Truman doctrine of containing Communism, the cost of air-dropping supplies into the region was becoming an intolerable burden. The French High Command finally concluded that their position in the Viet Bac was no longer tenable and began to draw up plans for the abandonment of Cao Bang. Before these plans could be implemented, however, the Viet Minh launched a surprise attack on Dong Khe, capturing the post. Taken aback by this bold move and desperate to secure the speedy and safe retreat of its Cao Bang garrison, the French High Command ordered the post's commander, Colonel Charton, to withdraw to Lang Son.

Leaving Cao Bang on 3 October 1950, Charton's column made it no further than Nam Nang, 17 km south of the town, before running into a Viet Minh ambush. Travelling northwards from That Khe to rendezvous with Charton, Lepage's forces were also intercepted in the vicinity of Dong Khe. The subsequent battle in the hills to the west of Highway 4 resulted in a resounding Viet Minh victory, in the aftermath of which, on 8 October, some 8000 French troops had been either killed or taken prisoner. Within days the French had abandoned all their remaining posts on Highway 4.

The Viet Minh victory on Highway 4 was a major turning point in the war, which threw the colonial forces throughout the north into complete disarray. During the following two weeks the French were obliged to withdraw all their forces from Lang Son, Thai Nguyen and Tuyen Quang, while in the northwest, the French garrisons at Hoa Binh and Lao Cai were also driven out. Thus was the scene set for the final stage of the First Indochina War, which would culminate four years later in the momentous battle at Dien Bien Phu (see page 78).

Lang Son and around → *For listings, see pages 114-116.*

The town of Lang Son lies on the Ky Lung River in a small alluvial plain surrounded by 1000-m-high mountains. Like Cao Bang, Lang Son was badly damaged during the border war of 1979 and has since been substantially rebuilt. But, the old quarter of the town, south of the Ky Cung River still contains a number of interesting historic buildings as well as the town's markets.

Ins and outs

Getting there and around Lang Son is 155 km northwest of Hanoi on Highway 1. The direct route from Hanoi is along Highway 1A via Chi Lang and Bac Giang, 154 km, 3½ hours. (Chi Lang Pass is the site of Le Loi's historic victory over 100,000 Ming invaders in 1427, effectively bringing to an end 1000 years of Chinese hegemony.) The longer, more scenic route is along Highway 1B via Bac Son and Thai Nguyen, 237 km, seven hours. The road passes through some delightful highland countryside settled by Tay, Nung and Dao. There are early morning bus departures from Hanoi. One train runs daily from Hanoi and back – at 1830, arriving 2240, returning 0350, arriving 0810 – to Dong Dang (Border Gate) and to Lang Son at 0540 arriving 1100. There are plenty of taxis and *xe ôm* in Lang Son. ▸▸ *See Transport, page 115.*

Best time to visit It is fairly temperate all year round. The best time is spring or autumn.

Tourist information **Lang Son Tourism and Export company** ⓘ *9 Tran Hung Dao St, T25-381 4848*. It arranges a good selection of tours within the vicinity. Staff have a good command of English. Friendly and helpful.

History

Lang Son rose to prominence as early as the Bronze Age, when emergent trade routes between India and China turned it into an important transit stop on the main road from the Red River Delta through Nanning to Guangzhou.

Between 1527 and 1592 the Mac devoted considerable attention to the task of fortifying the strategically important Lang Son border region. Vestiges of a number of Mac Dynasty fortifications may still be seen today in Lang Son Province, the best preserved of which is the citadel, which lies on a limestone outcrop to the west of the present town.

By the time of its seizure by French troops in 1885 Lang Son had developed into a sizeable and prosperous market town. In subsequent years it became a French military base second in importance only to Cao Bang.

Sights

The rebuilt **Dong Kinh Market** is chock-full of Chinese consumer goods brought through Dong Dang. Although rebuilt many times and finally sidelined by the gleaming new structure at Dong Kinh, **Ky Lua Market** is the oldest in Lang Son and still sees a trickle of trading activity every day. Members of the Tay and Nung are regular visitors here. **Lang Son Citadel** comprises a large section of the ancient city walls, dating back to the 18th century. The former **Lang Son monastery**, which once stood on the other side of the city walls, is south down Nguyen Thai Hoc Street from the old quarter to My Son junction.

The east- and west-facing walls of the imposing 16th-century **Mac Dynasty Citadel** are located on a limestone outcrop west of Lang Son. To get there, head out of town past the six-way junction on the Tam Thanh Road.

At the **Tam Thanh Cave** ⓘ *on the road to the Mac Dynasty Citadel, 10,000d*, there are three chambers; the outer one functions as a pagoda with two shrines and the second one contains a fresh water pool. A poem by Ngo Thi Sy (1726-1780), military commander of the Lang Son garrison who first discovered this and other caves in the area, is carved on the wall near the entrance.

Nhi Thanh (10,000d) perhaps the best known of Lang Son's caves, is located south of Tam Thanh Cave (from the six-way junction take the Nhi Thanh road). There are in fact two separate caves here – the one on the right contains the Tam Giao Pagoda, established in 1777 by Ngo Thi Sy, in which are six shrines, while the one on the left follows the Ngoc Tuyen stream deep into the mountain: the latter is particularly dramatic. More of Ngo Thi Sy's poetry adorns the walls here. The ladies who sit in front of the pagoda are very friendly and will offer visitors tea and bananas.

Dong Dang and the Chinese border

Some 18 km north of Lang Son is the border with China at Dong Dang. The Chinese border town is Ping Xiang. It is possible to cross by road and by train. The road crossing is at Cua Khau Huu Nghi Dong Dang (the Friendship Pass). It is a couple of kilometres between the two international border posts. You will need to obtain a Chinese visa at the embassy in Hanoi and specify the Dong Dang crossing. For Chinese visa costs see page 93. Entering Vietnam, you will have needed to obtain a Vietnamese visa in Beijing or Hong Kong as these are not available at the border.

Bac Son → *For listings, see pages 114-116.*

Settled mainly by members of the Tay and Nung ethnicity, this small market town has two important reasons to claim significance in the history of the Vietnamese nation. The first derives from the very large number of prehistoric artefacts unearthed here by archaeologists. The so-called Bac Son period (5000-3000 BC) was characterized by the development of pottery and the widespread use of refined stone implements, including distinctive axes with polished edges known as Bacsonian axes.

The second is the Bac Son Uprising. In September 1940, revolutionaries detained in Lang Son prison, seized the opportunity afforded by the Japanese attack on the town to escape, heading northwest across the mountains to Bac Son. With the support of the local Communist Party organization they fomented a general insurrection in the town, disarming the fleeing French troops and taking over the district centre to set up the first revolutionary power base in the Viet Bac.

The following year French forces responded by launching a campaign of terror in the Viet Bac, forcing the leaders of the uprising to retreat into the mountains. The Bac Son uprising did, however, prove to be an important milestone in the revolutionary struggle and, in the years which followed, the tide turned steadily against the French throughout the region.

On the way into the town the road passes an unmarked white building on stilts with a Vietnamese flag fluttering on its roof – this is the **Museum of the Bac Son Rebellion** ⓘ *0700-1600, free*, which contains a collection of prehistoric axe-heads and other tools dating from the Bac Son period plus a large display of artefacts relating to the Bac Son Uprising. These include the weapons and personal effects of those involved in the uprising, plus letters and other documents written by Ho Chi Minh and revolutionaries such as Hoang Van Thu.

Cao-Bac-Lang listings

For Sleeping and Eating price codes and other relevant information, see pages 10-13.

Sleeping

Bac Can *p106*

$ Huong Son, T281-387 0375. Better rooms have a/c and adjoining shower/toilet; cheaper rooms have fan and shared outside facilities.

Ba Be National Park *p107*

$$-$ Ba Be Hotel, Nguyen Cong Quynh St, Cho Ra, T281-387 6115, about 15 km east of Ba Be National Park. Twin, fan rooms with hot water, shower/toilet. The hotel manager can arrange a whole-day trip including 2 hrs on the river to the lake passing a small ethnic community homestead where you will be fed and filled with rice wine. Opposite the hotel is a 5-day market for Dao and Tay people, some of whom will have walked through the night to get there.

$ Ba Be National Park Guesthouse, T281-389 4026. 62 nice and comfortable a/c rooms with adjoining bathrooms with hot water. Meals available in the park office.

$ Hoanh Tu Homestay, T281-389 4071, T1688-472446 (mob). A lovely homestay with balcony overlooking the lake. Bathrooms are not next to the living quarters.

Cao Bang *p107*

$ Bang Giang Hotel, Kim Dong St, T26-385 3431. New 70-room building, 1st floor a/c, 2nd floor fan, all with adjoining bathroom.

$ Giao Te Hotel, Hoang Nhu St, T26-385 1023. 28 rooms a/c and fan.

$ Phong Lan, K83 Kim Dong St, T26-385 2260. 50 rooms, better ones a/c, cheaper fan and shared facility.

Lang Son *p112*

$$ Bac Son, 41 Le Loi St, T25-387 1849. 22 rooms, all with adjoining bathroom; pricier rooms have a/c.

$$ Kim Son, 3 Nguyen Minh Khai St, T25-387 0378. Chinese joint-venture hotel, 29 rooms all a/c, adjoining bathroom. Quang Chau Chinese restaurant on the premises.

$ Dong Kinh, 25 Nguyen Du St, T25-387 0166. Near market, better rooms with own bathroom, a/c, fridge, etc, cheapest rooms shared facilities, basic but comfortable accommodation, restaurant.

$ Hoa Binh, 127 Tran Dang Ninh St, T25-387 0807. Comfortable accommodation, 15 rooms all a/c, adjoining bathroom.

Eating

Bac Can *p106*

Lac Lon restaurant. Simple fare.

Thin Vien Restaurant, in the the Huong Son hotel (see Sleeping, above), T281-387 0375. Serves simple local fare. Shuts early.

Cao Bang *p107*

Bac Lam, K025 Hoang Nhu St, T26-385 2697. Local dishes, open 1000-2000.

Huong Sen restaurant. Good place to try the local speciality of roast duck.

Thanh Truc, 133 Xuan Truong St, T26-385 2798. Serves basic fare from 0800 until 2000.

Lang Son *p112*

Cua Hang An Uong, corner of Le Loi and the market street, looks like a 1970s English clubhouse, but serves fantastic *lau* (steamboat) at good prices.

Transport

Bac Can *p106*

Bus

The bus station is on Duc Xuan St. There are buses to **Ha Giang**, **Cao Bang** and **Hanoi**. Hanoi is about 288 km away, 9-10 hrs.

Cao Bang *p107*

Bus

The bus station is on Kim Dong St. Buses to **Hanoi**, 10 hrs; to **Thai Nguyen**, 7 hrs. To **Nguyen Binh**, **Tinh Túc**, **Bao Lac**, **Bao Lam** on Route 34, 1 bus leaves between 0530-0700, another at 1400 and the last leaves at 1500.

Lang Son *p112*

Bus

The bus station is at 28A Ngo Quyen St, T25-371 5975. A main highway links Lang Son with **Hanoi** and public buses travel along this route, 5 hrs. Hoang Long Co operates frequently.

Car and motorbike

It is possible to return (on a Minsk) via Halong Bay and the coast; the road to **Tien Yen** is a shocker and carry lunch and spare fuel with you as there are no supplies en route. From Tien Yen the road improves.

Train

To **Hanoi** on the Dong Dang line.

Dong Dang and the Chinese border *p113*

Minibuses and *xe ôms* travel from Lang Son to the Friendship Pass for the Chinese border, 30 mins. The train to **Nanning** and **Beijing** runs through Dong Dang from Hanoi. You change trains at Dong Dang. Some travellers say it is cheaper to get a ticket from Hanoi to Ping Xiang, just inside the Chinese border and then change trains. The Hanoi train departs at 1830 Tue and Fri, arriving in Ping Xiang at 0141, in Nanning at 0700, and in Beijing at 1209. The train leaves Dong Dang for Hanoi at 0350 on Tue and Sat arriving 0810.

In China From Ping Xiang, catch a minibus near the main bus station to the border. Tell the driver you want to go to YuteLarm GorGwarn (Cantonese for Vietnam border). At the drop-off point you will be greeted by a crowd of willing motorbike drivers one of whom can take you to the border, a 5- to 10-min drive. He will take you to the policed border-gate leaving you to walk the 500 m or so down an almost deserted road before reaching the Chinese Immigration Building. After paying ¥10 for the privilege of leaving China and other obligatory stages of red tape, you have to continue, unescorted, down the same road for another 5 mins with the occasional truck going past, but little else. The silence is quite eerie and out-of-place for a border point.

Bac Son *p114*

Bus

Connections with **Hanoi** and **Lang Son**. The best method is to return to Lang Son and get a bus from there.

Directory

Bac Can *p106*

Banks Agriank, Phung Chi Kien St. **Internet** Minh Khai St. **Post office** Phung Chi Kien St.

Cao Bang *p107*

Bank Agriank, Kim Dong St. **Post office** on Be Van Dan St.

Lang Son *p112*

Banks Agriank, 1 Tran Hung Dao St. Vietcombank, 1 Quang Trung St. **Post office** 49 Le Loi St.

Haiphong and around

Haiphong is still the Vietnam of yesteryear. There are beautiful old French buildings, a peaceful but busy city life where men still pedal ancient cyclos, and sidecars are in generous abundance. There is little to attract the tourist other than an authentic glimpse into life without tourism.

The port of Haiphong was established in 1888 on the Cua Cam River, a major distributory of the Red River. It is the largest port and the second largest city in the north. Over and above its natural attributes Haiphong is blessed with a go-ahead and entrepreneurial People's Committee (no surprises that the district sports Vietnam's first casino) and this attitude is reflected in the bustle in the streets and the industry and vitality of the population. Haiphong's prosperity looks set to redouble with heavy investment in port and communications infrastructure and major investment from overseas in manufacturing plants. Despite this (from the tourists' viewpoint) seemingly inauspicious framework, central Haiphong remains remarkably attractive and its people open and warm. » *For listings, see pages 121-122.*

Ins and outs

Getting there As the north's second city after Hanoi, and the region's premier port, Haiphong is well connected. Cat Bi, Haiphong's airport, is 7 km from the city and there are flights from Ho Chi Minh City. The road from Hanoi is now excellent (for Vietnam) and there are frequent bus and minibus connections. Choose a big bus in the interests of comfort and safety. There are trains each day in either direction between the two cities. Haiphong is the departure point for Cat Ba Island and from there with Halong Bay. The 100 km road from Hanoi to Haiphong, the north's principal port, passes through the flood-prone riceland of the Red River Delta. In places the land lies below sea-level and a system of dykes and bunds has been built up over the centuries to keep the river in place. » *See Transport, page 121.*

Getting around Central Haiphong is sufficiently compact for most sights to be visited on foot. But a journey from, for example, the railway station to the port, or a trip to the outer temples, merits a taxi, cyclo or *xe ôm*. Because Haiphong does not receive many Western tourists it is not normally possible to rent a motorbike for independent exploring. From Haiphong it is a one-hour hydrofoil ride to Cat Ba Island, one of Vietnam's more accessible national parks, see page 126.

Tourist information Vietnamtourism ⓘ *57 Dien Bien Phu St, T31-384 2989, www.hptourism.com.vn, Mon-Sat 0800-1100, 1400-1700*. Your hotel should be able to provide you with information too.

Haiphong

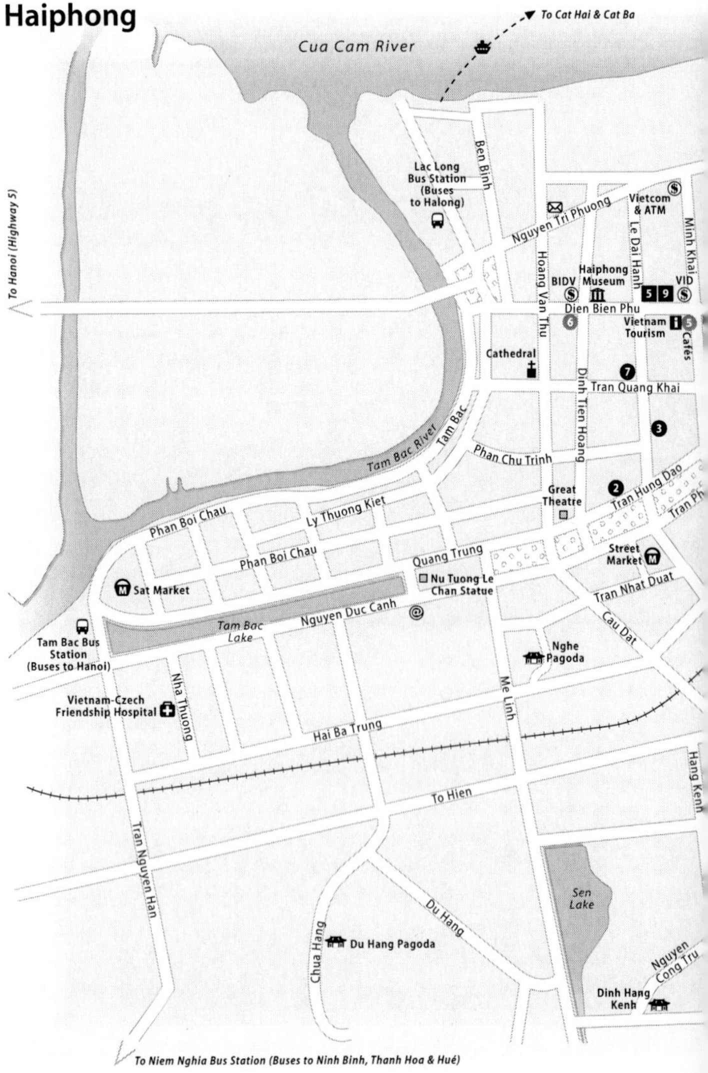

History

Haiphong witnessed the initial arrival of the French in 1872 (they occupied Hanoi a year later) and, appropriately, their final departure from the north at 1500 in the afternoon of 15 May 1955. As the major port of the north, it was subjected to sustained bombing during

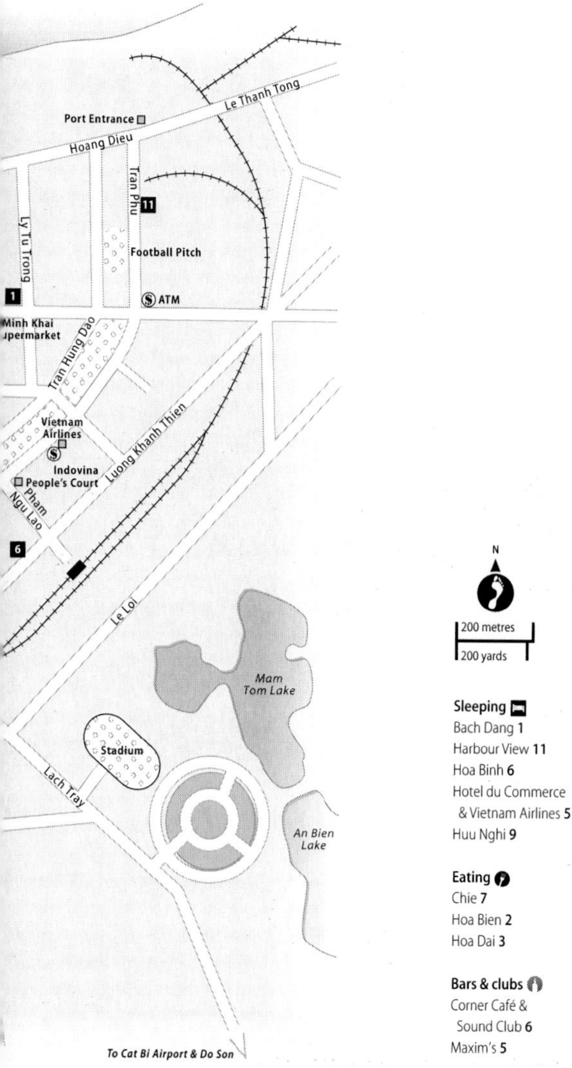

the war. To prevent petrol and diesel fuel reaching the Viet Cong, nearly 80% of all above-ground tanks were obliterated by US bombing in 1966. The US did not realize that the North Vietnamese, anticipating such action, had dispersed much of their supplies to underground and concealed tanks. This did not prevent the city from receiving a battering, although Haiphong's air defence units are said to have retaliated by shooting down 317 US planes.

Sights

Much of outer Haiphong is an ugly industrial sprawl that will win no environmental beauty contests. But, considering the bombing the city sustained, there is still a surprising amount of attractive **colonial-style architecture** in the city centre. Central Haiphong is pleasantly green with tree-lined streets.

Right in the heart of town is the **Great Theatre** ⓘ *corner of Tran Hung Dao St and Quang Trung St*, built in 1904 using imported French materials, with a colonnaded front, and facing a wide tree-lined boulevard. In November 1946, 40 Viet Minh fighters died here in a pitched battle with the French, triggered by the French government's decision to open a customs house in Haiphong. A plaque outside commemorates the battle. The streets around the theatre support the greatest concentration of foodstalls and shops.

Other colonial architecture includes the **People's Court** ⓘ *31 Tran Phu St*, a fine French building with shutters; the **post office** ⓘ *5 Nguyen Tri Phuong St*, in an attractive building, and the **bank (Vietcombank)** ⓘ *11 Hoang Dieu St*, a handsome yellow and cream building.

Haiphong Museum (Bao Tang Thanh Pho Hai Phong) ⓘ *66 Dien Bien Phu St, Tue and Thu 0800-1030, Wed and Sun 1930-2130, 2000d*, is an impressive colonial edifice in a wash of desert-sand red, and contains records of the city's turbulent past (some labels are in English).

There are a number of **street markets** and **flower stalls** off Cau Dat Street, which runs south from the theatre, along Tran Nhat Duat and Luong Khanh Thien streets. **Sat Market** is to be found in the west quarter of town, at the end of Phan Boi Chau Street. A market has stood on this site since 1876. The present building is a huge six-storey concrete edifice that has never quite taken off.

Near the centre of town on Me Linh Street is the **Nghe Pagoda** built at the beginning of the 20th century. The pagoda is dedicated to the memory of heroine General Le Chan who fought with the Trung sisters against the Chinese. A festival is held on the eighth day of the second lunar month to commemorate her birthday and offerings of crab and noodles, her favourite foods, are made. There is also an enormous statue of her in front of a cultural building diagonally opposite the Great Theatre.

Du Hang Pagoda ⓘ *1 km south of the city centre on Chua Hang St (take a* xe ôm*)*, was originally built in 1672 by wealthy mandarin-turned-monk Nguyen Dinh Sach. It has been renovated and remodelled several times since. Arranged around a courtyard, this small temple has some fine traditional woodcarving.

Dinh Hang Kenh (Hang Kenh communal house or *dinh*) ⓘ *2 km south of the centre at 51 Nguyen Cong Tru St*, dates back to 1856. Although built as a communal house, its chief function today is as a temple. The main building is supported by 32 columns of ironwood and the wood carvings in the window grilles are noteworthy. From the outside, the roof is the most dramatic feature, tiled in the fishscale style, and ornamented with a number of dragons. The corners of the roof turn up and it appears that the sheer weight is too much, as the roof is now propped up on bricks. There are a number of *dinh* in and around Haiphong, reflecting the traditional importance of Chinese in this area. Today Taiwanese businessmen are counted among the major investors in Haiphong.

Haiphong and around listings

For Sleeping and Eating price codes and other relevant information, see Essentials pages 10-13.

Sleeping

Haiphong *p117, map p118*

Haiphong offers plenty of accommodation to meet the demands of industrialists and expats rather than travellers; standards tend to be fairly good but prices a little high.

$$$$ Harbour View, 4 Tran Phu St, T31-382 7827, www.harbourviewvietnam.com. Haiphong's most luxurious hotel. Near the river, this under-utilized 127-room hotel has 2 restaurants and a bar. It is well managed and comfortable but watch out for overcharging in the bar. Daily buffet lunch.

$$$ Huu Nghi, 60 Dien Bien Phu St, T31-382 3244. Central and, with 11 storeys and 162 rooms, one of Haiphong's largest. It's efficient enough although overpriced. Rooms are fully equipped and quiet. Staff are helpful. Gym, pool and tennis court on site. Popular with Chinese tour groups; breakfast included. From the top storey the view of the port and French colonial buildings is incredible.

$$-$ Bach Dang, 40-42 Dien Bien Phu St, T31-384 2444. Newly renovated with 35 comfortable rooms at a range of prices in a central location, restaurant. Steam baths.

$ Hoa Binh, 104 Luong Khanh Thien St, T31-385 9029. Conveniently opposite the station with 31 standard a/c rooms.

$ Hotel du Commerce, 62 Dien Bien Phu St, T31-384 2706. Attractive colonial style, renovated but still atmospheric, large rooms, restaurant.

Eating

Haiphong *p117, map p118*

Foreign business influence is reflected in the form of Japanese, Chinese and Taiwanese restaurants. See also under Bars and clubs, below, for eating premises.

ΨΨΨ-Ψ Chie, 18 Tran Quang Khai St, T31-382 1018. Open 1100-1400, 1630-2200. This small Japanese restaurant seems out of place in Haiphong but in fact it's a must. Totally delicious sushi and sashimi are served up by staff in maroon and white kimonos. The sushi platter with 14 dishes is very good value; the spaghetti bolognese is incongruous.

Ψ Hoa Bien, 24 Tran Hung Dao St, T31-374 5633. Excellent Vietnamese fare with Chinese influence in a street-side setting. All dishes served fresh and piping hot.

Ψ Hoa Dai, 39 Le Dai Hanh St, T31-382 2098. Popular with well-off locals. Good Vietnamese food, particularly busy at lunchtime, and welcoming staff.

Bars and clubs

Haiphong *p117, map p118*

Corner Café and Sound Club, 107 Dien Bien Phu St, T31-374 6970. Open 0700-1300. The former **Saigon Café** is a bar, café and restaurant with good ice cream and drinks.

Maxim's, 51B Dien Bien Phu St, T31-382 2934. Bar/café with live music in the evening. Also serves Asian and European food; drinks prices rise after 1830.

Shopping

Haiphong *p117, map p118*

The large **Minh Khai** supermarket, Minh Khai St, will supply all your needs.

Transport

Haiphong *p117, map p118*

Air

Cat Bi, Haiphong's airport, lies 7 km southeast of town; the only air connections are with HCMC.

Airline offices Vietnam Airlines, 166 Haong Van Thu St, T31-381 0890.

Boat

Check all ferry information before setting out as timetables are liable to change. Connections with **Cat Ba** from the wharf on Ben Binh St where there are a number of ticket offices. Services may take motorbikes depending on ferry size. **Transtour Co** runs the Haiphong-Cat Ba ferry, T31-384 1099, www.transtourco.com.vn. To **Cat Ba** at 0700, 0900, 1100, 1330 (a/c express boat), 45 mins, 100,000d, children 50,000d; slow boat at 0630 and 1230, 80,000d, 2 hrs 10 mins. Should you miss the boats or want another route, **Hoang Long Co**, 5 Pham Ngu Lao St, T31-392 0920, www.hoanglongasia.com, runs buses from Hanoi (Luong Yen bus station, T4-3987 7225) and Haiphong to the **Dinh Vu** ferry terminal (30 mins) and a boat from here to Cat Ba (1 hr 30 mins), 100,000d. Buses leave at 0800, 1000, 1400 and 1600. There is also a ferry to **Cat Hai** from **Ben Binh wharf** at 0650, 40,000d.

If it is not running late the 0600 train from Hanoi will get you to Haiphong just in time to *xe ôm* across town to catch the morning boat.

It's worth weighing up the pros and cons of taking a tour or making your own way to Cat Ba. While the do-it-yourself method is easy and cheap, by the time you add in all the little incidental costs and the cost of a boat excursion from Cat Ba it may be just as cheap to take a tour.

Bus

Highway 5 is a fast motorway connecting capital with coast. There are regular bus departures to **Hanoi** leaving from Tam Bac bus station in front of Sat Market. **Hoang Long bus company** leaves Tam Bac station 42 times a day from 0455-1925.

Buses to **Halong** leave from the Lac Long bus station every 15 mins. Buses to **Ninh Binh**, **Thanh Hoa** and **Hué** leave from the Niem Nghia bus station.

Taxi

Mai Linh Taxi, T31-383 3833.

Train

5 departures daily in either direction between **Hanoi** and Haiphong, T31-392 0026. Trains depart from Long Bien station on Gam Cau St, Hanoi, or from the Central Station.

Directory

Haiphong *p117, map p118*

Banks BIDV, 68-70 Dien Bien Phu St. Cash major currencies but no TCs. Visa ATM. **VID Bank**, 56 Dien Bien Phu St. Changes US and Singapore dollars and Malaysian ringit, TCs and cash. **Vietcombank**, 11 Hoang Dieu St. Cashes TCs, has an ATM. **Hospitals** **Vietnam-Czech Friendship Hospital**, 1 Nha Thuong St, T31-384 6236. **Internet** On Tuyen Sinh Tin Hoc St and at 8 Tran Quang Khai St. **Post office** 5 Nguyen Tri Phuong St.

Halong Bay

Halong means 'descending dragon', and an enormous beast is said to have careered into the sea at this point, cutting the fantastic bay from the rocks as it thrashed its way into the depths. Vietnamese poets (including the 'Poet King' Le Thanh Tong) have traditionally extolled the beauty of this romantic area with its rugged islands that protrude from a sea dotted with sailing junks. Artists have been just as quick to draw inspiration from the crooked islands seeing the forms of monks and gods in the rock faces, and dragon's lairs and fairy lakes in the depths of the caves. Another myth says that the islands are dragons sent by the gods to impede the progress of an invasion flotilla. Historically more believable, if substantially embellished, the area was the location of two famous sea battles, in the 10th and 13th centuries (see box, page 78).The bay is now a UNESCO World Heritage Site. ›› *For listings, see pages 129-134.*

Ins and outs

Getting there There are two bases from which to explore Halong Bay: Halong City or Cat Ba. Traditionally, visitors went direct to Halong City from Hanoi and took a boat from there. This is still a valid option, especially for those who are short of time. But Cat Ba is becoming increasingly popular as a springboard to Halong Bay, largely because Cat Ba itself is interesting. Many people, however, take an all-inclusive tour from Hanoi, and if you are short of time, this is your best option.

Getting around Boat tours of the bay can be booked at the Bai Chay Tourist Wharf in Halong City and Cat Ba Town. To see the bay properly allow four to five hours but an overnight trip is enjoyable and preferable. One option is to buy a day ticket for a boat trip and get off at Cat Ba town when it docks thus allowing you a few hours in the bay too. Tour operators in Hanoi, see page 122, also offer tours of the bay of varying duration. ›› *For boat tours and transport details, see pages 132-133.*

Best time to visit It can be stormy in June, July and August. July and August are also the wettest months. Winter is cool and dry. The bay is no fun in the rain or fog so get a weather forecast if you can. If there are warnings of cyclones, stay away. Several tourists died in 2009 when boats took risks in this dangerous weather.

Tourist information Quang Ninh Tourism Information Promotion Centre ⓘ *C29 Royal Park Area opposite the Halong 1 Hotel and near the Novotel, T33-362 8862, www.*

halongtourism.com.vn, Mon-Fri 0730-1630, is super helpful and can provide a whole heap of advice about boats and hotels. It advises only to book boat trips through its tourist office, the Bai Chay Tourist Wharf and the larger hotels and tourist companies. It advises against staying at and booking tours with the Phuong Vi guesthouse at 25 Vuon Dao St and advises paying at least US$50 for a boat trip or US$15 for a day trip. For rescue services contact the **Halong Bay Management Department** ⓘ *166 Le Thanh Tong St, on T33-362 2761/091-326 3474 (mob).*

Karsts and caves in Halong Bay

ⓘ *Grotto of Wonders, Customs House Cave and Surprise Grotto all charge 30,000d (the Ti Tov cave is 10,000d) and are open 0730-1700. Fees for cave visits and boats to enter caves will not be included in the price of your boat tour. Many are a disappointment with harrying vendors, mounds of litter and disfiguring graffiti. Many are lit but some are not so bring a torch. Rocks can be treacherously slippery, so sensible footwear is advised.*

Geologically the tower-karst scenery of Halong Bay is the product of millions of years of chemical action and river erosion working on the limestone to produce a pitted landscape. At the end of the last ice age, when glaciers melted, the sea level rose and inundated the area turning hills into islands. The islands of the bay are divided by a broad channel: to the east are the smaller outcrops of Bai Tu Long, see page 129, while to the west are the larger islands with caves and secluded beaches.

Among the more spectacular caves are **Hang Hanh**, which extends for 2 km. Tour guides will point out fantastic stalagmites and stalactites that, with imagination, become heroes, demons and animals. **Hang Luon** is another flooded cave that leads to the hollow core in a doughnut-shaped island. It can be swum or navigated by coracle/canoe. **Hang Dau Go** is the cave wherein Tran Hung Dao stored his wooden stakes prior to studding them in the bed of the Bach Dang River in 1288 to destroy the boats of invading Mongol hordes. **Hang Thien Cung** (Heavenly Palace) is a hanging cave, a short 50-m haul above sea level, with dripping stalactites, stumpy stalagmites and solid rock pillars. A truly enormous cave and one of those most visited is **Sung Sot Cave** (Surprise Cave).

Halong City and around → *For listings, see pages 123-134.*

The route from Hanoi passes newly industrializing satellite towns whose factories, petrol stations and houses spill onto what were recently paddy fields. After Uong Bi, the scenery improves with the limestone hills which rise out of the alluvial plain giving a foretaste of the better things to come. Following the admission of Halong Bay to UNESCO's hallowed roll of World Heritage Sites, the two small towns of Bai Chay and Hon Gai were, in 1994, collectively elevated in status by the government and dubbed Halong City, a moniker largely ignored by locals. Halong City is an unattractive place with little to recommend it. What appeal it does have is strung along the seafront, which is being spruced up. For reasons unknown, the **Novotel** has opened and the **Sheraton Four Points** is to open.

Ins and outs

Getting there There are regular bus connections from Hanoi's My Dinh terminal to Bai Chay, across the water from Hon Gai, four to five hours. The Bai Chay station has moved from the waterfront to 5 km west of the city. ▸▸ *See Transport, page 133.*

Getting around Given the paucity of sites in the town, pretty much anywhere of relevance can be reached on foot. For venturing further afield, the town has the usual gangs of *xe ôm* drivers.

History

It was at Halong that, arguably, Vietnam's fate under the French was sealed. In late 1882 Captain Henri Rivière led two companies of troops to Hon Gai to seize the coal mines for France. Shortly afterwards he was ambushed and killed and his head paraded on a stake from village to village. His death persuaded the French parliament to fund a full-scale expedition to make all of Vietnam a protectorate of France. As the politician Jules Delafosse remarked at the time: "Let us, gentlemen, call things by their name. It is not a protectorate you want, but a possession."

Sights

The twin towns, Bai Chay to the west and Hon Gai to the east, separated by a river estuary and now linked by a huge new 903-m-long bridge (10,000d toll), could not be more different. Few visitors made the short ferry crossing to Hon Gai which, with its port and adjacent coal mines, could fairly be described as the industrial end of town.

Bai Chay has made great efforts and not a little progress towards turning itself into a destination rather than merely a dormitory for those visiting Halong Bay. At huge expense a narrow beach has been constructed in front of the hotels; casuarina, palm and flame trees have been planted along the prom, old hotels renovated and new ones built. There is no denying the effect of the plans to create the feel of a seaside town. But the charm is not likely to work its magic with travellers from abroad in the same way that it does with Vietnamese who are drawn in huge numbers, rapidly swamping the little beach every weekend. And, in any case, UNESCO officials have instructed the Vietnamese to stop building new resorts in the area before the unlimited developments threaten the protected bay area. Several large and attractive modern hotels have been built, including the **Halong Plaza**, one of the most luxurious in the country. But quite who is going to occupy all these junior and executive suites is a problem the marketing men appear to have overlooked.

Hon Gai, connected to its neighbour by a US$134 million bridge since December 2006, is, as mining areas go, quite a nice one, but it does not live up to the 'natural wonderland' image Quang Ninh Tourism is trying to promote. The port of Hon Gai is busy with plenty of little bamboo and resin coracles (*thung chai*) which are used by the fishermen as tenders to get out to their boats and to bring ashore the catch.

There is a thriving market and near the ferry dock is the 106-m-high **Poem Mountain** (Nui Bao Tho), so named following a visit in 1486 by King Le Thanh Tong who was so taken by the beauty of Halong Bay that he composed a poem celebrating the scenery and carved his verse into the rock. It is quite a scramble up the hill and finding the right path may require some help. At the foot of the mountain nestles the little **Long Tien Pagoda** which dates from the early 20th century. Twenty minutes' walk north up from Hon Gai is a **ruined colonial church** damaged by a bomb in 1972 but the site affords lovely views.

Yen Tu Mountains

The Yen Tu Mountains are 14 km northwest of Uong Bi and climb to a maximum elevation of 1068 m. Peppered with pagodas from the 13th to 16th centuries, much has been lost to the ravages of war and climate but stupas and temples of more recent foundation survive. The site has attracted pilgrims since the 13th century when King Tran Nhan Tong abandoned the throne in favour of a spiritual life. He washed the secular dust from his body in the Tam stream and entered the Cam Thuc (Abstinence) Pagoda. His 100 concubines traced him here and tried to persuade him of the folly of his ways but despite their undoubted allure he resisted all appeals and clung to his ascetic existence. Distraught by their failure, the poor women drowned themselves. Tran Nhan Tong later built a temple to their memory. Climbing the hills, visiting the temples and admiring the views can take a full day.

Cat Ba Island → *For listings,see pages 125-134.*

Cat Ba occupies a stunning setting in the south of Halong Bay. Much of the island and the seas around are designated a national park and, while perhaps not quite teeming with wildlife (already eaten), it is pleasantly wild and green. Cat Ba's remoteness has been steadily eroded (it only plugged into mains electricity in 1999) and it now represents a handy weekend break for many Hanoians. Despite the growth in numbers of karaoke-loving weekenders, Cat Ba remains an attractive place (minus a few of the uglier buildings) but best of all it is a great springboard into the surrounding waters of Halong Bay and an increasingly popular alternative to Halong City. The chief advantage is that there is a lot to see on the island including the stunning scenery of the interior. Cat Ba, however, will come under intense tourism and ecological pressure with the proposed building of a bridge from Dinh Vu on the mainland to Cat Hai Island (improving the links between the island

Cat Ba Island & Halong Bay

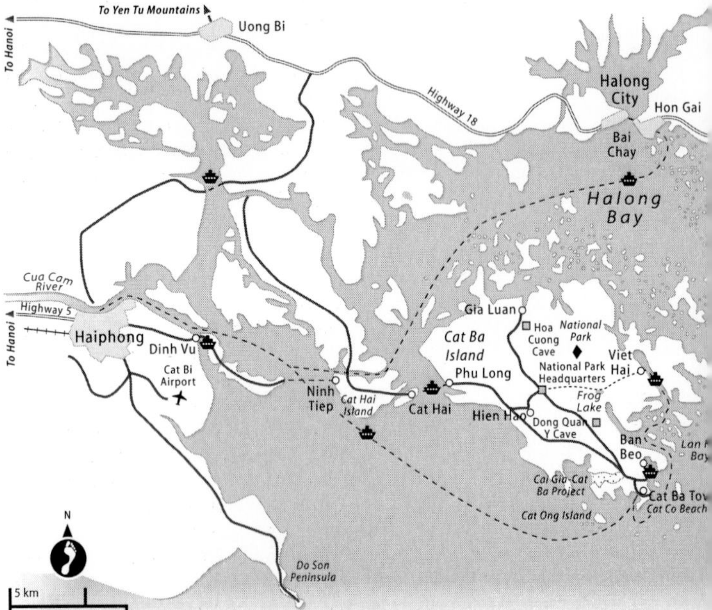

and the mainland) and the building of the US$600 million 72-ha Cai Gia-Cat Ba urban project for people from Cat Hai Island along with villas, hotels, shopping centres, a marina and entertainment attractions.

Ins and outs

Getting there There are direct hydrofoils from Haiphong or via the Dinh Vu ferry from Haiphong. Boats also leave Bai Chay and Tuan Chau 'Island' in Halong City for Gia Luan in the north of Cat Ba Island where a bus transports you to Cat Ba Town in the south. It is also possible to get a one-way ride with a tour leaving from the tourist wharf at Bai Chay (Halong City) direct to Cat Ba Town where tourist boats dock. Alternatively, organize a tour from Hanoi. ▸▸ *See Transport, page 126, and Haiphong Transport, page 121.*

Getting around Either by tour organized by a local hotel or tour operator in Hanoi, or by *xe ôm* or hire a motorbike. There is a bus service between Cat Ba town and Phu Long where the Haiphong ferry docks along the new road and to Gia Luan where the Bai Chay and Tuan Chau 'Island' boats dock. Tourist boats use the new Cat Ba pier in the middle of town but when strong westerly winds are blowing they use the old harbour. From the old harbour (Ban Beo) it is a 10-minute *xe ôm* ride to the hotels.

Best time to visit Cat Ba is at its wettest from July to August, and driest and coolest (15°C) from November to January. The busiest and most expensive time is during school summer holidays from May to September, when hotel rates double.

Tourist information The **Cat Hai District People's Committee Tourism Information Centre** ⓘ *along the seafront, T31-368 8215, www.catba.com.vn*, offers free travel information as well as tours. Most of the hotels also offer information and tours.

Exploring the island

Cat Ba is the largest island in a coastal archipelago that includes more than 350 limestone outcrops. It is adjacent to and geologically similar to the islands and peaks of Halong Bay but separated by a broad channel as the map illustrates. The islands around Cat Ba are larger than the outcrops of Halong Bay and generally more dramatic. Cat Ba is the ideal place from which to explore the whole coastal area: besides the quality of its scenery it is a more agreeable town in which to stay, although the countless new hotels springing up are slowly eroding the difference. The island is rugged and sparsely inhabited. Outside

Cat Ba town there are only a few small villages. Perhaps the greatest pleasure is to hire a motorbike and explore, a simple enough process given the island's limited road network. Half of the island forms part of a national park, see below.

For an island of its size Cat Ba has remarkably few **beaches** – only three within easy access, creatively named **Cat Co 1**, **Cat Co 2** and **Cat Co 3**. It's a 1-km walk to the first and a further 1-km to the second which is quieter, cleaner and more secluded; Cat Co 2 is accessible by a walkway from Cat Co 1 or by boat. Cat Co 1 and 2 feature the **Cat Tien Tourism Complex**: there's food, sun loungers for hire, showers, toilets, lockers, campground and bungalows for hire on Cat Co 2, see Sleeping, page 135. The **Catba Island Resort & Spa** on Cat Co 1 is also open to non-guests to use the pool and water slides, US$10; see under Sleeping. There's also a restaurant and drinks here on the beach. Cat Co 3 (home of the Sunrise Resort) is also accessible by walkway from Cat Co 1 and by road and then stairs also.

These lie just to the east of town behind a steep hill in the southern fringes of the national park. They are popular with locals and visitors, especially in the late afternoon and at weekends but are also tending to attract tourist paraphernalia and litter, national park status notwithstanding.

On the way to the national park is the Dong Quan Y cave built between 1960 and 1965 and used by the Americans as a hospital. It has 17 rooms and three floors; 20,000d. Near **Gia Luan** village is **Hoa Cuong Cave**, 100 m from the road. From the park headquarters to Gia Luan the scenery is increasingly dramatic with soaring peaks rising out of the flat valley floor. It is so outstandingly beautiful it is almost other-worldly. Gia Luan harbour is used by Halong boats; there's plenty of mangrove, karst scenery, a fishing village (black oysters and snails) and no services. Heading west, passing pine trees, you will arrive at **Hien Hao**, a village of 400 people where water is collected from wells. There's a small temple on the village outskirts; homestay is possible, see Sleeping, page 136.

Behind the town winds a road, right, up to a peak from where the views of Cat Co 2 and Lan Ha Bay are utterly spectacular. You could walk but the heat may see you on the back of a moto.

Offshore **Monkey Island** can be visited. It is close to Cat Ba and can be combined within a day-long cruise of Halong Bay or shorter four-hour excursion in a small boat. Accommodation is available here.

Cat Ba National Park

ⓘ *Park office, T31-388 8741, open 0700-1700; 3 km trek, 15,000d (with guide, 65,000d); 15 km trek 35,000d (with guide 135,000d); park accommodation, 50,000d; 15,000d per meal. Town to park gate, 15 km, is 30 mins on a motorbike.*

The national park (**Vuon Quoc Gia Cat Ba**), established in 1986, covers roughly half the island and is some 252 km sq. Of this area, a third consists of coast and inland waters. Home to 109 bird and animal species, and of particular importance is the world's last remaining troupe of **white-headed langur** (around 59 animals). Their numbers dropped from around 2500 in the 1960s to 53 in 2000; the primate is critically endangered and on the World Conservation Union 2006 Red List (www.catbalangur.org). These elusive creatures (*Trachypithecus poliocephalus poliocephalus*) are rarely spotted and then only from the sea as they inhabit wild and remote cliff habitats. There are also several types of rare **macaque** (rhesus, pig-tailed and red-faced) and **moose deer**. Vegetation ranges from mangrove swamps in sheltered bays and densely wooded hollows, to high, rugged limestone crags sprouting caps of hardy willows. The marine section of the park is no less bounteous: perhaps less fortunate is the high economic value of its fish and crustacea populations, which keeps the local fishing fleet hard at work and prosperous. In common with other coastal areas in the region the potential for snorkelling here is zero.

Visitors are free to roam through the forest but advised not to wander too far from the path. Many hotels arrange treks from the park gate through the forest to **Ao Ech** (Frog Lake) on to the village of **Viet Hai** for a light lunch then down to the coast for a boat ride home. This takes the best part of a day (six to 10 hours) and costs around US$10. It is a good way to see the park but those preferring solitude can go their own way or go with a park guide. A short trek leads to the **Ngu Lam Peak** behind the park headquarters. July to October is the wet season when leeches are a problem and mosquitoes are at their worst. Bring leech socks if you have them and plenty of insect repellent. Collar, long sleeves and long trousers advisable.

Bai Tu Long and towards the Chinese border → *For listings, see pages 128-134.*

Bai Tu Long is east of Halong Bay in the Gulf of Tonkin stretching towards the Chinese border. The group of islands makes up the Bai Tu Long National Park, covering 15,783 ha. **Quan Lan Island**, a remote island just south of Bai Tu Long is home to a very small community, some guesthouse accommodation, small restaurants, beaches and wild, untamed land. Bicycles can be hired at guesthouses as well as small boats.

Mong Cai

Mong Cai is located on the Gulf of Tonkin and is next to Dong Xing, China. The main point of interest in Mong Cai is the plethora of cheaply made Chinese goods available. It would also be the sensible place to cross if you are planning to go to Hainan Island. Apart from that there is not a lot to do or see. The border crossing is open from 0730 to 1630. The Chinese entry visa must be issued by the embassy in Hanoi and specify the Mong Cai crossing. For costs, see page 93.

The only tourist attraction is **Tra Co Beach** which is 7 km from Mong Cai itself. It is a delightful sandy peninsula and, as it is 17 km long, you are bound to find a quiet spot. The best time to vist would be anytime except May to August; also avoid the Vietnamese holidays if possible as it will be crowded.

Halong Bay listings

For Sleeping and Eating price codes and other relevant information, see pages 10-13.

Sleeping

Halong City *p128*

The past few years have seen an explosion in the number of hotels and guesthouses in Bai Chay and Hon Gai; this reflects the popularity of Halong Bay as a destination for both Vietnamese and foreign visitors. Many of the newer hotels are badly built and, apart from the fact that some of the taller ones look structurally unsound, are quite frequently damp and musty; check the room first.

There are few hotels in **Hon Gai** but they tend to be more competitively priced than those in Bai Chay. In **Bai Chay** there are 2 main groups of hotels, 2 km apart. Most are to be found at the west end on the way in to town, set back a little from the seafront, and include Vuon Dao St composed entirely of 5- to 8-room mini hotels. 2 km further on, nearer the bridge, is a smaller group, some of which have good views. Their main advantage used to be that they were close to the bus station but as this has moved they are rather isolated from the bulk of restaurants, tourist office, post office and night market.

$$$$ Halong Dream, 10 Halong Rd, T33-384 9009, www.halongdreamhotel.com. A huge, characterless place but it's quiet and close to all the local services. It's also got a pool and spa and the breakfast is reasonable.
$$$$ Halong Plaza, 8 Halong Rd, Bai Chay, T33-384 5810, www.halongplaza.com. A Thai joint venture with 200 rooms and suites and fantastic views over the sea, especially from upper floors, luxuriously finished, huge bathrooms, every comfort and extravagance, pool, restaurants and engaging staff; a lovely hotel by any standards. The evening dinner buffet at US$22 and half price for children aged 12 and under represents good value.
$$$ Saigon Halong, Halong Rd, Bai Chay, T33-384 5845, www.saigonhalonghotel.com. Run by **Saigontourist** with 23 rooms in 'villas' and 205 rooms; comfortable, all mod cons, set back from the road on the way into town; relaxed and attractive surroundings.
$$ Ha Long 1, Halong Rd, Bai Chay, T33-384 6321. A converted French villa with stacks of charm set among frangipani and raised up on a hill overlooking the sea. Some of the 23 rooms have sea outlook, huge bathrooms, bathtubs, bidets, etc but in now in need of a bit of a spruce up. The exterior and wooden shutters have recently been renovated.
$$ Viethouse Lodge, Tuan Chau Island, T33-384 2233, www.viethouselodge.com. With rooms scattered around a hillside this can be a more pleasant alternative to staying in the city. There's a restaurant, bar, games and transport to hire. The island is now connected to the mainland by a bridge.
$$-$ Bach Dang, 2 Halong Rd, Bai Chay, T33-384 6330, www.bachdanghotelqn.com. Next to the Halong Plaza, an older but well-kept establishment, a/c, sea views and restaurant.
$ Halong Guesthouse, 80-82 Le Thanh Tong, Hon Gai, T33-382 6509. 16 a/c rooms with hot water and private bathroom; clean and good value. Fairly close to the bridge near cafés and small restaurants. Several other guesthouses on Le Thanh Tong St.
$ Minh Tuan, Ho Xuan Huong St, Bai Chay, T33-384 6200. Up a quiet lane off the main road in a low-key Vietnamese neighbourhood. 14 a/c rooms with bathroom, clean, well managed but bargain hard as the rooms are looking a little neglected. No longer convenient for the bus station but recommended for its position in a quiet local street with a small market nearby.
$ Peace Hotel, 39 Vuon Dao St, T33-384 6009. A mini-hotel offering reasonable rooms. 1 hr free internet for guests.

Cat Ba Island *p126*

While in summer prices may be slightly higher than those listed, as far as possible the price ranges below give a fair indication of seasonal variations. It may still be possible to negotiate discounts in quieter periods. There are no addresses, and to confuse matters further, many hotels claim the same name.
$$$$ Cat Ba Island Resort & Spa, Cat Co 1, T31-368 8686, www.catbaislandresort-spa.com. There are 109 pleasant rooms decorated with white rattan furniture across 3 buildings facing the bay with a lovely out- look and fronting right on to the beach. The obtrusive water slides cannot be seen from the 2nd and 3rd building. 3 restaurants provide Western and Asian food and there are 2 pools, water slides, jacuzzi, massage, billiards and a tennis court. Trekking and Halong Bay tours are offered. Eagles, for some reason, find it an attractive spot.
$$$$ Sunrise Resort, Cat Co 3, T31-388 7360, www.catbasunriseresort.com. An attractive low-keyish resort on a beach linked by road to the town and by footpath to Cat Co 1. It has beach loungers and thatched umbrellas, a pool, jacuzzi, massage, 3 restaurants and travel services. Note that you cannot drive to the door of the hotel. You must walk around 50 m up and down stairs to reach the reception and beach.
$$$ Holiday View Hotel, T31-388 7200, www.holidayviewhotel-catba.com. A hotel this size should never have been allowed to be built; it dominates the Cat Ba seafront. Rooms are furnished with all mod-cons.

$$$ Princes, T31-388 8899, www.princeshotel-catba.com. The rooms are nice and light and airy and, unlike all the vertical shoebox hotels, this one has made an effort to look decent and has an open courtyard at the back. Well-furnished rooms and friendly reception. It is quite large, 80 rooms, takes credit card and breakfast is included in the price. It also rents motorbikes, bikes and kayaks.

$$ Family (Quang Duc), just west of the pier, T31-388 8231. The original 'Family' hotel, a/c, hot water, 7 spotlessly clean rooms, views from most, a very well-run little hotel, owners are knowledgeable on local matters and helpful, newly renovated and now offers a range of watersports. Recommended.

$$ Gieng Ngoc, east of the pier, Cat Ba town, T31-388 8286. Among the best of the budget hotels. Quiet, front rooms overlook sea. There are 59 rooms that are basic, clean and come with a/c.

$$ Ocean Beach Resort, Cat Ong Island, 3.5 km southeast of Cat Ba town, T4-3210 2727, www.oceanbeachresort.com.vn. 7 bungalows with fans and mosquito nets situated on 2 beaches on this island getaway.

$$ Sun and Sea, past the post office on the right, T31-388 8315. One of the plushest in town, 32 rooms, all mod cons including satellite TV, tall; seaview from some rooms.

$$-$ Cat Tien Tourism Complex, Cat Co 1 and 2, T31-388 7988, giathanh@flamingovietnam.com. Cat Co 2 is more beautiful but Cat Co 1 is more accessible from town. There are 7 fan-cooled small bungalows and 2 large ones on Cat Co 2; camping (**$**) with your own tents is possible.

$ Homestay, Hien Hao Village, on the west coast of the island. Hien Hao People's Committee office, T31-888 732/90-8693 4099 (mob). Hien Hao is 12 km from Phu Long, 20 km from Cat Ba town and 4 km from the National Park HQ. If you get the Hoang Long bus, it can drop you there on its way to and from Phu Long. Meals provided on request.

$ Monkey Island. The **My Ngoc** hotel, see below, will rent tents and arrange boat transfer. There are no washing facilities.

$ My Ngoc, quite central, not far from the ferry pier, T31-388 8199. 23 rooms, a/c, hot water. Restaurant and tours arranged.

$ Noble House, T31-388 8363. Overlooking the pier with 5 comfortable and well-appointed rooms. A/c and fridge, good views, more expensive rooms include breakfast. Popular bar and restaurant serving reasonably priced Vietnamese and Western dishes. Tours are offered.

Cat Ba National Park *p128, map p126*

$$ Park guesthouse, Viet Hai Village, Viet Hai Community Based Tourism Association, T31-388 8836. Homestays have beds with mosquito nets. A mattress and bed sheets can also be provided.

Bai Tu Long and towards the Chinese border *p129*

There are a couple of hotels and guesthouses on Quan Lan Island. Go direct from Hon Gai or Bai Dai (see Transport) or arrange through **My Ngoc** hotel.

$ Quan Lan Resort, Son Hao Beach, T33-387 7316. Wooden huts with en suite showers. A restaurant is available.

Mong Cai *p129*

$ Nha Nghi Hai Van, 2 Thang Loi St, T33-388 6479. A relatively new hotel. The rooms are well equipped but more importantly the staff are friendly and helpful. It is centrally located and 3 mins' walk to the market.

Eating

Halong City *p130*

Seafood is fresh and abundant and fairly priced. **Le Qui Don St** in Hon Gai has good seafood restaurants. Other than the hotels (see **Halong Plaza** especially), **Halong Rd**, near the junction with Vuon Dao St, Bai Chay, is lined for several hundred metres with restaurants all of which are pretty good.

¥¥¥-¥¥ Co Ngu, Halong Rd, beyond the Post Office, T33-351 1363, www.halongcongu.com. A new restaurant in a building over 3 floors. Everything from fried chicken and salmon dishes to sautéed bladder.

¥¥ Emeraude Café, Co/Royal Park, T33-384 9266. Open 0900-2100. An oasis of comfort food close to the main hotels and restaurants. Free internet and Wi-Fi. Expensive shuttle bus arranged to Hanoi.

¥ Lavender, 99 Halong Rd, Bai Chay, near the junction, T33-384 6185, does a good squid with chilli and lemongrass.

Cat Ba Island *p126*

After dark there is a charged atmosphere along the front as tanned Westerners crowd into small restaurants to quaff bottles of chilled beer, consume fresh seafood and strike up lively conversations. Some hotels listed above have restaurants.

¥¥ Green Mango, T31-388 7151. This is an outstanding addition to Cat Ba cuisine. The sesame-encrusted *ahi* tuna on a bed of cellophane noodles is worth the ferry trip to Cat Ba alone. Other culinary delights include home-smoked duck with vindaloo rice, green mustard and pomegranate jus and warm chocolate pudding, raspberry purée and cream. Indoor and outdoor seating is available. Highly recommended.

¥ Truc Lam or **Bamboo Forest**, T31-388 8654, truclamrestaurant@yahoo.com. Mr Dau, the owner, is a relative newcomer to Cat Ba, but knowledgeable and can arrange tours; he also rents rooms (**$**). His restaurant serves the usual seafood and also vegetarian dishes as well as rice wines.

Bars and clubs

Cat Ba Island *p126*

Flightless Bird, on the seafront, T31-388 8517. Run by Graeme Moore, a New Zealander, the only real pub in town. See also **Noble House**, Sleeping, above.

Activities and tours

Halong City *p131*

Boat tours

Boat tours can be booked from hotels in Halong and in Hanoi, see below, although it may be cheaper to organize the trip independently; to do so go to the Bai Chay Tourist Wharf and visit the ticket office only, not the 'tourist office' in the compound. Prices displayed on a board start from 180,000d. Children under 5 are free; those aged 5-10 are half price. On Sat, Sun and holidays, prices are reduced by 20%. Foreign-language speaking guides can also be hired here. The wharf has snack places, an ATM and internet. There's a taxi stand and bus stop right outside. Or, go direct to the **Quang Ninh Tourism Information Promotion Center**, which regulates the boats, see Tourist information, page 123. Because it takes about 1 hr to get into the bay proper, 1 long trip represents better value than 2 short ones. A tour of the bay including a cave or 2 and a swim needs 4-5 hrs. A number of day trips are on offer: **Route 1** goes to Thien Cung Grotto, Dau Go Cave, Dinh Huong islet and Ga Choi islet (4 hrs); **Route 2** follows the same route plus Sung Sot Grotto and Ti Tov Beach (6 hrs); **Route 3** follows the same route as Route 2 but is longer (7-8 hrs); **Route 4** sails to Me Cung Cave and the floating villages of Cua Van and **Route 5** goes to Bai Tu Long: Ngoc Vung Island, Quan Lan Island and Minh Chau Island (2 days). Trips leave between 0730-0900. Tickets for visits to the cave can be bought at the tourist wharf or at the caves. It's also possible to charter a boat if you are a large group.

Buffalo Tours, 94 Ma May St, Hanoi, T4-3828 0702, www.buffalotours.com, operates the luxury *Jewel of the Bay* boat. This comfortably furnished boat with capacity for 10 includes children's toys, a deck for sunbathing and star-watching; enormous quantities of superb food are served and the staff are welcoming. Kayaks can be used to explore from the boat.

Cruise Halong Co, Suite 328, 33B Pham Ngu Lao St, Hanoi, T4-3933 5561, www.cruisehalong.com. The *Halong Ginger* is a luxury junk cruising the waters and is a beautiful sight on the bay with its proud orange sails. It has 10 cabins, restaurant, lounge, 2 bars, shop and a library. Kayaking, snorkelling and cooking classes are available.
Emeraude Classic Cruises, 46 Le Thai To St, Hanoi, T4-3935 1888, www.emeraude-cruises.com. Also at Royal Park, Halong Rd, Bai Chay, T33-849 266. The best way to see Halong Bay in style is on the reconstructed French paddle steamer, the *Emeraude*. There are 39 cabins with extremely comfortable beds and nice touches (gift-wrapped biscuits) and old-style fans although the bathrooms are on the tiny side. There's a sumptuous buffet lunch and more delicious food than you can eat for dinner. Entertainment includes a Vietnamese spring roll demo, swimming off the boat, squid fishing, t'ai chi exercise on the sun deck at dawn and a massage service. There's a sundeck and bar. **Emeraude** is also now offering day trips: 1130-1700 for US$100 per person (for 2 people); cheaper if there are more people. Shuttle service arranged from Hanoi. Worth pitching up at the Halong City office for last-minute options.
Life Heritage Resort Halong Bay, www.life-resorts.com. 22 private deluxe boats with a living area, sun deck, DVD player and TV and their own captain and staff. Therapy treatments are available on board.

The **Huong Hai Junk Halong Company** (www.halongdiscovery.com) also operates in the bay.

Cat Ba Island *p126*

Boat tours

Halong Bay is the most famous excursion from Cat Ba. Almost all hotels in Cat Ba offer tours as do the touts along the seafront. It is better to use a service provided by a reputable hotel (as listed in Sleeping, above), as you are less likely to be left stranded or charged extra for lunch.

Kayaking

Kayaking in Halong Bay and Lan Ha Bay are now regular features, especially in the summer months. It is best to go via one of the established tour operators in Hanoi, such as **Handspan** and **Buffalo Tours** but **Family Hotel** and **My Ngoc Hotel** in Cat Ba also have kayaks. These are best taken out on a larger boat and paddled from the open sea. **Family Hotel** is the place to ask about watersports.

Rock climbing

Climbing the rock karst limestone faces and towers on Cat Ba and Halong Bay is now possible with experienced, licensed and enthusiastic climbers, see Tour operators below. At least 140 climbing routes have been established.

Tour operators

The Cat Hai District People's Committee Tourism Information Centre, along the seafront, T31-368 8215. Daily 0700-2200, runs guided tours to the national park and Halong Bay; organizes *xe ôm* to park HQ; 1-hr boat trip to Lan Ha Bay; boat charter; car hire; motorbike hire; bicycle hire.
Slo Pony Adventures/Asia Outdoors, 222 1/4 St, Group 19, Ward 4, T31-368 8450, www.slopony.com. Rock climbing, kayaking, trekking, environmentally conscious boat cruises and other adventures. Slo Pony works directly with the local community on Cat Ba Island, employs both domestic and international staff and assists the national park with efforts to protect the endangered langur as well as with the park's conservation efforts.

Transport

Halong City *p132*

Bus

Halong City bus station is now 5 km west of Halong city, near Halong train station. Local bus No 3 runs to and from the centre of town, 5000d. There is a bus stop right outside the Bai Chay Tourist Wharf. There are regular connections from Bai Chay bus station to **Hanoi** from 0700, last bus departs 1600. Buses are slow, crowded, uncomfortable and full of pickpockets. Regular connections with **Haiphong**'s Lac Long bus station 0900-1500. There are also buses to **Mong Cai** every 15 mins and to **Bai Dai** (for ferries to **Quan Lan**), every 15 mins, 13,000d.

Boat

To Cat Ba Jump on a tourist boat for a 1-way (4-hr) ride for 200,000d from the **Bai Chay Tourist Wharf** (Halong Rd, T33-384 6592) open daily 0730-1700; get there early as last group departures (ie cheaper leave around 1230) and get off at the port of Gia Luan which is in the north of Cat Ba. A bus runs from Gia Luan to Cat Ba Town, 10,000d. Ferries also run from Tuan Chau 'Island' to Gia Luan in the summer at 0730, 0930, 1100, 1330, 1600, and in the winter at 0800 and 1400, 30,000d.

From Hon Gai (Halong City) boat station (98 Ben Tau Road near Long Tien pagoda) to **Quan Lan Island** at 1000, 140,000d, 2½ hrs. There is an 0700 boat service to **Mong Cai**, 300,000d, 3 hrs.

Cat Ba Island *p126*

Boat

It would be wise to check all ferry information before setting out as timetables change.

To Haiphong Transtour Co runs the Cat Ba–Haiphong ferry, T31-388 8314, office on the seafront. Express boat to Haiphong, 0700, 1445, 120,000d, children 60,000d; slow boats at 0545 and 1230. Hoang Long Co, T31-388 7244 (Cat Ba), with an office on the seafront, runs a bus to **Phu Long** on Cat Ba and then boat to the **Dinh Vu ferry terminal** (1½ hrs), and then bus (30 mins) to Haiphong. Several buses a day. You can also continue the journey to **Hanoi**'s Luong Yen bus station.

To Tuan Chau 'Island' (Halong City) From Gia Luan at 0900, 1100, 1330, 1500 and 1700 in summer, 30,000d. In winter at 0900, 1500. A bus runs from Cat Ba Town to Gia Luan, 10,000d.

Bai Tu Long and towards the Chinese border *p129*

Boat

Daily boat service from Mong Cai to **Hon Gai** (Halong City) at 1330, 300,000d, 3 hrs From Quan Lan Island to Hon Gai at 1500, 140,000d, 2½ hrs. From Bai Dai (northeast of Halong City) to **Quan Lan Island**, 0900 returning 1500 in summer, 0815 in winter, returning 1415, 80,000d. 1½ hrs. This Bai Dai ferry also goes on to **Minh Chau Island**.

Bus

Mong Cai is 360 km from **Hanoi**. There are 5 departures between 0530-0730, 10 hrs. There are many buses between Mong Cai and **Halong City** from 0500-1700, 6 hrs. There is also a 5-hr journey to **Lang Son** but this schedule is erratic. The buses will only leave if there are sufficient people on board.

Directory

Halong City *p133*

Banks Vietcombank, Halong St, Bai Chay, with ATM. Agribank, 2 Vuon Dao St, Bai Chay, also with ATM. **Hospitals** Bai Chay Hospital, T33-384 6557. **Internet** Many hotels and cafés provide email services at reasonable prices. **Post office** In Bai Chay at junction of Halong Rd and Vuon Dao St. Internet service also.

Cat Ba Island *p126*

Banks Agribank, T31-388 8227, on the back road will change dollars. ATM on seafront. Hotels will exchange US$ cash at poor rates. Alternatively there are a couple of gold shops at the west end of the town. Vu Binh, T31-388 8641, will give cash on Amex, Visa and MasterCard. **Internet** A couple of hotels have email as does the tourist information place. **Post office** In town centre, opposite pier.

Mong Cai *p129*

Bank Vietcombank change TCs and there's an ATM. **Internet** Lots of internet cafés along Hung Vuong St. **Post office** Corner of Tran Phu and Hung Vuong St.

Ninh Binh and around

Ninh Binh is capital of the densely populated province of Ninh Binh. It marks the most southerly point of the northern region. The town itself has little to commend to the tourist but it is a useful and accessible hub from which to visit some of the most interesting and attractive sights in the north. Within a short drive lie the ancient capital of Hoa Lu with its temples dedicated to two of Vietnam's great kings; the exquisite watery landscape of Tam Coc, an 'inland Halong Bay', where sampans carry visitors up a meandering river, through inundated grottoes and past verdant fields of rice; the Roman Catholic landscape around Phat Diem Cathedral, spires and towers, bells and smells; and the lovely Cuc Phuong National Park, with its glorious butterflies, flowers and trees. The town of Nam Dinh is a centre for visiting several pagodas in the area. » *For listings, see pages 140-141.*

Ins and outs

Getting there It is a three-hour journey from Hanoi by bus or by train. From Hanoi, the route south runs through expanding industrial towns which, in the last few years have been convulsed with change: road widenings, demolition of old buildings to make way for industrial zones and factories gobbling up 'ricefield' sites. Communities which for centuries were divided by nothing more than a dirt track now find themselves rent asunder by four-lane highways, but ancient ties of kith and kin and tradition have yet to adjust. Beyond Phu Ly the limestone karsts start to rise dramatically out of the flat plain. » *For further details, see Transport, page 141.*

Getting around Visitors can get to the places around Ninh Binh as a day trip from Hanoi through tour agencies or by taking tours or hiring transport from the hotels in Ninh Binh.

Tourist information **Ninh Binh Tourism** ⓘ *www.ninhbinhtourism.com.vn*. The hotels all have good information.

Hoa Lu

ⓘ *US$1.*

Hoa Lu lies about 13 km from Ninh Binh near the village of **Truong Yen**; it is a couple of kilometres signposted off the main road and can be reached by bicycle or *xe ôm* (6 km north of Ninh Binh and 6 km west of Highway 1, follow signs to Truong Yen).

It was the capital of Vietnam from AD 968 to AD 1010, during the Dinh and Early Le dynasties. Prior to the establishment of Hoa Lu as the centre of the new kingdom, there was nothing here. But the location was a good one in the valley of the Hong River – on the 'dragon's belly', as the Vietnamese say. The passes leading to the citadel could be defended with a small force, and defenders could keep watch over the plains to the north and guard against the Chinese. The kings of Hoa Lu were, in essence, rustics. This is reflected in the art and architecture of the temples of the ancient city: primitive in form, massive in conception. Animals were the dominant motifs, carved in stone.

A large part of this former capital, which covered over 200 ha, has been destroyed, although archaeological excavations have revealed much of historical and artistic interest. The two principal temples are those of Dinh Bo Linh, who assumed the title King Dinh Tien Hoang on ascending the throne (reigned AD 968-980), and Le Hoan, who assumed the title King Le Dai Hanh on ascending the throne (reigned AD 980-1009).

The **Temple of Dinh Tien Hoang** was originally constructed in the 11th century but was reconstructed in 1696. It is arranged as a series of courtyards, gates and buildings. The inscription on a pillar in the temple, in ancient Vietnamese, reads 'Dai Co Viet', from which the name 'Vietnam' is derived. The back room of the temple is dedicated to Dinh Tien Hoang, whose statue occupies the central position, surrounded by those of his sons, Dinh Lien (to the left), Dinh Hang Lang and Dinh Toan (to the right). In the 960s, Dinh Tien Hoang managed to pacify much of the Red River plain, undermining the position of a competing ruling family, the Ngos, who accepted Dinh Tien Hoang's supremacy. However, this was not done willingly, and banditry and insubordination continued to afflict Hoang's kingdom. He responded by placing a kettle and a tiger in a cage in the courtyard of his palace and decreed: 'those who violate the law will be boiled and gnawed'. An uneasy calm descended on Dinh Tien Hoang's kingdom, and he could concern himself with promoting Buddhism and geomancy, arranging marriages, and implementing reforms. But, by making his infant son Hang Lang heir apparent, rather than Lien (his only adult son), he sealed his fate. History records that the announcement was followed by earthquakes and hailstorms, a sign of dissension in the court, and in AD 979 Lien sent an assassin to kill his younger brother Hang Lang. A few months later in the same year, an official named Do Thich killed both Dinh Tien Hoang and Lien as they lay drunk and asleep in the palace courtyard. When Do Thich was apprehended, it is said that he was executed and his flesh fed to the people of the city.

The **Temple of King Le Dai Hanh** is dedicated to the founder of the Le Dynasty who seized power after the regicide of Dinh Tien Hoang. In fact Le Dai Hanh took not only Hoang's throne but also his wife, Duong Van Nga. Representations of her, Le Dai Hanh and Le Ngoa Trieu (also known as Le Long Dinh), his fifth son, each sit on their own altar in the rear temple. Near this temple the foundations of King Dinh's (10th century) royal palaces were found by Vietnamese archaeologists in 1998.

A short walk beyond Le Dai Hanh's temple is **Nhat Tru Pagoda**, a 'working' temple. In front of it stands a pillar engraved with excerpts from the Buddhist bible (*Kinh Phat*). Opposite Dinh Tien Hoang's temple is a hill, Nui Ma Yen, at the top of which is **Dinh Tien Hoang's tomb**. Locals will tell you it is 260 steps to the top. There are boat trips on the river to **Xuyen Thuy cave** ⓘ *15,000d*, less spectacular than Tam Coc (see below).

Tam Coc and Bich Dong

ⓘ *Daily 0700-1700, 60,000d (1-2 people) for the boat, 30,000d for the grottoes including Bich Dong (a tip and purchase will be requested on the boat). The turning to Tam Coc and Bich Dong is 4 km south of Ninh Binh on Highway 1. A small road leads 2-3 km west to Tam Coc.*

Tam Coc can easily be reached by bicycle or xe ôm *from Ninh Binh or by car from Hanoi (on a day trip). It's possible to go from Bich Dong to Xuyen Thuy cave by boat, 20,000d. There are a couple of hotels and restaurants.*

Tam Coc means literally 'three caves'. The highlight of this excursion is an enchanting boat ride up the little Ngo Dong River through the eponymous three caves. Those who have seen the film *Indochine*, some of which was shot here, will be familiar with the nature of the beehive-type scenery created by limestone towers, similar to those of Halong Bay. The exact form varies from wet to dry season; when flooded the channel disappears and one or two of the caves may be under water. In the dry season the shallow river meanders between fields of golden rice. You can spot mountain goat precariously clinging to the rocks and locals collecting snails in the water. Women row and punt pitch-and-resin tubs that look like elongated coracles through the tunnels. It is a most leisurely experience and a chance to observe at close quarters the extraordinary method of rowing with the feet. Take plenty of sun cream and a hat. The villagers have a rota for rowing and supplement their fee by trying to sell visitors embroidered table cloths and napkins. On a busy day the scene from above is like a two-way, nose-to-tail procession of waterboats; to enjoy Tam Coc at its best make it your first port of call in the morning.

A short drive to the south is Bich Dong. This is much harder work, so not surprisingly it is a lot quieter than Tam Coc. Bich Dong consists of a series of temples and caves built into, and carved out of, a limestone mountain. The temples date from the reign of Le Thai To in the early 15th century. It is typical of many Vietnamese cave temples but with more than the average number of legends attached to it, while the number of interpretations of its rock formations defies belief. The lower temple is built into the cliff face. Next to the temple is a pivoted and carved rock that resonates beautifully when tapped with a stone. Next see Buddha's footprints embedded in the rock (size 12, for the curious) and the tombs of the two founding monks.

Leading upwards is the middle temple, an 18th-century bell, a memorial stone into which are carved the names of benefactors and a cave festooned with rock forms. Here, clear as can be, are the likenesses of Uncle Ho, a turtle and an elephant. More resonant rock pillars follow and a rock which enables pregnant women to choose the sex of their baby: touch the top for a boy and the middle for a girl. But best of all scramble right to the pinnacle of the peak for a glorious view over the whole area. Unfortunately, the view has been marred by a horrible new orange and sickly green concrete building.

Phat Diem Cathedral

ⓘ *24 km southeast of Ninh Binh in the village of Kim Son, daily 0800-1700, English and French guidebook; 15,000d; there are several services daily. The journey takes in a number of more conventional churches, waterways and paddy fields. Take a motorbike from Ninh Binh or hire a car from Hanoi. Hoa Lu, Tam Coc and Phat Diem can all be comfortably covered in 1 day; there are souvenir shops selling* nuoc mam *(fish sauce) and Virgin figures side by side.*

Phat Diem Cathedral is the most spectacular of the church buildings in the area, partly for its scale but also for its remarkable Oriental style with European stylistic influences. Completed in 1899, it boasts a bell tower in the form of a pagoda behind which stretches for 74 m the nave of the cathedral held up by 52 ironwood pillars. The cathedral was built under the leadership of parish priest Father Tran Luc between 1875 and 1899. He is buried in a tomb between the bell tower and the cathedral proper. Surrounding the cathedral are several chapels: St Joseph's, St Peter's, the Immaculate Heart's, the Sacred Heart's and St Roch's.

In 1953 French action in the area saw artillery shells damage the eastern wing of the cathedral causing part of the roof to collapse.

The cathedral was bombed in 1972 by Americans who despatched eight missiles. St Peter's Church was flattened, St Joseph's blown to an angle, the cathedral forced to a tilt, the roof tiles hurled to the floor, and 52 of the 54 cathedral doors were damaged. Restoration of different parts of the complex is ongoing.

The approach to the cathedral is impressive: you drive down a narrow valley to be confronted with a statue of Christ the King in the middle of a huge square pond; behind are the cathedral buildings.

The Red River Delta was the first part of the country to be influenced by Western missionaries: Portuguese priests were proselytizing here as early as 1627. Christian influence is still strong despite the mass exodus of Roman Catholics to the south in 1954 and decades of Communist rule. Villages (which are built of red brick, often walled and densely populated) in these coastal provinces may have more than half-a-dozen churches, all with packed congregations, not only on Sundays. The churches, the shrines, the holy grottoes, the photographs of the parish priest on bedroom walls and the holy relics clearly assume huge significance in people's lives.

Cuc Phuong National Park

ⓘ *Nho Quan district, T30-384 8006, www.cucphuongtourism.com, daily 0500-2100, 40,000d, children 20,000d; botanic garden 5000d. 1- to 6-day treks can be arranged with a guide; short treks of a couple of hours are also available (trail to silver cloudy peak and ancient tree; trail to Muong village; wildlife experience tour; night spotting; bicycle tours can also be arranged as well as a tour to Van Long Nature Reserve, see page 139). Mr Hai who is head of the tour guide section is very helpful and has worked at the park for more than 10 years. A visit to the park can be done as a day trip from Ninh Binh or from Hanoi. Direct access by car only. An organized tour from Hanoi may be a sensible option for lone travellers or pairs, otherwise charter a car or hire a motorbike. See also Transport, page 141, for independent travel.*

The park, which is around 120 km south of Hanoi and 45 km west of Ninh Binh, is probably the second most accessible of Vietnam's national parks, and for nature lovers not intending to visit Cat Ba Island, it is worthy of consideration. It is also Vietnam's oldest park, established in 1962. Located in an area of deeply cut limestone and reaching elevations of up to 800 m, the park is covered by 22,000 ha of humid tropical montagne forest. It is home to an estimated 2000 species of flora including the giant parashorea, cinamomum and sandoricum trees. Wildlife has been much depleted by hunting; only 117 mammal and 307 bird species and 110 reptile and amphibian species are thought to remain. The government has resettled a number of the park's 30,000 Muong minority people, although Muong villages do remain and can be visited. April and May see fat grubs and pupae metamorphosing into swarms of butterflies that mantle the forest in fantastic shades of greens and yellows.

The **Endangered Primate Rescue Center** ⓘ *www.primatecenter.org, 0900-1100, 1330-1600, limited entrance every 30 mins, 10,000d*, is a big draw in the park. There are more than 30 cages, four houses and two semi-wild enclosures for the 130 animals in breeding programmes; there are some 15 different species and sub-species. The centre is repsonsible for discovering a new species in Vietnam, the grey-shanked douc langur (*Pygathrix cinereus*), in 1997. The centre's work is extremely interesting and it is well worth a visit.

There's also the **Turtle Conservation Center**. Visitors can arrange tours to visit the 16 species kept there. Cuc Phuong also has a botanical garden that is excellent for birdwatching in the early morning as well as listening to the nearby primates' dawn chorus!

Visitors can take a number of trekking tours in the park and also spend the night at homestays with the Muong. Night spotting could enable you to see black giant squirrel,

Indian flying squirrel, samba deer and Loris. Birdwatchers could see the rare feathers of the silver pheasant, red-collared woodpecker, brown hornbill and bar-bellied pitta. Two lucky tourists and their guide saw an Asiatic black bear in early 2007.

Facilities at the park headquarters include accommodation, a restaurant, visitor centre and guides' headquarters; a museum is planned. From here you can trek 15 km (two to three days) to the Muong village or trek for 25 km camping, accompanied by a guide From headquarters to the park centre is 20 km. The drive will take you past Mac Lake, the path for the walk to the 45-m-high Ancient Tree (*Tetrameles nudiflora*), and Cave of Prehistoric man. At the park centre you can walk the 7-km paved hike through forest to the 1000-year-old tree (45 m high and 5 m wide) and a 1000-m-long liana (*Entada tonkinensis*) and palace cave. The centre area has accommodation and a restaurant. ▸▸ *See Sleeping, page 140.*

Van Long Nature Reserve and around

ⓘ *The Van Long-Ninh Binh Tourist Ecological Area ticket office, T30-386 8798, is just beyond the Van Long hotel; boat and entrance ticket, 35,000d; daily 0700-1700.*

The 3000-ha Van Long Nature Reserve is 17 km north of Ninh Binh and 8 km from Highway 1 towards Cuc Phuong (take a right down the road on the corner of which is a restaurant). It is the home to the endangered Delacour's langur (*Trachypithecus delacouri*), one of the 25 most endangered primates in the world. The species is endemic to Vietnam. Less than 320 are said to be living in northern Vietnam with just 40 at Van Long. The best time to spot the primates known as Vooc Mong Trang in Vietnamese, is early morning or just before sunset. Several caves can also be visited. Boat tours last around two hours. The **Van Long Restaurant**, Gia Van, Gia Vien, T30-364 1248, on the main road, organizes buffalo rides in the area.

Kenh Ga floating village is 21 km north of Ninh Binh on the Hoang Long River and 3 km from the main road. Visitors can paddle 3 km to Kenh Ga past the yellow Roman Catholic church and watch village life go by amid limestone towers. The boat operation (0600-1600, 40,000d) is run by **Ninh Binh Tourism Joint Stock Co** ⓘ *T30-386 8560*, and it takes you to a cave and other villages.

Nam Dinh

Nam Dinh is a large and diverse industrial centre, with a reputation for its textiles. The Nam Dinh Textile Mill was built by the French in 1899, and is still operating.

Thien Truong and **Pho Minh pagodas** – both highly regarded – are to be found in the village of Tuc Mac (My Loc district), 3 km north of Nam Dinh. Also here are the few remains of the Tran Dynasty. Thien Truong was built in 1238 and dedicated to the kings of the Tran family; Pho Minh was built rather later, in 1305, and contains an impressive 13-storey tower. You can get to the pagodas either by *xe ôm* from Nam Dinh or as part of a day trip by car from Hanoi or Ninh Binh.

Doi Son and **Doi Diep Pagodas** are situated on two neighbouring mountains (Nui Doi Son and Nui Doi Diep). The former was originally built at some point during the early Ly Dynasty (AD 544-602). When the Emperor Le Dai Hanh (AD 980-1005) planted rice at the foot of the mountain, legend has it that he uncovered two vessels, one filled with gold and the other with silver. From that season on, the harvests were always bountiful.

North of the main channel of the Red River, 10 km southwest of Thai Binh, is the site of the 11th-century **Keo Pagoda**, which was destroyed in a flood. The present building dates back to the 17th century but has been remodelled several times. Its chief architectural attraction is a wooden, three-storey campanile containing two bronze bells.

Ninh Binh and around listings

For Sleeping and Eating price codes and other relevant information, see Essentials pages 26-31.

Sleeping

Ninh Binh *p135*

$$ Hoa Lu, Tran Hung Dao St, T30-387 1217, hoaluhotel@hn.vnn.vn. On Highway 1 towards Hanoi. 84 rooms at a range of prices for a range of standards. Cars and motorbikes for rent and tours arranged. English not spoken at reception.

$$ Thanh Thuy's Guesthouse, 128 Le Hong Phong St, T30-387 1811, www.hotelthanhthuy.com. A friendly place with cheap rooms and newer, more expensive rooms; most bathrooms have bathtubs.

$$ Thuy Anh, 55A Truong Han Sieu St, T30-387 1602, www.thuyanhhotel.com. 37 rooms, with fridge, etc in this spotless hotel in the town centre; the deluxe rooms come with a view. Breakfast included. Will arrange tours and are a useful source of information. The restaurant is good and there is the **Lighthouse Café** and rooftop garden.

$ Hoang Hai Hotel, 36 Truong Han Sieu St, T30-3871 5177, www.ninhbinhhotel.com.vn. The 11 rooms are divided into 3 types; the bigger rooms are more expensive.

$ Queen, Hoang Hoa Tham St, T30-387 1874, luongvn2001@yahoo.com. Near the station. Simplerooms; the more expensive ones are larger, have a/c and bathtubs. There's also a dorm with TV, fan and shared bathroom. Transport, tours and internet offered. Restaurant.

Hoa Lu *p135*

$$$-$$ Van Xuan, just off Highway 1 towards Hoa Lu and on the right, T30-362 2617. This hotel has a/c, hot water and a restaurant.

Cuc Phuong National Park *p138*

Four different areas with accommodation: at the park HQ; 1 km from the main gate, at Mac Lake; 2 km from the park HQ; at the park centre (20 km from the main gate); and at the Muong village, 15 km from the park HQ.

$$ Park centre concrete bungalows with en suite and a/c but more expensive than at HQ. The 4 bungalows, are set around a lawn. Electricity only available 1800-2200.

$$-$ Headquarters concrete bungalows with en suite facilities, TV and a/c and fan. These are lined up across the road from the restaurant and are clean and comfortable.

$ Headquarters detached bungalow. One bungalow with en suite facilities, hot water and a/c and fan.

$ Headquarters stilt house. These rooms have fan and shared bathrooms with hot water. **$** per person.

$ Homestay with ethnic minorities in the park. Price per person.

$ Mac Lake Bungalow. 4 bungalows with a/c and private bathroom.

$ Park centre stilt houses. These are near the start of the 1000-year-old walk. They have shared bathroom facilities and no hot water. **$** per person.

Van Long Nature Reserve *p139*

$$-$ Van Long Resort, Gia Van, Gia Vien, Ninh Binh (coming from Hanoi, turn right off Highway 1 at the Gian Khau crossroads towards Cuc Phuong. After 5 km turn right to Van Long and drive for 2 km), T30-364 1290, www.resortvanlong.vn. The 47 rooms are spacious and there's a pool and tennis courts. It is next door to the ticket office at the entrance to the Van Long Reserve. The **Van Long Restaurant**, Gia Van, Gia Vien, T30-364 1248, on the main road, 1.5 km away.

Nam Dinh *p139*

$$-$ Vi Hoang, 153 Nguyen Du St, T350-384 9290. Somewhat uncared for, restaurant.

Eating

Ninh Binh *p135*

Hoang Hai Hotel, 36 Truong Han Sieu St, T30-3871 5177. Open 0800-2200. This centrally located restaurant has zero atmosphere but service is prompt. Breakfast, lunch and dinner served.
Thanh Thuy's Guesthouse (see Sleeping, above). The portions are plentiful.
Thuy Anh (see Sleeping, above). A choice of Vietnamese fare across a range of prices.

Cuc Phuong National Park *p138*

There are 2 restaurants in the national park, one at the main gate, the other 1 km further in. Both serve a limited, and sometimes unavailable, range of food. Drinks available.

Activities and tours

Ninh Binh and around *p135*

Queen, see Sleeping, above, runs tours to the local attractions.
Thanh Thuy's Guesthouse, see Sleeping, above, organizes a recommended 3-day trip to the Pu Luong Nature Reserve near Mai Chau. Also trips to the local attractions.
Thuy Anh, see Sleeping, above, runs tours to Tam Coc, Bich Dong, Hoa Lu, Kenh Ga, Van Long reserve, Phat Diem and Cuc Phuong. Can also arrange trips to Haiphong, Cat Ba and Halong and trekking.
Vic Travel, 17 Pham Ngu Lao St, T30-388 3438/91-230 1640 (mob), http://victravel.net. Recommended.

See also Hanoi tour operators, page 140.

Transport

Ninh Binh *p135*

Bus

From Ninh Binh's bus station at 207 Le Dai Hanh St to **Hanoi**'s southern terminal, Giap Bat, hourly, 3 hrs, 30,000d and also to **Haiphong**, 4 a day, 40,000d; minibuses to Hanoi, 2 hrs. To **Phat Diem**, 1 hr; to **Kenh Ga** at 1000, 30 mins; then get a motorbike at the turn-off for the final 2 km. Take the same bus for **Van Long** and take a moto at the turn-off to the reserve. Some **Open Tour Buses** stop here on their way to Hanoi and **Hué**.

Car, motorbike and bicycle

Hoang Hai Hotel (see Sleeping, above) rents cars, motorbikes and bicycles. Queen rents too and Thuy Anh rents all these services at slightly cheaper prices and offers English- or French-speaking guides. Thanh Thuy's Guesthouse also rents bikes and motorbikes at similar prices. To get to **Cuc Phuong National Park** independently of a tour, take a *xe ôm* or hire a car for the day.

Cuc Phuong National Park *p138*

Bus

For independent travel: buses depart Giap Bat terminal in Hanoi for **Nho Quan** at 0800, 0900, 1200, 1300, 1500, 1600 and return at 0700, 0800, 1100, 1200, 1300 and 1400. From Nho Quan take a *xe ôm*. There's also 1 daily return bus direct from Hanoi to Cuc Phuong.

Nam Dinh *p139*

Bus

Regular connections with **Hanoi**'s Southern terminal, 3 hrs, and with **Haiphong** on Highway 10, 4 hrs.

Taxi

Ninh Binh taxi, T30-387 6876.

Directory

Ninh Binh *p135*

Bank Vietcombank, Tran Hung Dao St. Cashes TCs, ATM. **Internet** Thuy Anh Hotel. **Post office** Tran Hung Dao St.

Nam Dinh *p139*

Post office 4 Ha Huy ap St.